AUTISM AND MASKING

of related interest

Camouflage
The Hidden Lives of Autistic Women
Dr Sarah Bargiela
Illustrated by Sophie Standing
ISBN 978 1 78592 566 5
eISBN 978 1 78592 667 9

Working with Girls and Young Women with an Autism Spectrum Condition
A Practical Guide for Clinicians
Fiona Fisher Bullivant
ISBN 978 1 78592 420 0
eISBN 978 1 78450 784 8

Girls with Autism Becoming Women
Heather Stone Wodis
Foreword by Erika Hammerschmidt
ISBN 978 1 78592 818 5
eISBN 978 1 78450 907 1

Spectrum Women
Walking to the Beat of Autism
Edited by Barb Cook and Dr Michelle Garnett
Foreword by Lisa Morgan
ISBN 978 1 78592 434 7
eISBN 978 1 78450 806 7

Women and Girls with Autism Spectrum Disorder
Understanding Life Experiences from Early Childhood to Old Age
Sarah Hendrickx
ISBN 978 1 84905 547 5
eISBN 978 0 85700 982 1

Autism and Masking

How and Why People Do It, and the Impact It Can Have

Dr Felicity Sedgewick,
Dr Laura Hull and Helen Ellis

Jessica Kingsley Publishers
London and Philadelphia

First published in Great Britain in 2022 by Jessica Kingsley Publishers
An Hachette Company

6

Copyright © Felicity Sedgewick, Laura Hull and Helen Ellis 2022

The rights of Felicity Sedgewick, Laura Hull and Helen Ellis to be identified
as the Authors of the Work has been asserted by them in accordance with the
Copyright, Designs and Patents Act 1988.

Front cover image source: Shutterstock®.

A CIP catalogue record for this title is available from the British Library and
the Library of Congress

ISBN 978 1 78775 579 6
eISBN 978 1 78775 580 2

Printed and bound in Great Britain by Clays Limited

Jessica Kingsley Publishers' policy is to use papers that are natural,
renewable and recyclable products and made from wood grown in
sustainable forests. The logging and manufacturing processes are expected
to conform to the environmental regulations of the country of origin.

Jessica Kingsley Publishers
Carmelite House
50 Victoria Embankment
London EC4Y 0DZ

www.jkp.com

The authorised representative in the EEA is Hachette Ireland, 8 Castlecourt
Centre, Dublin 15, D15 XTP3, Ireland (email: info@hbgi.ie)

Contents

Acknowledgements

There have been an immeasurable number of people to whom we owe thanks for their part in this book coming together: our contributors and the multitude of autistic people who have taken part in the research we cite have given their time and personal experiences to move autism knowledge forwards; our employers, who have been understanding of us taking time to work on this totally separate project outside our paid roles; and, of course, the team at Jessica Kingsley Publishers who have shared their expertise and insights with us, making this book better than it would ever have been without them.

We also have some people we would like to acknowledge individually:

Felicity: Writing and editing this book has been an experience – mostly a good one. For support during the times that it was not so good, I want to thank my parents, who have listened to me sketch out ideas and complain about tricky sections on far too many phone calls. To my co-authors – who have made this a much more interesting and enjoyable process than it could ever have been doing it on my own – we have earned a celebration together, having done the entire thing through virtual communication! For the insights shared, I want to thank the autistic people in my life both personally and professionally.

You have made this book possible, and it is an honour to share your stories and experiences with the world. Finally, I owe heartfelt thanks to my partner, who has kept me going throughout, known when to drag me away from the computer screen, was an excellent sounding board for ideas and generally improves my life hugely.

Laura: I am so grateful to have been able to contribute to this book – which involves reflecting on my entire academic career so far – and trying to improve upon the parts I wish I had done differently! Thanks to Felicity and Helen for making the whole experience truly enjoyable and collaborative, despite taking place during a global pandemic. I want to thank my colleagues at UCL, my friends and my family; in particular my partner Max, for listening to my enthusiastic summaries and motivating me with hot chocolate during those late-night writing sessions. And finally, thanks to everyone who has shared their insights on masking with me, whether directly or indirectly, through research, collaboration, or just on Twitter. All interesting and useful opinions in this book are thanks to you; any misinterpretations are my own.

Helen: This book has been a true labour of love; it's been emotionally draining to be so open and exposed about something that impacts so much of my life. My sincere thanks to my co-authors for taking my rambling personal explanations and pseudo-therapy sessions and shaping them into something that we hope will be useful to autistic people, family members and professionals across all fields! I'm also grateful to my employers, the National Autistic Society, who have supported me in writing this book independently of my job. It's not easy knowing where 'work me' finishes and 'autistic individual me' starts sometimes, but we seem to manage it okay mostly! To the Wolfpack and my Tribe – thank you for being the joy in my life. And finally, my everlasting gratitude to my family – you have each played such key parts in helping me to find the ways to feel like I can lower my various masks and be myself, and indeed give me the confidence to share the hard-won wisdom I have earned, whatever it takes.

Preface

It is always good to know a little about the people who wrote a book as you read it, so each of the authors has written a short introduction to themselves and how they came to be involved in this project.

Felicity Sedgewick

I am an academic whose work focuses on the overlap between social and developmental psychology, rather than sitting in one specialism. I am non-autistic, though I have friends, family members and colleagues who represent a range of neurodiverse conditions, and have done my entire life. I have carried out research into gender differences in autism, autism and relationships, and autism and mental health, as well as how these areas all interact. Although rarely the focus of these projects, camouflaging has been a common theme in nearly every study I have done, as it has such an impact on relationships and mental health and because it is used differently by people of different genders. Understanding the impact of theorized constructs (such as camouflaging/masking) on the everyday lives of autistic people is central to all my interests. I care deeply about sharing that knowledge with those who are best placed to use it to improve autistic people's lives, and do a lot of outreach work to try to make this happen. I see this book as the next part of that passion project, and am excited about the chance for more people to learn about masking among autistic people.

Laura Hull

I am an academic who looks at factors impacting autistic people's wellbeing and access to support. I am non-autistic and have friends, family members and colleagues who are autistic or otherwise neurodivergent. My previous research focused on understanding the concept of masking and developing ways to measure masking (or camouflaging), and I am currently conducting research into the mental health of autistic children and teenagers, and how autistic adults are diagnosed. I am passionate about exploring individual experiences of masking and how it can affect people in different ways. I am thrilled to be able to contribute towards this book, which I hope will empower autistic people and those around them to think about how they mask and how it impacts them.

Helen Ellis

Helen is an autistic adult who was first identified at the age of 15 and received a clinical diagnosis a week before her 22nd birthday. She works for the National Autistic Society in the Human Resources team, with responsibilities for diversity and inclusion, as well as leading on the internal mentoring scheme, co-ordinating autistic representation on interview panels and delivering the Understanding Autism session to MPs when they ask!

Outside of work, Helen is a dedicated fan of Saracens Rugby Club, including being the elected disabled supporters' rep on the club's Supporters' Forum, and is a passionate advocate of autistic people sharing the joy they get from special interests and stims, as the world always needs more unmasked happiness.

Helen is keen to stress that she is not writing this book on behalf of the National Autistic Society or as part of her job there, nor is she attempting to speak for all autistic people in this book: personal opinions and experiences shared are noted as such for clarity.

Introduction

This book came about because the topic of masking is somewhat like the moral of the elephant. If you place three blindfolded people at the trunk, leg and tail of an elephant, they will respectively tell you that an elephant is a long snake-like creature; a thick, tall cylinder; or a short, thin, whip-like being. They all have elements of the whole, but they must work together (and get the outside view of some other people) in order to get an overall and more accurate idea of what an elephant *actually* is.

Hopefully, we, the authors of this book, are not quite so blindfolded as the people in the metaphor. We were all individually interested in masking – but felt that we each held only pieces of the wider picture, rather than any one of us being able to speak to the whole. We bring lived experience, specific research knowledge, and years of work with autistic people who mask and live with the consequences of masking in a myriad of ways.

Our book is an attempt to combine those different areas and types of expertise, to share them with an (assumedly) interested audience, and to bring in the voices of lots of different autistic people to share their thoughts and experiences of masking. It is organized into chapters with questions as titles, which we then try to answer. Each chapter contains an overview of research into the topic, interspersed with quotes from autistic people as well as longer accounts of specific lived experiences. They all also have an 'Other things to think about' box which takes on a key issue in the world of autism and masking.

The first chapter of the book looks at 'What Is Masking and Who Does It?' This is an overview of the earliest research into masking. It will look at how masking is defined and identified, and who engages in masking to different extents. 'Other things to think about' looks at some of the reasons why there might be differences in how much and the ways people mask.

The second chapter of the book is titled 'How Do People Mask?' This part talks about the masking strategies that people employ, how they learn to use these strategies (including learning how to lie) and, importantly, some of the differences between introvert and extrovert approaches to masking. 'Other things to think about' looks at the experience of needing to mask with other autistic people, and the impact this can have.

The third chapter is called 'Why Do People Mask? And Where?' It looks at some of the reasons identified in research to date, and how these link to wider theories of the psychological drives and social pressures that contribute to it. It will also consider different situations where people mask, and how those contexts might affect the kind of masking people use. 'Other things to think about' looks at differences between autistic and non-autistic culture, and how this might influence masking.

The fourth chapter is titled 'What Are the Consequences of Masking?' This chapter looks at the many ways masking plays out in people's lives, including many of the negative impacts. It ranges from how masking affects the diagnostic process through mental health and work impacts, to what happens when people can no longer maintain the mask. 'Other things to think about' discusses the concept of masking among non-autistic people, and whether neurotypical people are masking too.

The fifth, and final, chapter, 'How Can One Help around Masking for Different Groups?', is about practical guidance around masking. This is not to encourage people to mask, but to think about when and how much to mask can be useful, and how to navigate stopping masking. There are also sections for the families of autistic people, for education and healthcare professionals, and for employers, among others. These sections will look at how to recognize when an autistic person may be masking, and how to support the autistic people in their lives to either not need the mask or to avoid the negative consequences of doing so. 'Other things to think about' looks at the ways in which other neurodiverse people mask, giving an overview of some other ways in which people use masks to help them navigate the world.

There is also a glossary at the end of the book for terms readers may be unfamiliar with.

CHAPTER 1

What Is Masking and Who Does It?

When we say that someone who is autistic is 'masking', we mean that they are using strategies (whether or not they are aware of this) to hide their autistic differences from other people, or to find ways around things that they struggle with because of autism. For example, this could involve forcing themselves to make eye contact with someone when they don't want to, putting on a smile when they are experiencing sensory overload, or practising how to chat to someone new they meet.

In this book we are talking about masking of autistic characteristics. As we will discuss later, people can mask all sorts of different things about themselves – such as their sexuality, mental or physical health difficulties, or even just aspects of their personality. In many cases, this is because that characteristic is associated with stigma, or is otherwise seen as undesirable by other people. We will describe how masking of autism can be different to other types of masking, because of the strategies used, the effort involved, and the impact that it has for the person doing the masking. Autistic people can mask their autism as well as other things about them, and non-autistic people can mask different things about them, including autistic-like traits they might have. Later in the book we will talk about the similarities and differences of masking by autistic and non-autistic people.

A note on language

There are quite a few different words that people use to describe these behaviours. You might hear or see people talking about 'masking', 'compensation' or 'camouflaging'. We (the authors of this book) think that all these words refer to the same idea of hiding aspects of autism and finding strategies to overcome difficulties or differences, but they might be focusing on different strategies or approaches. For instance, 'compensation' is often used to talk about more 'successful' strategies, which produce a difference in behaviour compared to what other people might expect. 'Camouflaging' often refers to all the behaviours involved in changing a person's autistic presentation – whether they are successful or not.

Helen explains her interpretation of the differences between 'camouflaging' and 'masking' as:

> camouflaging is very much about hiding in the background and not being noticed, shying away from the spotlight and 'blending in' with the scenery. Not speaking up, not standing out, not being called upon, not being different. Masking is what takes place when camouflaging isn't possible and instead the survival strategy is about not being recognized as 'different' or 'struggling' and hiding true emotions and responses.

In this book we use the term 'masking' because this is one of the words used most often by autistic people themselves. But a lot of the research and discussion we talk about here uses alternative words. We believe that all these words refer to the same underlying concept, and so we include sources using these words interchangeably.

This book was written during the 2020/21 global COVID-19

pandemic, and during this time the word 'mask' became a lot more common in our everyday language! Many people may think first of protective face masks when they hear the word 'masking', and in the context of autism may think that this refers to the sensory difficulties which mean that some autistic people are not able to wear masks. Ironically, some could argue that by putting the [face] mask on, autistic people are able to take their [social] mask off to a greater extent, as there is less emphasis on facial expressions when talking to other people. However, we still believe that 'masking' is the most appropriate word to use in the context of autistic masking, and hope that our meaning will be clear to readers.

You will have already noticed that we tend to talk about 'autistic people' rather than 'people with autism'. Using this identity-first language is important because it reflects the preferences of the majority of autistic people themselves. Although many clinicians, practitioners, teachers and parents mostly use person-first language (person-with-autism), autistic people have described this as feeling as though they are being separated, or alienated, from autism as a central part of their identity. Although not all autistic people feel this way, and some will have no strong opinion or preference as to which is used to describe them, we want to make this book as respectful as possible and therefore will be using 'autistic person' throughout our writing. However we want to emphasize that when talking about or quoting individuals, we have asked them about their preferences regarding language and use the language they personally prefer, or use the language they use to describe themselves.

We also use the term 'non-autistic person' rather than 'neuro-typical person'. 'Neurotypical' refers to someone whose brain has developed in a typical way – that is, they experience the world in a similar way to most other people. In contrast, 'neurodivergent' refers to someone whose brain has developed in a non-typical way, so they experience the world differently to most people. Some use the term 'neurodiverse' to describe multiple people with multiple types of brain development. We use 'non-autistic' throughout the book because we feel it is important to recognize that autism is not the only form of neurodiversity, and so someone can be non-autistic without being neurotypical. When we are talking about those with other forms of neurodivergence, such as attention deficit hyperactivity disorder (ADHD), we will make this clear so as to avoid any confusion.

A brief history of masking in autism

Who first started talking about masking?

Autistic people have been talking about masking for a while – it took researchers and healthcare professionals a bit longer to start listening!

There have probably been discussions about masking among autistic people for many years. In 1999, Liane Holliday Willey published her book *Pretending to be Normal* (an expanded edition was published in 2015), which described her experiences of growing up and becoming an adult, with undiagnosed Asperger's syndrome. Liane described how she realized she was different to other people, especially other girls, and set about trying to learn how to hide her differences and pretend that she was 'normal' just like everyone else. For example, she describes how she watched other people to learn how they used their faces in interactions: 'I mentally recorded the way they used their eyes, how they would open them wide when they spoke loud and animated, or how they would cast them downwards if they spoke quietly or slowly' (Holliday Willey, 2015, p. 45). These are good examples of masking behaviours, which were sometimes developed on purpose and practised, and other times emerged without Liane even being aware of them.

Although pretending to be normal was sometimes helpful, there were also some unintended consequences for Liane. She found it very difficult to control when and how she masked her autism, and described it as 'very stressful and exhausting' (p. 131). When her younger daughter received an autism diagnosis, Liane realized that she herself experienced many of the same difficulties with understanding other people as her daughter did, and shared some of the sensory preferences and need for routine, which led to Liane receiving her own diagnosis of Asperger's syndrome. In the expanded edition of the book (Holliday Willey, 2015), Liane talks about being happier when she doesn't have to pretend, and much more comfortable with her 'Aspie' self now she has an official diagnosis. As we will discuss later, some autistic people who receive a diagnosis later on in life say that they don't feel as much pressure to mask once they have an explanation for why they are different.

These accounts were some of the first times that masking behaviours were described by an autistic person and shared widely with non-autistic people, although other autistic people have also talked about masking for a long time. Liane described feeling different to other people, and trying to watch them to work out how she was different and how to be less so. She did this even before she knew she was autistic – demonstrating that someone doesn't need to have a formal diagnosis of autism to mask. However, this book also shows that from the very beginning, autistic people have been aware of the demanding and stressful nature of masking. As we will discuss later, this might be one of the key aspects that makes autistic masking different to the social strategies everyone uses to some extent.

As the Internet and social media have developed, it has become easier for autistic people and those who live and work with them to discuss issues affecting them. There are many fantastic autistic self-advocates, many of whom also advocate on behalf of others, who have discussed the concept of masking; indeed, there are too many to mention here! However, if you are interested in learning more about how people talk about masking, we advise following #masking and other hashtags to see a whole range of perspectives on social media. Many autistic people have written blogs and articles, produced Twitter threads, and even made TikTok videos describing their experiences of masking. These are constantly changing and being updated, so rather than recommending specific examples, we suggest you have a look for yourself at what people are currently talking about. You will also see a range of different perspectives on masking, which demonstrates that, as with most interesting and complicated things, there is no single 'autistic opinion' on masking and its consequences.

The camouflage hypothesis

Although researchers and healthcare professionals didn't use the word 'masking' until relatively recently, there has been some awareness that autistic people can hide their autism (whether or not they are aware of doing so), and that this might impact their support and wellbeing. It's also important to emphasize here that some of the researchers and professionals looking into masking are themselves autistic, and so bring both personal and research expertise into their work.

As early as 1981, pioneering autism researcher Lorna Wing described what is known as the 'camouflage hypothesis': the idea that autistic girls might appear to have better social skills than they actually do, because of copying and practising behaviours from other people. This idea was taken up by other researchers, who thought that camouflaging or masking might explain why autistic girls and women can find it harder to receive a diagnosis compared to boys and men. In the 1990s, psychologists described how some autistic girls are able to show 'superficially' good social skills during a brief meeting such as a diagnostic assessment. This means that their true difficulties getting on with other people might not be obvious to someone who doesn't know them well. However, these girls would struggle to fit in with larger groups or other children over longer periods of time. For instance, one girl was described as 'say[ing] all the right things on first meeting new people. However, shortly thereafter she completely ignores them' (Kopp & Gillberg, 1992, p. 95). The researchers noted that these children were interested in meeting and talking to others, and showed some social behaviours, but lacked a 'deeper understanding' of social communication. In other words, they were able to mask some of their autistic characteristics when they first met people, but not for a long time or for more complicated interactions. Research at this time often assumed – whether explicitly or not – that neurotypical social communication and behaviours were the best or only way to interact with others, and therefore masking of autistic behaviours (to appear non-autistic) was a positive outcome. As we will discuss later in the book, this assumption is now challenged by autistic people and others who emphasize authentically autistic ways of communicating.

Other researchers have proposed behaviours through which girls might mask their autism, although until recently there were few attempts to actually look for masking or ask autistic people about it. Around this time there was emerging evidence that it was harder for girls to get an autism diagnosis compared to boys; for instance, girls tend to be diagnosed later on average, and girls with the same level of autistic traits are less likely to get an autism diagnosis compared to boys. Because of this, most of the discussions of masking took place in the context of trying to identify reasons why autistic girls were being missed in clinical settings, and so were focused on behaviours shown by girls and women. As will be discussed later in this chapter, there is still mixed evidence about whether girls and women mask more than boys or men, and whether this is the only reason for diagnostic biases in autism.

As researchers became more interested in understanding the lived experiences of autistic women and girls, descriptions of masking became more and more common. Interviews and focus groups which asked broader questions about late diagnosis, coping strategies, and mental health often brought up examples of masking behaviours. Most of the women and girls interviewed also described, often spontaneously, how exhausting it was to mask their autism. These studies helped to demonstrate to the academic and clinical communities that masking was a real, and relatively common, behaviour that autistic people used. However, there was still no commonly agreed definition of masking, or description of exactly what masking involved.

What is masking?

The descriptions of masking included here are taken from interviews with autistic people (with and without a formal diagnosis of autism), or parents of autistic children, including people who answered questions specifically for this book. We have included the source wherever any direct quotes from published studies are used, and a full list of sources is included at the end of the book. There is also a list at the end of the book of everyone who contributed their experiences, and we have added details about the people we interviewed if they agreed to this. However, it's important to emphasize here that these are just some examples of masking which have been described by some autistic people. Not everyone will do all of these strategies if they do mask, and most people will probably have other strategies that they use when masking which we don't describe here. Throughout the book we will see many examples of how different people mask, and how these may change depending on the situation, the person and who they are with. For now, we will mention some of the more commonly described examples, which can give you a sense of what masking involves.

Different types of masking

There are different types of masking, such as instinctive, subconscious, ingrained, and active masking, among others. Below, we discuss some of these types of masking and how they can be experienced by autistic people. It is worth noting that these subtypes of masking have not all been explored in autism research yet, and these distinctions come more from lived experience accounts than anything else at this point.

Instinctive masking is when a fear response deep in the brain sets off a survival instinct. It can be seen as similar to the way trauma survivors may be hyper-aware of other people nearby, or be hyper-vigilant to possible threats in their area. Some people liken it to the 'freeze' response (of the 'fight, flight, or freeze' trope): the instinct to become still if we see a predator, to not draw attention to ourselves and to wait until the danger has passed. For autistic people, this can be an instinctive move to hide their distress or pain when they are in a position of stress or risk.

Subconscious masking is developed in reaction to someone's life history – it is the mask that they have created and internalized to a point that they don't think about it, particularly around specific triggers. These are often related to a historical trauma (something that happened to them or something they witnessed), which does not have to fit the traditional concepts of 'trauma' for neurotypical people. Examples could include being reprimanded or belittled for stimming in school by a teacher, or having a meltdown in public resulting in a negative reaction from an authority figure, which are then embedded in memory. When the autistic person later sees a teacher, or a similar authority figure, this can act as a trigger for a flashback, which reinforces the perception that to (re)act authentically is 'Not A Good Idea'. This can lead to reactions becoming stilted and frozen as the autistic person fights their natural actions, smothering them and creating the first 'blank' mask.

Ingrained masking can be mistaken for instinctive masking, but it is essentially a learned response – something that was at one point a conscious choice, but which has become an embedded 'subroutine' in an autistic person's brain. This leads to it becoming their default response to a situation or trigger. Ingrained masking of natural behaviour or response is something that can be led by social expectations – the supressing of a burp, the polite smile when a drunken person tries to make conversation, the projected calm of a driver pulled over by the police. It is likely that a lot of the long-term impacts of masking on autistic people's mental health come from a combination of this ingrained masking and the conscious masking described below.

Conscious masking is the active recognition that the current situation is not comfortable, does not feel like a safe place to be your authentic self, or requires a specific way of presenting yourself for some reason. An autistic person may then feel that that they need to engage with masking strategies to get through the situation until they can leave and get to somewhere they feel safe to drop that mask. This type of masking involves processing and reflecting on the situation, recognizing that it is in some way difficult, actively choosing what masking strategies to deploy, and working out how to extract themselves without drawing unwanted attention – often the whole point of the mask in the first place.

Hiding your autism

One of the main ways people can mask is simply by trying to hide aspects of their autism from other people. This might be done consciously or without even being aware of it; as we will learn in the next chapter, many autistic people may have learned to mask automatically, even before they knew they were autistic. We will see more of the reasons why autistic people might feel the need to mask later in the book.

Hiding your autism can involve stopping yourself from doing things that make you seem autistic, or just seem different to other people because of your autism. Autistic people often act or interact in ways which are different to non-autistic people, and so just by being yourself you can seem different. For instance, some people have described stopping themselves from stimming (moving their body in repetitive ways which can be calming, exciting, or express emotion). Some people try to keep their body still when they want to stim, or find other ways to meet sensory needs, such as fiddling with their hair. Many people might use fiddle toys or other stimming toys because these are seen as more appropriate or acceptable ways to stim, even if they would rather be moving their body differently. Others change the way that they are stimming so that it draws less attention to them.

> If I start to stim or move 'oddly' I stop myself, and I remember how others move and act and try and do that myself. Even things like using hand movements when I speak or the intonation of my voice. I'm so self-conscious of every little movement I make and what others will think of it. (Hannah, female, 31)

> This [demonstrates hand flapping], works a lot better but it gets people's attention a lot more so we don't do this [hand flapping], we do this [demonstrates hand-wringing], it's a lot more socially acceptable. (Quoted in Cook *et al.*, 2021, p. 5)

Some people describe how they need to hide their sensory responses to the environment, because the way they react is different to other people and so draws attention. For example, if the noises in a classroom are distracting or disturbing to a child, they might want to cover their hands with their ears. But if they do this, other children, or even teachers, might point out that they are reacting differently to other people, or tell them off. Instead, they pretend not to be distracted by the noise, even if it causes them pain or distress. Using tools such as earplugs or noise-cancelling headphones can also serve as a mask, as they might not be visibly obvious to other people (e.g. earplugs), or could look like things that non-autistic people also use (e.g. wearing noise-cancelling headphones without music playing, but which make it look like the person is just listening to music). Other people want to hide any kind of difference from people around them, such as not telling people they are autistic or trying to hide the support and adaptations they might need.

> During adolescence I started to try to hide my autism. Even if all the class knew, I still tried not to let them see me getting help. Not letting them see that if I miss class, the assistant will make photocopies for me. I would even pay money to photocopy, only to avoid getting help from the assistant. (Quoted in Schneid & Raz, 2020, p. 4)

Who do you want me to be?

Many autistic people have described masking as 'putting on a character': hiding behind the behaviours and characteristics of someone who isn't autistic. This could be a real person who the autistic person is mimicking or copying, or a persona that they have developed of how they think other people want them to be. The characteristics of the character or role might change depending on the situation, so that the autistic person feels they have the skills or characteristics needed for that particular situation.

> I honed something of a persona which was kind of bubbly and vivacious, and maybe a bit dim, because I had nothing to say other than adult novels. So I cultivated an image, I suppose, that I brought out to social situations as my partner's girlfriend, that was not 'me'. (Quoted in Bargiela, Steward & Mandy, 2016, p. 3278)

> When I am in a group there is no stillness. I have to be the alpha male. Like, taking the role of the actor, or the instructor, or the Emcee, or the mediator. And to take over. Or I reduce myself, like, to the point of suppressing my reactions. (Quoted in Schneid & Raz, 2020, p. 4)

As this person describes, another way to mask through a character is just to shut down your responses – so to replace everything with a 'blank mask'. This might be something that the person does without being able to control it, similarly to a burnout or shutdown; they might not even be aware that they are doing this. However, it can be a masking strategy to stop people responding negatively to that person looking autistic.

One parent described how her daughter would mask this way at school, changing from her more authentic and emotional self to wearing a calm, quiet mask:

> The minute she got in the [school] door I remember that Jane would immediately change, you could see her physically change from being upset and angry to being almost like these mannequins. (Quoted in Anderson *et al.*, 2020, p. 1550)

And this has also been described by autistic people themselves, putting on a smile no matter how they are feeling because other people don't understand their actual emotional experiences:

> I do hide many of my emotions and I'm used to like having a smile on my face. (Quoted in Tierney, Burns & Kilbey, 2016, p. 79)

> I still think what I like, but mask it behind a smile. (Quoted in Baldwin & Costley, 2016, p. 490)

This character or mask can be something that involves the whole body, or it can just apply to some parts of behaviour. For instance, many autistic people describe copying how other people talk or move their bodies, in order to present themselves in ways which seem less autistic. Again, this might not be something that they are consciously aware of, until they talk to other people and realize that this is not something that non-autistic people tend to do, or until someone else points it out to them.

> I honestly didn't know I was doing it until I was diagnosed, but when I read about it, it made perfect sense. I copy speech patterns and certain body language. (Quoted in Bargiela *et al.*, 2016, p. 3287)

Mimicking of other people's characteristics can be as specific as copying the way someone else laughs, smiles, or walks. Some autistic people who mask will use television, films or books to try to learn about specific behaviours that they can incorporate into their character.

This person talked about how they identified a colleague's laugh as a characteristic that people seemed to like, and so mimicked it even though they didn't like the sound of the laugh themselves:

> I used to hate her laugh because it used to give me a headache but everyone seemed to really like her and they always used to say things like, 'Oh, she's so happy, she's so funny,' and I thought, 'Oh, maybe I will try and make myself a bit more like her.' So I changed my laugh and I started practising my laugh to make it a bit more like hers. (Quoted in Cook *et al.*, 2021, p. 6)

Some people also mask by not talking about things that could 'give them away' as being autistic – such as their interests, if these are more intense or focused on more unusual topics that most non-autistic people's interests. They might pretend to find it less interesting than they do, or use a mental 'timer' to stop talking about that interest after a certain amount of time, even if they want to keep on talking.

> I don't often feel able to talk about the things that interest me so I have to try to adapt to other people's interests and conversations. (Helen, female, 54)

Compensating for difficulties or differences

Another way that many autistic people have described masking their autism is by identifying aspects of social interaction they struggle with, and trying to find ways around these difficulties. Some people may not feel they have social difficulties, but their methods of communication and interaction might be different to those of most non-autistic people and so they feel the need to adapt what they do to make others happy.

One of the most common examples of this is making eye contact when talking to someone – this is something that many non-autistic people expect to happen automatically. However, many autistic people find this hard or painful, or just don't do it automatically. Often autistic people have been told by others from a young age that they 'should' be making eye contact, and so they will put a lot of effort into forcing themselves to look people in the eye, or finding ways to give the impression of making eye contact without actually having to do this.

> Someone said to me, you never make eye contact, you look really shifty. So, I had to train myself to do eye contact. (Quoted in Cook *et al.*, 2021, p. 6)

> I look in people's eyes when I first meet them...even though I wouldn't naturally, because I know you're supposed to. (Quoted in Hull *et al.*, 2017, p. 2526)

Some autistic people might find themselves doing this without ever being aware that it is a 'mask', but still notice that they have to change the way they would naturally make eye contact because it is different to other people. As one anonymous contributor to the book said:

I'm pretty sure that my use of eye contact, in everyday living, is unusual… I'm aware of having to think about eye contact, deliberately, and prefer not to deliberately make eye contact.

Similarly, autistic people's facial expressions can sometimes be different to non-autistic people's, appearing more or less expressive when feeling a specific emotion. Some autistic people try to mask this by practising their facial expressions, often spending hours in front of the mirror trying to look 'right'. In some cases, people have told them that they look rude, or bored, or uninterested because they don't show the same facial expressions as most non-autistic people. As a response, they might make a conscious effort to smile, nod or change facial expressions regularly in order to look more like a non-autistic person.

They might also pay attention to their body language, holding themselves in certain positions which are considered appropriate (such as sitting cross-legged when they would rather spread their legs wide), or try to mirror the body language of the person they are talking to as a cue for what is acceptable. For instance, if the autistic person isn't sure what to do with their arms when talking to someone, they might use the other person's body language as a guide, only crossing their arms or using gestures when the other person has done so first. Some people have described masking using gestures, for example by learning gestures that are common in a certain culture and putting them into movements (whether or not they are aware of doing this consciously at the time).

It is important to point out here that this might be something that is uncomfortable or tiring for the autistic person, and in some cases could even lead to misunderstandings with others, because the autistic person is showing an emotion that they don't actually feel. One interviewee for our book said:

> I've been asked if I'm drunk or 'slow' or if I'm a cop or attracted to someone, because I tend to watch the people around me. (Cheyenne, female, 29)

We will discuss this more later in the book, when we consider some of the unintended consequences of masking. Other people may not mind putting the effort into making these deliberate facial or body language expressions, except that it is not what they would naturally do in that situation.

Sounding different

In addition to masking by trying to look more typical, some autistic people also mask how autistic they sound when talking to others. In many cases this involves developing lists or rules to follow during conversations, such as only talking for a certain amount of time and then waiting to see if the other person speaks.

> I'm not good at knowing when it's my turn and I also tend to just blurt out things or keep talking when I should have stopped, so I prep myself always in social situations to have a reminder...about not speaking too much and trying to do more listening, nodding, agreeing. (Quoted in Hull *et al.*, 2017, p. 2526)

Some people have developed rules about what they are willing to talk about, such as not going into too much detail about things they are interested in. This might be because having strong interests is seen as a characteristic of autism, and so others might think that the level of detail is unusual. There are also 'safe topics' which can be discussed. In Britain, the weather is usually a safe topic for small talk! Some autistic people are happy to stick to these topics in order to not have to worry about sharing too much information about themselves. Others, however, find these topics boring or pointless and so might choose a few specific topics that they enjoy talking about, but which are still unoffensive to the other person.

Non-autistic people often assume that others are interested in them and might be upset if an autistic person doesn't respond in an empathic or compassionate way. As one interviewee describes, they mask by saying what other people expect from them:

> When masking I tend to say things I don't mean, like trying to empathise with someone when I really don't care (!) but I know it's the right thing to say or do. (Jessica, female, 36)

Many autistic people have described asking questions as a way to remove the focus of a conversation from themselves, or as a reminder in case they have been talking for a long time without the other person contributing.

> I did my usual party trick of she asks me a question and I just flip it back and I give her answers and flip it back say, 'and you?' It's my way of keeping the conversation going. (Quoted in Cook *et al.*, 2021, p. 6)

This can mask some of the awkwardness or uncertainty felt during a conversation, and also has the 'bonus' of demonstrating that the autistic person is a great listener! However, there is a risk that if the autistic person always asks questions about other people, they are not able to share things that are important or meaningful for themselves.

Some people who mask will go as far as thinking about the sound of their voice when talking to others. Sometimes this is because of comments from other people that they 'sound like a robot', or because the person is aware of the stereotype that autistic people talk in a monotone. One person in a study described trying to control the tone of their voice to better fit non-autistic communication styles:

> What I'm trying to do is to smooth my tone of voice out...and make it sound less choppy which seems closer to what most neurotypical people do. (Quoted in Cook *et al.*, 2021, p. 6)

If an autistic person struggles to think of what to say during a conversation, or gets panicked when under pressure, they might also mask this by preparing anecdotes, questions for others, or just phrases to respond with.

> I repeat myself or use tv/film phrases and sometimes say things which are out of place. (Quoted in Livingston, Shah & Happé, 2019, p. 771)

This can sometimes work well, if the 'script' they have prepared is appropriate for the situation. In other cases it can create more issues in communication. For instance, an autistic person might have prepared some phrases to use in a certain situation ('What a beautiful day for a wedding, everyone looks so happy.'). If the person they are talking to suddenly starts talking about something else ('Did you hear that Auntie Beth is getting divorced?'), the prepared phrase is no longer relevant but the autistic person might not have the capacity to think of something else to say in that instant.

As with many of the examples described here, masking during conversations requires a lot of effort to plan, remember what is happening, and adapt if the situation changes or the masking strategy is no longer appropriate.

Using autistic strengths

A final category of masking behaviours is using one's natural skills to help overcome one's difficulties. Many autistic people have fantastic memories and so rely on learning and remembering information about social interactions in order to think of what to do in a certain context.

> I have a very good memory so I can...relate that to a situation the other person's in... I sort of used that memory and just associated with what she knew. (Quoted in Tierney *et al.*, 2016, p. 79)

For some people, using these memorizing skills can work so well that they may not even realize they are using memorized information during social interactions. These learned behaviours might be easier and less effortful to use, compared to behaviours that require a lot of active thought to achieve. However, even if someone has been using a learned behaviour for a long time, if it doesn't feel authentic or genuine for that person they may still feel uncomfortable using the behaviour.

Another skill that can be used when masking is observation – a common autistic strength is being very observant and able to identify small details that others may not notice. Some autistic people use their skills in observation to watch other people interact and work out the details of how they are doing this. When they have understood the components of an interaction, they might then try using some of the strategies previously described, such as mimicry of certain behaviours, developing rules to follow, or putting on certain facial expressions, in order to try the interaction for themselves.

[I mask by...] Attempting to match my responses to studied and memorized patterns of NT [neurotypical] behaviour informed by reading about human psychology and social behaviour and asking NT friends to explain and propose useful 'stock' responses to be used in future following failures in challenging situations. (Paula, autistic non-binary person, 64)

One mother who was interviewed described how her daughter would watch other children playing and observe all the components of their game and how they interacted before trying to use some of these herself:

They really do they learn how to be a chameleon...if the kids were playing a game Victoria would stand on the edge watch, work out the rules like social rules as well as the physical rules and then go into the situation. (Quoted in Anderson *et al.*, 2020, p. 1551)

The behaviours we have described here are just a few examples of the kinds of masking strategies that people might use. Some of them may be familiar to you, and some may be strategies that you have never thought of, or don't consider to be part of masking. Every person's experience of masking is different, and so rather than trying to list every possible masking behaviour, we think it is more important to understand what masking means for a certain person within a specific context. However, examples of masking can be useful when trying to explain what masking is to someone who might not have considered it before, or when looking at similarities and differences across multiple people. This, however, relies on being able to measure masking which, as we will see, is not as straightforward as it sounds...

How to identify when and how much someone is masking

In order to understand more about masking and its impact on people, it is important to be able to measure masking behaviours. The most obvious, and easiest way to tell when and how much someone is masking is to ask them! The person themselves may have a very good sense of when they mask, how much they do it and the different ways they mask their autism. This is particularly helpful if they want support in managing their masking behaviours, because that support can be targeted to their individual needs and experiences. However, some people might not be able to tell others how much they mask. This could be because they don't communicate in ways that can express masking behaviours fully (for instance, if they have little spoken or written language), or because they aren't aware of all or some of their masking behaviours. In addition, people have different definitions of what masking is, and so some people might describe behaviours or strategies which they think of as being part of masking, but that others don't. For instance, one person might say that they mask by pretending to be happy even if they are feeling overwhelmed. Another person might disagree and say that, for them, masking just involves hiding their stimming behaviours when they are in public. Neither of these people is wrong, as masking is a very personal behaviour – but their own definitions might not apply to each other. As with other aspects of autism, one person's experience can't necessarily be used to represent other people's experiences, so it is useful to talk to a wide range of people to try to understand what masking 'is'.

Therefore, it is helpful to have ways to measure masking other than asking a person about their masking behaviours. These measurements should be accurate (they definitely measure masking, and not other behaviours) and reliable (they measure masking in the same way across different people and different situations). Accuracy and reliability are two of the most important characteristics of any measurement, so that we can trust what we measure. For instance, a thermometer needs to be accurate (it should tell you the correct temperature) and reliable (it should give you the same result each time you measure the same thing). If you have a thermometer which tells you that a pot of boiling water is 25 degrees Celsius, but tells someone else that the boiling water is 300 degrees Celsius, it's not a very useful thermometer! This is why we need to test that the ways we measure masking are accurate and reliable, so the measures can be used to help people.

Measurement: Internal versus external

There are two main ways to measure masking that have been developed by doctors and researchers so far. One is to look at the difference between someone's internal autistic experiences (how autistic they feel inside) and their external behaviours (how they appear to other people). If someone experiences a lot of autistic characteristics, but these aren't always visible to other people, that is evidence that they are masking their autism. In contrast, someone who shows a lot of behaviours associated with autism, and also reports high levels of thoughts, feelings and experiences that we associate with autism, might not be masking much or at all. This is similar to measuring temperature by looking at what happens when two substances are combined: if a frozen ice lolly melts when put into a mug of hot water, this suggests that the difference in temperature is pretty big. In contrast, if a cold sauce is added to a bowl of ice cream there might be no change to either, suggesting that the temperature difference is very small.

Several researchers have come up with different methods for measuring autism in this way. For instance, one study by Meng-Chuan Lai and colleagues (2017) measured masking by comparing how many autistic traits someone reports, using a questionnaire and a task to measure emotion recognition abilities, and the number of autistic behaviours a doctor identified when interviewing them. The greater the difference between the internal experience (number of autistic traits) and the external behaviour (autistic behaviours identified by a doctor), the more someone is masking. If someone has no difference, or reports fewer autistic traits compared to the amount of autistic behaviours they displayed, this suggests they do not mask their autism.

Measuring masking by looking at the difference between internal and external experiences is often known as a 'discrepancy' method of measurement, because any discrepancy between internal and external experiences is evidence of masking occurring. This can be used to measure masking in a very broad sense, such as demonstrating a discrepancy between autistic characteristics displayed by a person across different situations. If they show more autistic characteristics in one situation than another, this suggests they might be masking their autism in one of those situations. For instance, you could compare how many autistic characteristics a child's parents describe them as having to the number of autistic characteristics reported by that child's teachers. If the teachers tend to report lower autistic traits than the parents, that might be because the child is masking their autism at school and feels able to drop the mask when they get home.

The discrepancy method can also be used to measure particular types of masking. For instance, researchers measured typical use of language in speech, and found that that some autistic girls showed evidence of masking by using 'filled pauses' (saying 'um' and 'uh' during a conversation) in the same way as non-autistic girls, even though they had higher levels of parent-report communication difficulties than the non-autistic girls. Using filled pauses is a way to keep the conversation going that many non-autistic people do without thinking (for instance, if you want to indicate to the other person that you haven't finished what you were going to say yet), but it is less common in autistic people. This suggests that although their overall experience of autism was high (as identified by their parents), these girls were masking some aspects of their autism when talking to other people (as measured by how they used 'um' or 'uh'). Masking, as measured through the discrepancy method, can represent very specific strategies as well as the entire way a person presents themselves.

The discrepancy method is helpful because it can measure masking strategies that people might not even be aware of, such as changing behaviour in different situations or using specific communication strategies. This suggests that it is accurate (one of the key features of any good measurement tool), because it isn't impacted by the additional factor of the person's self-awareness. Some early evidence suggests that this method is also reliable, as it produces similar results to other methods of measuring camouflaging.

However, the discrepancy method also assumes that we have an accurate and reliable way to measure how autistic someone 'really is', compared to how autistic they look at a surface level. At the moment there are no ways to identify autism biologically (e.g. from someone's brain activity, or by testing their blood). We can only identify how autistic someone is from what they tell us about their experiences (which can be tricky if they have communication difficulties, or they are a very young child), or by looking at their behaviour (including asking someone else about their behaviour, such as a parent or teacher). If someone is not aware of their autistic experiences, for example because they do not realize they are different to most other people, they might not tell anyone about them. Similarly, if someone is masking their autism (whether or not they are aware of what they are doing), their behaviour might not look 'autistic enough' to be identified as such. This creates an issue for measuring masking in this way; we don't know for sure how autistic someone 'really' is, so we can't tell how different their behaviour might be to their 'true' autism. At the moment, we can only use proxies for measuring how autistic someone truly is – and these proxies may not be completely accurate or reliable themselves. That means that the accuracy and reliability of the discrepancy method is still unknown.

Another issue is that this method only measures successful masking strategies; that is, those that make someone appear less autistic to others. Many autistic people say that although they try to mask a lot, it's not always successful. People might also change how, and how much, they mask across different situations, and so behaviour in one situation (such as a doctor's office) might not reflect the person's masking in another situation (such as at school). It is therefore also important to measure attempts to mask, since they can still take a lot of effort and have an impact on people's wellbeing.

Measurement: Self-report

One way to measure masking that takes into account unsuccessful masking attempts is to ask people to report their own masking behaviours using a questionnaire. The answers can be compared across different people and times, but also allow autistic people to share their individual experiences of masking. One such questionnaire which has been used in research and by healthcare professionals is the Camouflaging Autistic Traits Questionnaire (CAT-Q; Hull *et al.*, 2018). The CAT-Q was developed by Laura as part of her PhD – but it is freely available for everyone to use, and other questionnaires are available! You can add up the person's answers to get an overall 'camouflaging score', which will tell you how much the person masks compared to other people. You can also use the CAT-Q as the start of a discussion about masking, to identify which masking behaviours the person uses and the impact these have.

The CAT-Q has been shown to have good reliability. It was first tested in adults with and without a diagnosis of autism, and was found to measure masking in the same way in both groups. This is important because (1) it means that people don't need to have a formal diagnosis of autism to measure their masking behaviour, and (2) it means scores on the CAT-Q can be compared between autistic and non-autistic people. Autistic people do score higher on the CAT-Q overall, but the ways in which they answer the questions seem to be the same as for non-autistic people. This measure also has good test-retest reliability, meaning it produces similar scores when the same people complete it at different time points. Finally, initial research suggests that the CAT-Q is also accurate. The amount of masking identified by the CAT-Q for a person is similar to the amount of masking identified through a discrepancy method for that person, which suggests that they are both measuring the same underlying concept of masking (this research has not yet been peer reviewed). There are also other questionnaires to measure masking, and more research is needed to compare and improve different methods of measurement.

The CAT-Q and other questionnaires can be helpful to get a (relatively) quick estimate of someone's masking behaviours, and can be used to compare masking across many different people and draw broader conclusions.

However, the main problem with using any questionnaire to measure masking is that the person completing the questionnaire has to be aware of their masking behaviours, and able to communicate them on the questionnaire. If someone has very little spoken or written language, or has an intellectual disability, they might not be able to describe the masking behaviours they use to other people. There might be other people who, despite having very good language abilities, are not at all aware of their masking strategies and so can't describe to other people what they are doing.

Because of this, it might be helpful to combine different ways to measure masking. However, this is often time-consuming, and some of the methods, which involve brain scans or behavioural assessments, can be expensive to complete. For now, we suggest that people use whichever methods they think are best to identify when, how and how much they are masking their autism. For many people, this might just involve talking about masking with someone else.

No matter how masking is measured, it can be helpful to have a record of how much someone masks in different situations, and which strategies they use. As we will discuss in Chapter 5, this can be used by an autistic person to evaluate their own masking behaviours and have more control over how much they mask and when. It can also be helpful for healthcare professionals, including those who are involved in the autism diagnostic process. If a person doesn't 'look' very autistic during an assessment, but reports that they are masking a lot of autistic characteristics, healthcare professionals should evaluate them more carefully. By measuring masking we can also identify people who might be at greater risk than others of mental health problems – either because they mask more than they want to, or because they experience negative consequences of not masking. This will be discussed further in Chapter 4.

Who masks? (What we know and what we don't)

As we previously described, researchers and healthcare professionals first became interested in masking as a possible explanation for the under-diagnosis of autism in women and girls. This means that most of the early research focused on masking by girls and women with a formal diagnosis of autism. Participants in these studies were usually people who did not have intellectual disability or difficulties with spoken language, and who had received a formal diagnosis of autism in adolescence or adulthood. For instance, in some of the first interview studies, participants were women who had been diagnosed with autism in adulthood, or adolescent girls who had mostly been diagnosed in later childhood/adolescence, and their parents. However, as researchers became more interested in understanding what masking is, they conducted research across a variety of different groups. At the same time, researchers and healthcare professionals began to listen more to what autistic people from many different groups and identities were saying about masking – although a lot more listening still needs to take place!

We now know that many different autistic people mask. Online surveys which have included both formally diagnosed and self-diagnosed autistic people demonstrate that a large proportion of people who respond to the survey say that they mask, or have masked their autism, at some time. As described at the beginning of this chapter, people use many different words to describe what they do, including 'masking', 'camouflaging', 'compensating' and many others. People have also identified masking using a range of different strategies, some of which they might only identify as masking retrospectively. So the strategies that some people use might not be considered as masking by other people, which can make it hard to compare between different people.

The largest online surveys so far suggest that up to 94 per cent of autistic people who took part have masked their autism at some point. However, it is important to emphasize that these studies only include people who can complete online surveys, and who can identify and describe their own behaviours. There are probably more people who mask their autism without being at all aware of it, or who have not yet been able to communicate how they mask to researchers. On the other hand, there are also some people who say that they do not mask their autism at all. This might be because they don't feel the need to, because they have deliberately chosen not to mask, or because they don't know how to mask, even if they want to. It is important that we also think about autistic people who do not mask, and consider how their experiences and outcomes are different to people who do mask.

In particular, we still know very little about how much masking is done by people who are autistic and have an intellectual disability. People with very high levels of support needs are less likely to mask those specific needs, partly due to it being harder to mask those needs (such as support needs around caring for yourself), and because they might find it harder to mask in general. However, we don't know how much autistic people with high support needs, including intellectual disability, might mask other aspects of their autism, or might use masking behaviours to some extent. More research and enquiry are essential to make sure we are including a broader range of autistic people in our understanding of masking.

It is also important to include people who have limited verbal or written communication. These people might mask some of their communication difficulties or differences, or might mask other aspects of their autism in similar or different ways to autistic people with good verbal and written communication. One way to do this is to make sure we are measuring masking through a variety of different ways. Some people might show their masking behaviours if they can't express them verbally, while other people might describe (through any form of communication) masking attempts that have a significant impact on them, but aren't visible to other people. As we will discuss in Chapter 5, it is important that those who are supporting an autistic person with high support needs also consider how much that person might be masking some aspects of their experiences.

Are there differences in masking across genders?

To be clear, here when we talk about 'gender' we mean the social identities that are constructed by people and by society, based on socially shared gender norms. People who are raised as or perceived as being one gender might identify as another, but still experience gendered social norms. For many people, their gender identity is consistent with the way they were identified at birth, usually based on their physical characteristics (their 'sex') – these people would be described as cisgender. If someone's gender identity is different to the way they were identified at birth – including having a fluid gender identity, or not identifying as any specific gender – they might be described as transgender. Most of the research in this area looks either at sex (without asking people about their gender identity), or gender (where people are asked about and grouped by their gender identity). But in all cases it is impossible to quantify exactly how much different people have been influenced by gender norms, and so we have to acknowledge that both sex and gender likely play a role when we talk about gender differences.

There has been a lot of research comparing masking across different genders, and there is no clear answer as to whether people of different genders mask at different levels. When people are asked to report whether or not they mask at all, most studies find no difference between males and females. However, some studies have found differences in how much people of different genders mask in specific ways. For instance, autistic women self-reported more masking than men in one study, although another study found no difference between male and female self-reported masking. Other studies that look at the impact of masking on behaviour have found that autistic women and girls tend to show behaviours more similar to non-autistic women and girls, despite having similar levels of autistic traits to autistic men and boys. Although most studies so far have only included people who identify as either male or female, some research by Laura and others suggests that people who identify as a non-binary or fluid gender also mask at high levels, similar to or even higher than those of women and girls.

Currently there is not enough research to give a definite answer to the question of gender differences in masking. If there are differences between males' and females' masking, these are likely to be relatively small. Autistic men and boys still mask at higher levels than non-autistic people, and so are still likely to experience the consequences of masking, including the impact on mental health and wellbeing (which will be discussed in Chapter 4).

Personal piece: Jack Howes, on masking, society and masculinity

Society's expectations around masculinity have been both a curse and a blessing.

I have had the remarkable good fortune to be a sport obsessive from the day I was born. I am a lifelong Tottenham fan and my very earliest memories consist of being surrounded by Spurs memorabilia: posters, duvet covers, videos, books, T-shirts – you name it, I had it. Sport was always on TV and radio in my house. I developed my literacy skills and vocabulary from reading weighty encyclopaedias about football, dull cricketers' autobiographies, the sports section in *The Times* every day, even Teletext. I can still tell you the Teletext page numbers for football, cricket and rugby (302, 340 and 370 respectively).

This has brought with it huge advantages throughout my life. As a collective, men are not always the most sociable, perhaps because we are under less gendered pressure to be social creatures. As an autistic person of course, socializing and making friends is often an even harder task, given our neurological and communicative differences.

Having a love of football was a huge help, especially when I was at school. While I may not have possessed easy charm or Wildean wit, a football and some shirts and jumpers for goalposts were all I needed to make friends with people. Being autistic didn't matter when you scored the winning goal before the bell rang for the end of lunchtime. At primary and secondary school, I made almost all of my friends through impromptu games of football and happening to join in.

A few years ago now, I was in of all places a minibus, travelling from Bergamo airport to Milan city centre at around midnight, cursing the lack of public transport infrastructure in Northern Italy. I had got a late flight from Stansted and was hoping to reach my hotel in Milan at a not utterly ridiculous hour. On this minibus, speeding across dull Italian motorways, I heard English voices around me and could pick up words such as 'Yeovil', 'Colchester', 'Crewe', 'Accrington Stanley'. I started listening in, answered a question someone posed, and before I knew it I was engrossed in a conversation about that day's lower-league football results, on this dated minibus somewhere in the nether regions of Italy.

There is an expectation of men, particularly working-class

WHAT IS MASKING AND WHO DOES IT?

men, to enjoy sport and pints down the pub. I love sport and a few pints! My perfect day would consist of watching Spurs, and a few pints at the Antwerp Arms beforehand. Booze acts as a relaxant and social stimulant, also engendering a camaraderie and sense of togetherness with others. On a match day, walking up to the stadium, I'm not autistic – I'm simply a Spurs fan.

Football crowds are often cruel and prejudiced. Misogyny is one of those existing prejudices. However, at Spurs anyway, an autistic male with some masking capabilities is largely welcomed. While this is worthy of wider and more lengthy discourse, the whole essence of football supporting is incredibly autistic in nature. Football fans can recall obscure names, games and goals from decades ago with alacrity. In the lower leagues, many fans try to visit all 92 league grounds and develop remarkable knowledge of pubs, train stations, motorway service stations and more. Thousands of people's lives, up and down the UK, are reliant on the structure that football brings. Does that sound neurodivergent to anyone?

Where I wildly differ from the gendered norms is with my attitudes and feelings towards sex and romance. There of course exists the fundamentally sexist dynamic whereby women who are openly sexual and express sexual desire are perceived as sluts, slappers and worse while those who do not express their sexuality so explicitly are mocked and abused for being frigid. For men, being sexually active is good and normal, indeed acting as a badge of honour. Men are supposedly these priapic creatures, boasting the sexual sophistication of donkeys, aroused by the merest whiff of a breast or a bum. This is somehow seen as healthy and positive.

I have little interest in sex. I remember as a child playing football with other kids down my street, most of whom were a few years older than me. I remember a friend showing me some pictures of a naked woman, with the expectation I would find this hugely arousing. Well, it could have been a picture of a packet of Wotsits for all I knew or cared. To this day, pictures of naked women do absolutely nothing for me. I have had a few opportunities down the years to take things further with women and, on each occasion, my fears and anxieties overwhelmed any desires I may have had.

Sexuality, both statistically and anecdotally, is far more fluid among autistic people. While mostly straight, I did a few years ago drunkenly leave a rather racy note for a male bartender when England had just been knocked out of the World Cup by Croatia. I've always thought Fernando Torres was cute as hell. I have little desire to label myself, but whatever I am, I don't meet heterosexual norms.

I have always found this tricky. I've had to feign interest in women, often becoming more outrageous in conversation to somehow show my macho credentials when ultimately I have little interest in flirting or chatting someone up. At other points I have simply opted out of such conversations – when I'm surrounded by men discussing their dating lives and sexual conquests, I quite literally have nothing to add. I don't have a romantic or sexualized life and frequently have to give the impression I do, just to fit in and not seem like an oddball.

I can be autistic and that be fine. But not wanting to shag everything in sight? That is just too weird.

Looking at differences between broad groups, such as between different genders, may not be very useful at helping individuals who mask. This is because there is so much variation between individual people in terms of how they mask, how much and the impact it has on them. Group differences are interesting for research, and can be helpful for identifying groups who may be at risk for specific negative outcomes. However, for practical, day-to-day support, it is better to look at the individual person themselves to consider how best to support them.

When do people start masking?

The question of when autistic people start masking is one that doesn't have a definitive answer in the existing literature. And it is likely to be quite individual, with some people being unable to remember a time when they haven't done some masking, and some people starting it later in life as a conscious way to help them navigate the world. Both of these are legitimate autistic experiences of masking, and, similarly, some people will pick and choose how and when to mask strategically, to gain the most advantage in a given situation.

What we do know is that autistic girls show evidence of 'linguistic camouflaging' from as young as 5 years old. This is a term used by Julia Parish-Morris and colleagues (2017) to describe the act of autistic girls using the same type of 'filler words' ('um' or 'uh') when speaking as their female peers, whereas they found that autistic boys used filler words which were more unique to themselves than similar to non-autistic boys. This research did not investigate whether this was done consciously by their young participants, but it has been taken as a sign that girls may be more socially aware of how their peers are talking and want to fit in with them more. This is consistent with research, including some by Felicity (Sedgewick *et al.*, 2015), which has shown that autistic girls are more socially motivated (i.e. more driven to take part in social activities and relationships) than autistic boys.

Autistic people who mask often report that they began masking in childhood or adolescence. Some people say that they have been masking for as long as they can remember, while others can identify a specific age at which they began masking. For many people, this was around the time that they began to realize they were different to people around them. This might be because they noticed differences between themselves and others, or because other people told them that they were acting differently, and that this was a bad thing. For example, some adults say that they remember their parents telling them not to stim, or remember other children at school telling them they were weird. As a result, many autistic people describe how they became more aware of their own behaviours, and tried to change them in order to seem more normal, from very early on.

Other people say that they only started masking their autism later on in life. Some people say that they were aware they were different to other people, but didn't know how to change their behaviour until they were taught or shown examples of other ways to act. For example, some people say that having drama lessons at school showed them they could change the way that their bodies and faces move to express different emotions. Other people describe watching TV shows and films to try to learn how people act in different situations, or watching people around them, such as other children at school, to identify socially acceptable ways to behave. These people often said that they then spent a lot of time practising by themselves, rehearsing what to say and how to act, before trying to mask around other people.

Many autistic people who were diagnosed relatively early in childhood have had some sort of social skills training. There are many different types of social skills training, some of which are considered helpful by most people, such as teaching someone how to look after themselves and get around; while others are more controversial and may include behavioural learning and reinforcement of certain behaviours. We still don't know much about how social skills training relates to masking. Some autistic people who took part in social skills training say they have used some of the strategies they learned there while masking, whereas other people say that their masking behaviours developed separately. As we will discuss in Chapter 4, there are many potentially negative consequences of masking your autism. It is therefore important to be cautious about social skills interventions which try to change someone's behaviour to meet non-autistic social norms, as we don't know what kind of impact this might have for them in the longer term.

Most research into masking has included adults, and has either been focused on their current masking, or has asked them to try to remember masking from earlier in their lives. So we know that most autistic adults who take part in these research studies do mask, or have masked, at some point. There has also been some research including teenagers and younger children, which provides evidence of masking even if the children can't describe it themselves. For instance, one study by Dean, Harwood and Kasari (2017), looked at children aged 5–8 years in the playground and how they played with each other. The researchers found that autistic boys tended to play by themselves, and were very obviously separate to other children. In contrast, autistic girls would play next to or near other children, or would try to join in their games. This gave the impression, on first glance, that they were able to fit in and play with the other children. However, a closer look showed that the autistic girls were still struggling to integrate in the way that the non-autistic children did, as they were not actually being included in the games. The researchers suggested that this is evidence for autistic girls masking their autism, even if they weren't explicitly aware of doing so. We need more research looking at children from very early on as they grow up, to try to identify exactly when they might start masking their autism and what sort of impact it has on their development.

Throughout childhood and adolescence, masking can also be seen in things such as choosing similar interests to peers that an autistic young person wants to be friends with – because 'it gives you something to talk about with them' (Sedgewick, private communication). Whether or not you are autistic, being a teenager is often a time when you become more aware of being different from other people, and there can be even more pressure to fit in. One study, which asked autistic and non-autistic teenagers about how much they mask, found that autistic teenagers masked more than non-autistic teenagers. The study, by Courtney Jorgenson and colleagues (2020), compared teenagers aged 13–15 and those aged 16–18, and found that there were gender differences in how much each group masked. Autistic teenage boys aged 16–18 years tended to mask less than younger boys, whereas autistic girls carried on masking at high levels across all ages. Many people say that their masking increased from childhood to adulthood, often before or during adolescence. Changes in social groups or living situations, such as moving out of home or going to college/university, can also lead people to mask more, as they want to make a good impression on the new people they are meeting.

This pattern of increased masking with age holds true into early and middle adulthood as well. The original studies of masking were generally done with this age group, in contrast to the majority of autism research, which is done with children. Adults tend to report using masking strategies more often than teenagers – measures of self-reported masking seem to be higher in autistic adults compared to the emerging work with young people. Again, this may be because of the increasing complexity of situations people face in adulthood making them feel that they need to mask in order to succeed, especially combined with the increased economic pressures of needing to work and pay rent and bills which are typical of adult life. However, another explanation is that people become more aware of their masking as they get older, and so are better able to describe it to others.

As people move into older adulthood, however, we seem to see somewhat of a reversal of this trend. Some older autistic people talk about masking less as they age because 'I just don't give as much of a crap any more!' (anonymous). Caring less about what other people think of you as you age is a common and well-recognized phenomenon in the non-autistic population, and so it is unsurprising that it is also seen in autistic people. As discussed elsewhere in this book, considering that at least some masking is driven by a desire to fit in and influence what other people think of you, a reduction in how important that feels would logically contribute to a reduction in masking behaviours. There is some statistical evidence for this happening – when looking at levels of reported masking by age group, the over-50s said they engaged in fewer of the behaviours on the CAT-Q than younger groups. Some older autistic adults have described how their masks 'broke' as they got older, for instance due to physical and sensory changes resulting from menopause. In one study by Moseley, Druce and Turner-Cobb (2020), autistic adults who had been through menopause described how they experienced more sensory sensitivities, more emotional changes and more meltdowns, all of which meant it was harder to mask.

It is important to note, however, that lower levels of masking are not just associated with increased age – they are also associated with increased comfort and identification with being autistic. Following diagnosis, an event that is widely discussed in literature as transformative or a 'watershed' moment for autistic people and their families, people face a process of coming to terms with the label, and many choose to incorporate it into their sense of identity. Some people who received a formal autism diagnosis in adulthood say that, once they had an explanation for why they were different, they no longer felt the need to mask those differences.

There is a growing body of work that shows that people who identify more strongly with being autistic, and who are part of the autistic community, have better mental health, are more socially connected and have a greater sense of wellbeing. This increased sense of self-acceptance is also correlated with increased acceptance from the people around them, which in turn can lead to a reduction in masking, 'because I can be myself and don't need to hide how I naturally want to react' (anonymous). The self-knowledge that comes from getting an autism diagnosis also has an impact on masking in social relationships, because people feel that they can 'just say, I'm autistic and I need you to be clear, or this doesn't work for me'. Reduced masking can be associated with increased comfort with being autistic and asking for accommodations from the people and situations around you. It can become a positive thing in many autistic people's lives.

Is it only autistic people who mask?

In addition to academic and autism community discussions of masking in the context of autism, there has also been a long history of the concept of masking more generally. This can be thought of in terms of changing the way you behave depending on who else is there – for instance, behaving differently when talking to your grandmother compared to when talking to your closest friends. Another example might be students in a classroom chatting and laughing when no adults are there, but sitting up straight and being quiet when the teacher comes in, to show that they are ready to learn. This is often called 'impression management' or 'self-presentation'. Many non-autistic people will change the way they present themselves to make a different impression on different individuals, sometimes even without being fully aware of it.

One of the first thinkers to consider this idea of masking was Erving Goffman, who wrote *The Presentation of the Self in Everyday Life* (1991a) as an extended description of the different roles and personas shown by people across their lives. There is quite a bit of overlap between the general idea of masking, and masking by autistic people, for instance, the idea of there being an 'ideal self' that the person who is masking wants to present to other people in that specific situation. However, masking of autism involves some more specific strategies than the more general masking that is often described when people talk about impression management. We will see an example of the similarities and differences between autistic and non-autistic masking in Chapter 4, where we experience a day in the life of an autistic person and a non-autistic person attending a conference.

One of the key differences that we see with autistic masking is that it requires a lot more effort than non-autistic masking. Autistic masking might be performed in every social situation, so the 'true' self is rarely revealed, whereas non-autistic masking involves shifting between different versions of the self for a controlled period of time. Non-autistic masking is often performed deliberately, and in collaboration with other people, who are considered part of the same 'team' (such as the students in the example above). For many autistic people, masking is something that they cannot control or are not even aware of, and unless they interact regularly with other autistic people, they might never mask 'with' someone else. In fact, autistic masking can often be so difficult because it feels like everyone else is on the same team, and the autistic person is left out without understanding why.

As we said above, people don't just mask their autism. Many

people also feel pressure from society, others around them, or themselves, to hide or change things about themselves. Erving Goffman also wrote about this in his book *Stigma: Notes on the Management of Spoiled Identity* (1991b). For instance, in many societies and cultures, being LGBTQIA+ (lesbian, gay, bisexual, trans, queer, intersex, asexual and others) carries stigma and shame, and people within this group might want to hide their identity or 'pass' as another identity to avoid discrimination. In addition, many people with mental and/or physical health problems try to hide the impact these difficulties have for them. This might be to avoid being treated differently or being seen as a burden. Masking of these behaviours, identities or characteristics involves some similar and some different strategies to masking of autistic characteristics. In this book, as we have said, we are focusing on autistic masking; we have neither the space nor the expertise to explore other types of masking.

However, it is also important to acknowledge that many autistic people have other marginalized identities, including being LGBTQIA+, being from a minority ethnic or cultural background, and experiencing co-occurring mental and physical health problems. Many autistic people have additional forms of neurodiversity, such as ADHD, dyslexia or dyspraxia. When people mask their autism, they are often also masking these other identities at the same time, and this may impact how they mask their autism. It is therefore especially important for those supporting someone who masks to be aware that masking of autism can't necessarily be separated from other masking behaviours, and to think about the intersectionality of identities that affect how someone masks.

What about people who do not mask?

There are some autistic people who do not mask, or do so very little. Not much is known about their experiences from research – why they do not mask, whether they want to mask or think not masking makes their lives easier, what impact not masking might have on their mental health (just as we know masking has an impact). For this reason, we can't say much about not masking among autistic people, but to finish this chapter we do have a personal piece from an autistic woman who writes about how she feels she has not really masked throughout her life and the impact this has had.

Personal piece: Tabitha, a woman on the autism spectrum who did not mask before her diagnosis

I am a 54-year-old woman who was formally diagnosed with Asperger's syndrome (ASD level 1) at the age of 47. I may be unusual in that I do not feel that I masked my autistic traits very much before my autism diagnosis, but have both learnt to, and chosen to, mask more since receiving my diagnosis.

My pathway to an autism diagnosis was complicated. From ages 11–21 and 40–47 years I was in the mental health system being treated for anorexia nervosa (AN), obsessive compulsive disorder (OCD) and depression. In between those periods I was working as a university lecturer/researcher and was quite unwell, both mentally and physically. It was during my later time in the mental health system that a smart psychiatrist recognized autism and referred me for an autism assessment.

Prior to my AN diagnosis at age 11, I was described by my parents and schoolteachers as anxious, obsessive and 'highly strung', yet also 'gifted'. I knew I was different to most of my peers; something I found intensely painful emotionally. However, I didn't quite know why this was so. I was a definite 'tomboy' who had no interest in dolls or pretend play and was drawn towards 'functional' toys like LEGO® and Meccano®. I didn't particularly want to play with other girls because I wasn't interested in what they were doing. Therefore, there was no need for me to try to develop an alternative persona that might make me more popular with other girls. I had intense interests that brought me a lot of excitement and pleasure – but although I was content with solitary play, I did want companions to do some of my interests with.

Thankfully, I managed to make some acquaintances by engaging other children in my interests. I had a habit of inventing clubs that I thought they may be interested to join. At seven years old I invented a Wombles club whose members were to spend breaks at school picking up litter around the schoolyard and sports fields. I later invented a cat club (collecting cat photos) and a climbing club (climbing trees on a local disused golf course). Some kids told me I was weird, but others were happy to join me in my interests. I didn't attempt to copy anyone else to try to fit in to their modes of play and I didn't try to hide stims or tics. I felt no need to mask any part of me.

Apart from my intense, obsessional anxiety around a fear of vomiting, accompanying OCD rituals and a terror of eating any new foods, 'unmasked me' managed satisfactorily at primary school. It was moving to secondary school that triggered an inability to cope. I didn't deal well with the transition to a new school with a new set of children to try to get to know. Neither did I cope well with puberty. The bodily changes upset me, as did the change in my peers' behaviours – and both my anxiety and obsessiveness escalated. While my female peers were developing interests in fashion and make-up, I was still a tomboy, with interests that seemed unusual to my female peers. I was hounded and bullied by a pack of girls and depression sank in. I started to restrict food and to over-exercise, which in combination led to rapid weight loss and a diagnosis of AN. I withdrew from my peers due to depression and feeling I had absolutely nothing in common with them. So why mask to try to fit in with people I didn't understand, who bullied me and with whom I had nothing in common?

My treatment for AN was quite successful, in that I quickly reached a healthy weight and was able to return to doing the sports I loved. I achieved county-level standard in middle distance running and tennis; therefore, much of my life outside of schoolwork focused on these sports. But I never socialized outside of these sports and wasn't interested in doing so. There was simply no need to mask. I achieved good A level grades and attended university in my home city. I loved the study but didn't know how to make friends. By this time, I did want friends and would watch with dismay the ease with which other students seemed to communicate and socialize while simultaneously berating myself for being so socially inept. I didn't know how to socialize, and in addition, student social nightlife didn't interest me. I didn't drink alcohol and I didn't like parties, pubs or nightclubs. I felt lonely, yet it didn't cross my mind to try to mask in any way. I did very well academically at university and after my BSc degree I did an MSc and PhD at universities away from home. Incredible loneliness and absence of masking, combined with an inability to cope with noisy student accommodation, led to me relapsing into depression and AN.

At age 24 I got my first job: a university lectureship. I was unwell with AN, depression and OCD, but I felt I had to earn a living. I managed the job intellectually but found the amount of 'peopling' overwhelming. Thankfully, I had a constant timetable, so I always knew what was needed of me and I worked extremely hard at the job, doing especially well in research. I had little social life and I didn't mask, except for during teaching when I did adopt a persona – perhaps like many lecturers do? At age 34, still with chronic mental illness, I secured an academic research post back in my home city. Without a regular timetable, alongside an expectation to be adept at multitasking and to manage fellow staff as well as students, I crumbled mentally. My AN worsened and my weight plummeted so low that I became very physically ill. I needed hospital treatment for the physical consequences of chronic AN and by age 40 I was back in intensive psychiatric treatment and unable to work. Had I learnt to mask my autism? No. Did it cross my mind to try to mask? No.

Perhaps the very fact that I didn't mask meant that after I had reached a stable physical state and after many one-to-one meetings with my psychiatrist, he suggested I be assessed for autism. At the time I hadn't a clue what autism was and was surprised by his suggestion. But the more he and I talked about my characteristics, my communication style, and many years of loneliness and feeling different, it did all start to make sense.

Reading my autism diagnostic report was quite eye-opening. It fully described my mode of communication and how this differed from most non-autistic people. Because I wanted to manage better in life socially, I used the information in this diagnostic report to practise masking some of my autistic traits. This worked well in scenarios demanding only superficial communication. It helped me to get to know some people sufficiently to be able to explain to them that I am 'on the autism spectrum' (my preferred explanation of how I am...) and to make friends. This has been great because I now have friends to do some of my interests with!

In summary: I did not mask before my autism diagnosis because of an inability to recognize how/why I was different, and because mental illness and/or lack of interest in what my peers were doing meant that I did not choose to try to socialize. Since my autism diagnosis I feel that I have used the knowledge I have gained about myself and how my autism manifests to mask when I need to 'get by' socially. Nevertheless, my masking is not elaborate, and I do choose to tell people I would like to get to know better about my autism and how it affects me. I have generally found that people listen and are supportive. My life is infinitely better now, and I am delighted to have people in my life who I feel I can call 'real' friends!

Other things to think about: Why are there differences in how much people mask?

Why do some people mask more than others? The most obvious answer is that some people feel more need than others to mask their autism, whether or not they are aware of it. This could be because of many different factors. One example is gender norms. In many cultures, there are different social expectations for how people of different genders 'should' behave. In the UK, girls are often expected to be quieter, more polite, and less disruptive than boys. This might mean that girls who are experiencing difficulties because of their autism, or who want to express their autism in noisier ways, feel more pressure to mask their autism compared to a similar boy. Another factor is personality. Some people are more influenced by negative responses from others, and so might try to mask more if other people think their autistic behaviours are weird or 'wrong'. Others might not pay as much attention to what those around them think, and so might not feel as much pressure to mask.

However, it's important to emphasize that this does not necessarily apply to all people from these groups. There are many girls and women who are autistic and don't feel the need to mask at all, and there are also many boys and men who feel a huge expectation to mask their autism. Similarly, there are some people who care a lot about what other people think of them, but who still don't or can't mask their autism. The factors that influence each individual person's masking behaviours are often very different to the factors that affect group differences in masking. Researchers tend to focus on group differences because it is easier to draw grand conclusions about larger groups of people. However, the flip side of this is that those grand conclusions often don't apply to many individuals, or only apply to a very small extent. A constant trade-off in research is that in order to say that something is accurate, it often has to apply to a large group of people. But the things that apply to large groups of people tend to be relatively broad, and therefore fail to capture the variations that make something meaningful to any individual. Much of the research we describe here is based on relatively small groups of people (such as autistic women who were diagnosed later in life, or people who identify as autistic in an online survey). By combining similar findings across different groups, we can assume that some of these findings apply across broader groups in a more general, less nuanced, way.

We still don't know exactly how or why individual differences between people affect masking from a psychological point of view. Some initial research suggests that different personality traits might be associated with different amounts of masking. An online survey by Erin Robinson and colleagues (including Laura) found an association between neuroticism – being more emotionally volatile and viewing the world as unsafe – and masking in autistic adults (Robinson, Hull & Petrides, 2020). Unsurprisingly, autistic people who tend to be more anxious about the world report greater levels of masking. A small association between masking and extroversion was also found, suggesting that autistic people who are more extroverted mask more – perhaps because they spend more time interacting with others, and so encounter more situations that require masking. This study also examined participants' levels of trait emotional intelligence, or their awareness of their own and others' emotions. Interestingly, there was no association between masking and emotional intelligence in the autistic sample, although in non-autistic participants masking was associated with lower emotional intelligence. This suggests that masking might be something that most autistic people do, regardless of their level of emotional intelligence, but that non-autistic people might feel the need to mask differences in emotional intelligence. For instance, non-autistic people who struggle to identify others' emotions from facial expressions might practise learning what different emotions look like on the people they know. Autistic people might practise this, whether or not they find it naturally easy.

Another answer to the question about differences in masking is that some people might find it relatively easier to mask than other people. This might be because they have more awareness of their own behaviours, so it is easier to change them. It might also be because some people find it harder to plan, remember, and keep track of how they are masking while trying to interact with other people. As we will describe in Chapter 2, masking can involve trying to keep track of many different things at once (such as what your body is doing, the facial expression of the person you are talking to and what you are going to say next in the conversation). Some people might find it easier to manage all these different things at once, and so find it easier or less tiring to mask. Research is still continuing to try to identify which abilities are needed when masking, and which might help people control their masking as easily as possible. Some of Laura's research has found that autistic teenagers who mask more tend to have higher executive function abilities (high-level cognitive abilities such as problem-solving, memory and planning) (Hull, Petrides & Mandy, 2020b). This suggests that masking involves many of these abilities. If someone struggles with, for instance, keeping track of their progress towards a goal, they might mask less than someone who finds it easier to self-monitor what they are doing and adjust their behaviour as needed.

CHAPTER 2

How Do People Mask?

As we discussed in the previous chapter, there are as many ways of masking as there are people who mask. It would be impossible for us to list all the strategies that someone could possibly use, so instead we will talk about different types of strategies. We will include examples of all these types, but if you are reflecting on your own, or someone else's masking strategies, and can think of behaviours we have not described here, we would suggest that you think about what types of strategies these are. This might help you think more about how and why the strategies are being used, and the impact they have.

Mimicry

Throughout the book so far we have discussed the idea of masking as putting on a mask that makes someone fit in more easily, by appearing non-autistic and more like their peers. This is often done through mimicry of those same peers – copying their ways of talking, their interests, their ways of dressing.

Some people reported that they were aware they masked by mimicking other people, whether consciously or not. Here we should point out that when we say 'mimic', we don't mean copying someone in order to make fun of them – although sometimes the word is interpreted that way. Instead, we mean copying other people's behaviours or actions automatically, just as your reflection in the mirror 'mimics' what your body does.

Previously in the book we have given examples of how autistic people have described mimicking other people's voices, characteristics and interests. Common across all these examples is that the mimicry was a response to being seen or felt as different to other people. The people who gave these examples all described how the natural way they behaved, such as how they interacted with colleagues, didn't produce the responses they wanted from others. They therefore looked around for examples of other people who did get positive responses from others, to mimic those people's behaviour. The mimicry might be focused on one particular behaviour, such as smiling, or it might encompass a whole persona, from a person's interests to how they dress themselves.

In many cases these were friends, classmates or even TV characters who seemed to be popular, or made people respond in a way that the autistic person wanted. But it's also worth pointing out that some people mimic others in ways that might not produce a good impression, in order to achieve a specific aim when interacting with people. One woman interviewed in a study about late-diagnosed autistic women said, 'When I was being bullied, there's this book by Ellen Montgomery and the character Emily, whenever somebody is horrible to her...she just looks at them, and because of her expression they go away' (quoted in Bargiela, Steward & Mandy, 2016, p. 3287). This woman mimicked the expression used by a character in order to put on a more aggressive mask, in order to try to stop her bullies from attacking her more. As we will discuss in more detail later, masking is sometimes seen as helpful to get out of certain situations, even if it's not done with the intention of making people like you more.

For women (and others), make-up is itself often part of putting on their mask. This is not just the case for autistic women, but for non-autistic women as well. After all, a nickname for make-up is 'warpaint'! For women at work, wearing make-up is often part of looking, feeling and being considered 'professional' – if, of course, they do it 'right'. This often means avoiding brightly coloured eyeshadow, for example, although there are very different norms in different industries; the more creative or arts based a role is, the more variety is considered acceptable in appearance. Make-up can be used to help someone get into their persona, or overall mask, and for some people can provide a helpful boundary between when they are being themselves (no make-up) and when they are wearing a mask. Other people might want to wear make-up to express themselves fully, and find that they wear less or no make-up as part of their professional or adult persona.

Active versus instinctive masking strategies

Masking strategies can often be separated into *active* versus *instinctive* strategies. Active strategies are ones which are learned and performed consciously – the person is aware of how they use the strategy, and it might be practised and changed over time. An example might be coming up with a list of questions to ask each time you meet someone new; you can reflect on which questions resulted in helpful answers, and try out new questions that might lead to a conversation. Instinctive strategies are ones which the person might not even be aware of using. These strategies might be automatic responses to someone else, or behaviours which were reinforced from very early on so the person doesn't even remember learning them. An example of an instinctive strategy might be hiding stimming behaviours when you are around other people; you might not even be aware that you stop twisting your hands when someone walks into the room, even though you still want to stim.

Some masking behaviours involve both active and instinctive components, such as not talking about your special interests. Someone might instinctively avoid talking about an interest they have, because they were told from a young age that other people don't care about that interest. However, they might actively research other interests that they think people are more willing to talk about, and try to bring these up in conversation instead of talking about what really interests them.

As well as involving different behaviours, active and instinctive masking strategies can also have different levels of success. We will go through a detailed example of each type of strategy to explain more about this.

Active masking: Facial expressions

Some autistic people have described how they mask by putting on different facial expressions. Many of these people don't naturally express their emotions on their faces, or they do so in ways which are different from non-autistic people. However, they have often been told that they 'need' to show facial expressions, for instance, to smile and look interested when they are talking to someone, so that they don't come across as 'rude'. In this case, using facial expressions is a very active form of masking. Someone might watch television shows to learn more about the different kinds of smiles people use when talking to different people. They might then spend a long time in front of the mirror, practising their own smiles and trying to see how they can look more 'normal' – open your mouth, crinkle the skin around your eyes, where do you put your tongue?! Then it is time to try to practise with other people: using a particular smile, making a note of how people responded to it (did they smile back, or did they look confused?), introducing a different type of smile if the situation changes, and always monitoring how other people react.

Sometimes, all this practice pays off. Someone who masks their facial expressions might find that people around them stop telling them to smile, or they might notice that other people understand what they are trying to convey with their face. However, even after all of this active work, some people might still find that their facial expressions don't look 'right' when they see pictures of themselves, or other people might tell them this – in other words, the strategy has not been successful despite all the effort that has gone into it.

This is especially difficult for smiling, because researchers have found that most (non-autistic) people can tell whether a smile is real or if someone is forcing themselves to smile. Even if the autistic person is doing everything they can to produce a genuine-looking smile, there are some parts of the smile you can't control yourself, so a non-autistic person might still think the smile looks weird or fake.

Being unsuccessful with active masking strategies can be very frustrating, and it might lead someone to give up on using those strategies altogether. As one participant in a study said, 'I try to ask them about the things they like, question after question, to keep conversation going but sometimes it doesn't work and they leave me' (Hull *et al.*, 2017, p. 2527). As we will discuss later, unsuccessful masking strategies which require a lot of effort can lead to burnout and can make the person feel worse about themselves. On the other hand, some people say that if a strategy is successful and they keep doing it over time, it can become easier and easier to use. For those people, some active masking strategies become useful tools that they can put on when they need to – for instance, when they want to make a good impression by smiling at someone they've just met – with very little effort.

Instinctive masking: Mimicry

In contrast to active masking, there are many strategies that people feel they have very little, or even no, control over when or how they use them. One example is mimicking other people. Some autistic people have described how, in the past, they have found themselves copying the body language, gestures, movements and even speech of other people around them. They might mirror the body language of someone they are talking to – if you sit back in your chair, I'll also sit back in my chair – or start using a gesture that a popular child at school is using. This might be done without being at all aware of it, until it is pointed out by other people. Some people have even described copying the way that other people speak; for instance, if someone with a strong accent starts talking, they might reply using the same accent even if it's not their usual accent. This is something the autistic person can't control, even if the other person thinks they are making fun of them – it is an automatic response, adjusting behaviour to be similar to that of other people around them.

Instinctive masking often occurs when someone feels particularly stressed or under pressure. They might be so overwhelmed by the social situation that they find another person to copy as a way to get through it. Sometimes this can be helpful as it gets you through the situation. For example, an autistic person at a party might mirror the body language of their friend, and so won't stand out as being too different and can make a good impression on other people. However, as we will discuss in Chapter 4, if someone is not aware of the impression they give when they mask, they might communicate things to other people they don't want to, and could put themselves at risk.

It is often hard to determine whether instinctive masking is successful or not. As the autistic person themselves is often not aware that they are masking until other people point it out to them ('The way you laugh is just like that character from a TV show'), they might not notice any effects of masking. However, instinctive masking can be harmful because it still requires effort and energy. The person might not realize how much they are masking until they use up all their energy, and experience a sudden burnout, shutdown, or meltdown. Family members of autistic children often describe how a young child might seem to behave perfectly well at school all day, fitting in with friends and acting as though nothing is wrong, but as soon as they get home they have a meltdown or need to rest for several hours. This might be because (among other reasons) they have been instinctively masking all day in order to get through school and avoid being bullied, but they have used up all their mental and physical energy on this. As soon as they are able to take the mask off, they collapse or let all their frustration and hidden behaviours come pouring out.

Another problem with instinctive masking is that is harder to adjust. Someone might be instinctively copying the way someone else talks as an automatic response. If the other person's manner of speech is very different to the autistic person's, it might be seen as mocking the other person and they might get angry (for example, if they copy an accent or a speech impediment). However, as the autistic person isn't consciously doing this, they might not be able to stop speaking in this way – and so the other person might get even more angry. Deciding whether instinctive masking is 'successful' therefore means evaluating how much the person can choose when and how to use those masking strategies in the ways that are most helpful to them.

Extroverted masking: Making yourself into a character
Another form of masking to think about is *extroverted* masking. Whereas introverted masking – a lot of instinctive masking would fit with that description – is about discretion and hiding any anxiety or discomfort an autistic person is feeling, extroverted masking is different. It can be more like projecting a persona to distract from their instinctive reactions, or to give them a character to play who reacts in the 'right' ways that they wouldn't naturally use.

Some people have likened this to being undercover – trying to fully inhabit a role so that 'their' reactions become 'your' reactions, and this helps you to blend in. This doesn't mean that an undercover operative (or autistic person) stops being hyper-aware of potential threats to themselves and to being discovered, but that they create a system of how to respond to the world around them as this other person.

This kind of masking becomes about staying in that character as much as possible to 'hide' that you are autistic, and that requires knowing a lot about the person you are portraying. Undercover operatives can spend months developing their characters: 'First I had to prepare and do the requisite backstopping. Who was I in my undercover role? What were the details of my background?' (McGowan & Pezzullo, 2018, p. 194). Autistic people have often spent their lives developing their character and learning exactly which aspects of their mask will be useful in different situations.

Equally, autistic people who use this strategy will spend time working out how successful their mask is – whether other people are seeing through it, or whether they believe it is genuine. This information can be added to a 'mental library' for how to respond next time, or in a similar situation. Each social interaction might require slightly different behaviours (a slightly different 'character') to feel like it has gone well, and this is part of what autistic people describe as exhausting about masking:

> It's that you're never 'done'. You can't build a mask and stop, because people don't stop. You have a personality that is fairly stable, but everyone changes how they act and what they want based on what's happened before, so I have to keep changing based on you changing. (Anonymous, autistic non-binary person)

Research has also looked at how autistic people build and think about the masks they use, pointing out that they are developed in response to the social context someone lives in (Pearson & Rose, 2021). This means that often, autistic people are using some of the 'real' things about them and their lives to help create the mask they then rely on, which makes sense. That piece of research also emphasized that what the mask is normally a reaction to is the stigma that autistic people face, and so it may be that autistic people who grow up in different environments have different masks which reflect the social and cultural norms of those environments.

METHOD ACTING

This type of extroverted masking – using aspects of your authentic self and experiences to build your character – is known as method acting. One undercover FBI agent talked about it like this:

> It is acting, but by this point in my career I had decided that the agent's scam on the street works best if it touches something real in his or her makeup – method acting, if you will. (Ruskin, 2017, p. 205)

Method acting encourages emotionally expressive performances that appear sincere to the audience, and is based on the 'as if' approach.

This asks actors to use experiences and emotions from their own lives to help them act 'as if' their character was genuinely going through the events of the script. Using this 'as if' analogy, an autistic person may be able to mask their irritation or confusion when a colleague talks about their children by reacting as if they are an undercover police officer tasked with learning as much as possible from a suspect. That way the interest displayed seems genuine as, for that short interaction, the autistic person genuinely does want to hear more of the colleague's personal stories, even if they themselves are not interested.

NOT BREAKING CHARACTER

Another acting technique that can be linked to autistic masking is that of 'refusing to break character'. This is when an actor chooses to act as their character even when they are not being filmed or on stage, and some do this for the whole period of shooting a film, for example. If an autistic person adopts their masked persona all the time, rather than dropping the mask when they are at home, in a safe space or even on their own, it could feel like 'refusing to break character'. People may do this for a similar reason to those actors – if you are acting a certain way all the time, it becomes more instinctive and therefore easier to keep up that performance. However, it is also known to have an impact on the mental health of actors who use this approach – famously Heath Ledger struggled to return to his normal life after method acting to play the Joker in *The Dark Knight*. This is very similar to the negative mental health impacts masking has on autistic people (Cage & Troxell-Whitman, 2019), as it can feel like losing yourself underneath the character.

Autistic author and computational biologist Dr Camilla Pang describes a time in her life when she consciously adopted the persona of the 'basic' girls she wanted to be friends with, taking this all-encompassing approach:

There was a time, in my teens, when I thought I could train myself to be like everyone else: emulating the behaviour of my peers so I could adopt their interests, their mannerisms and their language. I wanted to infiltrate a group of girls – just for 'funsies', as they would have said – to do as they said, share the jokes they shared and get excited by the same things as them. I wanted to be basic, so badly... I bought the jacket, I drank the coffees and I watched *Dawson's Creek* and *Made in Chelsea*, hoping somehow that these would provide the camouflage and the connection. It was when I fell asleep in front of the second of these – the big craze at the time – that I realised it wasn't working. I ended up wearing a jacket I didn't like, which limited my arm movement; drinking something I didn't want to drink; and pretending to laugh at a lot of jokes I didn't find funny (laughing in the wrong places, of course). It was exhausting... Trying to blend in by mimicking my peers, I had ended up suppressing my own personality, an even worse feeling than that of being left out. (Pang, 2020, p. 44)

Some people could interpret this kind of masking as lying about who you are – hiding your true identity to manipulate the people around you into liking you more or treating you differently. The next section assesses this interpretation, and looks at the topic of lying in autism more broadly, to understand the similarities and differences, and how relevant they may be.

Learning to lie

Let us be clear – masking is not the same as lying.

Saying that – lying can be part of masking, or make it easier to maintain the mask. This is because autistic people who are masking may at times lie about how they are feeling, or what they are (or aren't!) interested in, in order to make the interaction go more smoothly. So, it is important for many autistic people who mask to learn to lie, to help them keep up some aspects of their masking behaviours.

So, when do we learn to lie?

Research has shown, and most parents can attest, that children are capable of lying from earlier than many people might expect. Two- and 3-year-old children will lie about whether they have looked at a toy while the researcher was not looking (Evans & Lee, 2013), with the likelihood of lying increasing with age gains of even a few months. Earlier work by Lee had shown that there are specific social and cognitive features which correlate with how much children lie, such as inhibitory control (being able to stop yourself telling the truth spontaneously) and understanding what the other person believes (to help you maintain the lie) (Talwar & Lee, 2008). Equally, 3-year-olds are capable of using lies strategically – another study showed that these very young children told the truth to a friend, but lied to a competitor about where stickers were hidden in order to win those stickers (Heinrich & Liszkowski, 2021). This research also showed that there was a connection between false-belief skill (the ability to identify when someone thinks or believes something that is not objectively true, based on the knowledge you know they have about the situation) and likelihood of lying, as the lies were explicitly relying on creating false beliefs in the competitor. False-belief skill is linked to theory of mind (Baron-Cohen, Leslie & Frith, 1985), which is the ability both to understand that other people have different knowledge, thoughts and feelings to you, and to guess what that knowledge, thoughts and feelings contain. It has historically been thought that autistic people 'lacked' this theory of mind skill, though more recent research has shown that this is not necessarily the case, such as Catherine Crompton's work on communication chains (Crompton et al., 2020). Interestingly, children as young as 4 years old have been shown to be able to tell what are known as 'second-order lies' (e.g. telling the truth to deceive someone because they think you will lie), again in a task where doing so won them a prize (Sai et al., 2018).

The lying described above is generally used by children for their own benefit, such as winning stickers. There are, obviously, many types of and reasons for lying, but another common category is the 'white lie', or a lie which is related to a politeness situation, for example to make the other person feel better, or to avoid giving offence. Children tend not to do this when they are very young, as they have not learned the social rules and norms which white lies aim to maintain and work around. Studies have shown, however, that neurotypical children start to do this from the age of 7, and use white lies more and more frequently as they reach the age of 11. In line with their increased use of white lies as they get older, they are more accepting of other people telling white lies as they age too, showing a link between their socio-moral knowledge and their actual behaviours in everyday interactions (Xu *et al.*, 2010). It has also been shown that in collectivist cultures (those that focus on the group rather than the individual), children learn to tell lies for the collective good (known as 'blue lies') at the same developmental rate as Western children learn to tell white lies for the interpersonal good, suggesting that this may be a core social skill (Fu *et al.*, 2008).

Although children learn to lie from a very young age, there is evidence that we lie less as we get older – 16- and 17-year-olds tell fewer lies than 10- and 11-year-olds, for example, and lies tend to become more focused on the consequences for both people rather than just for yourself (Glätzle-Rützler & Lergetporer, 2015). It has also been shown that older children require more self-justification to lie, meaning that they have to talk themselves into it more or think that they are more 'in the right' for telling the lie than younger children do (Maggian & Villeval, 2014). This trend continues into what is called 'emerging adulthood', the period from about 18 to 25 years old. Research has found that when you ask adolescents and emergent adults about lying to their parents, teenagers do this more than slightly older young adults do, though both groups emphasize that the lies are often told as a way of asserting their growing autonomy. It may therefore be that young adults who are over 18, and are more likely to have left home, feel less need to lie to their parents because they have already established independence (Jensen *et al.*, 2004).

A recent review paper found that theory of mind skill is consistently linked to lying ability, though with only small effect sizes (meaning that it has an impact, but not a big one), and is particularly important for being able to stick to a lie once it was told (Lee & Imuta, 2021).

Another review also found that executive function skills (things like working memory, short-term memory, being able to control your responses) have an impact on lying, but more so on telling a lie in the first place than on being able to maintain the lie successfully (Sai *et al.*, 2021). Considering this evidence, it is unsurprising that autistic people, who experience differences and difficulties both with theory of mind and with executive function, might have different lying experiences to neurotypical people.

Autism and lying

Autistic people are famously blunt and likely to 'tell it like it is' rather than lying, including not telling 'white lies'. In Felicity's research (Sedgewick *et al.*, 2019), she once had an adult autistic woman who was a participant in a study who explained that she had failed to make friends with the other mums at school because the first time she was invited shopping with them, the conversation in the changing room went like this:

> Other mum: Does this dress make me look fat?
> Participant: No, the dress doesn't make you look fat. Your fat makes you look fat.

The other mum felt embarrassed and upset, and assumed that the participant did not want to be friends with her or involved in the social life of the group of mums, because she had given an answer that was perceived as rude and deliberately hurtful. Because being rude is something people normally do to people they don't like, the other mum assumed the participant didn't like her, and didn't invite her to any other events or outings. The problem was that the participant did like her, and would have liked to be involved in the group – but she had been totally honest about the dress and the lady's body, rather than telling the kind of social 'white lie' that people normally use in those situations ('Oh no, you don't look fat, but I'm not sure it's the right shape/colour for you' or 'Not at all, I just think the other one suited you even better!'). These are aimed at making someone feel better, or to avoid hurting them, rather than lying for manipulation or malicious deception, and therefore are generally thought of as more acceptable.

Stories like the one above chime with the long-held assumption of researchers that autistic people who struggle with theory of mind must also struggle with, or be unable to tell, lies (because lying depends on understanding what the other person does and does not know, and what they want to believe). Some tests of theory of mind focus on whether autistic people can spot lies, white lies and sarcasm, which can sound like either a lie or the truth or a joke, depending on how it is used (for example, The Awareness of Social Inference Test; McDonald *et al.*, 2006). These often find that autistic adults are less accurate at identifying sarcasm and white lies than non-autistic people, and tend to classify lies and white lies as the same (Sedgewick *et al.*, 2018) – although interestingly, autistic and non-autistic teenagers score fairly similarly across the categories (Sedgewick, Hill and Pellicano, 2019).

Other work has found that it is possible to teach autistic children to be better at detecting lies, using what is called 'multiple exemplar training' – basically, working through lots of examples of situations where people told lies, doing role-play and giving them feedback about the scenario – and that these improved skills were generalized to other real-life situations (Ranick *et al.*, 2013). What is worth noticing about this study, though, is that only three autistic children were involved, they were all boys, and they were 6, 7 and 9 years old – meaning that we cannot know whether the training would be effective with a larger sample, with girls, or with anyone of a different age. Also, the training they received came from ABA (applied behavioural analysis) practitioners and was delivered using those principles, something that is highly controversial in the autism community (see Lynch, 2019; Devita-Raeburn, 2016), and, according to autistic adults, can be traumatic, with those who experience ABA having higher levels of post-traumatic stress disorder (PTSD) than those who do not (Kupferstein, 2018; McGill & Robinson, 2020). While this intervention did not use negative reinforcement or punishment, this does not mean we can ignore the problematic nature of the therapeutic approach overall while evaluating the usefulness of the findings.

What these studies described in the paragraphs above are doing, though, is researching how good autistic people are at working out when other people are lying, rather than whether and how good they are at lying themselves. This is an important distinction! There is surprisingly little work on autistic lies, and none to date exploring links between lying and masking. What has been shown is that, contrary to the long-held assumptions outlined above, and in line with what any autistic person or their family members or friends would say: autistic people can and do lie. But they approach it slightly differently to non-autistic people. Autistic children are less likely to lie than neurotypical children are – a study using the same 'peeking' methodology as mentioned earlier found that 96 per cent of neurotypical children lied about peeking at the toy, but only 72 per cent of the autistic children did – despite more or less the same proportion of children actually looking under the cover (Talwar *et al.*, 2012). The autistic children who lied the first time they were asked also found it harder to maintain the lie when asked again than the neurotypical liars did – this is consistent with other studies (Li *et al.*, 2011). This might be because, as suggested in other work mentioned earlier, maintaining a lie takes a lot of cognitive effort and relies on several different elements of executive function, which often differ for autistic people, so it makes sense that autistic children might find this harder. Also, other studies have supported a link between working memory and lying in autistic children (Ma *et al.*, 2019). Another finding that tied in with other research was that, as in neurotypical children, those with higher false-belief (theory of mind) scores were more likely to lie than those with lower scores on the same test. This suggests that the links between theory of mind and lying are also present in autistic children.

Similar to the above intervention that taught autistic children to detect lies, there has also been an intervention study seeking to teach three young autistic children (two boys, one girl; 5–7 years old) how to tell 'socially appropriate' lies, or white lies. This found that with examples and modelling of white lies being built into the existing behavioural sessions, all the children learned to tell socially appropriate lies, such as pretending to like an unwanted present (Bergstrom *et al.*, 2016). Again, there are the mentioned issues with ABA approaches with autistic people (though there was no punishment used here either), and the sample size is very small and cannot be generalized to the broader autistic population. However, as most autistic adults would attest, they can and do tell these white lies and have learned to do so throughout their lives, often as a consequence of negative reactions from those around them when they did not utilize this social tactic. The study simply shows that this can be taught formally, potentially avoiding some of those negative social interactions, but that teaching needs to come through supportive and positive learning methods.

There is also a crucial difference between learning to lie, and learning to lie *effectively*. Many of us will be able to think of a time when a toddler we know has promised that they were absolutely not the one who took the biscuits from the table, while the crumbs are still stuck to their cheeks! They are definitely lying, but they are not lying effectively, because it is too easy to prove that they are not telling the truth. An effective lie is one that is harder to detect, or which is never uncovered. Considering the wealth of evidence presented already that autistic children struggle to maintain lies plausibly, it is reasonable to assume on that basis that they are less likely to be able to lie effectively. Research has also shown that autistic people consistently judge situations more on the outcomes than on the intentions of the people involved (Bellesi *et al.*, 2018; Margoni & Surian, 2016), with an impact on how likely they were to forgive the transgressor (Rogé & Mullet, 2011). This may have an impact on how likely autistic people are to lie, as most people apply broadly similar moral standards to themselves as they do to other people. If autistic people are less tolerant of lying in others, it makes sense that they are less tolerant of it in their own behaviour too.

There have been even fewer studies of lying among autistic adults than there have of lying among autistic children. This is not surprising in the context of autism research generally, where the majority of work is done with those under 14 years old. One study that has directly explored deception among autistic adults found that they were just as likely as neurotypical adults to lie to win a game, were actually more likely to use complex deception strategies and were just as good at detecting when they were being deceived. They were less likely to lie to begin with, and took longer to spot when they were being lied to, but by the end of the session they were performing just the same (van Tiel *et al.*, 2021). This shows that, despite differences in childhood in terms of autistic and non-autistic lying, by adulthood autistic people are capable of using and spotting lies similarly to non-autistic people, at least in the controlled environment of a lab-based experiment. Whether this is also the case in real-life social interactions is more questionable; anecdotal evidence would suggest that autistic adults can find it difficult to spot deception in others, but this needs further investigation.

Where does this leave us when thinking about lying and masking? Children as young as 5 can distinguish between 'pretending' and lying, for example knowing the difference between taking on the role of someone else or lying that you are that person (Taylor, Lussier & Maring, 2003). If we see masking as a type of pretending to be someone else (as we discussed in the Extroverted masking section earlier in the chapter), then it is possible that autistic children are similarly aware of 'putting on the mask' from a similar age, though this has not yet been investigated. If so, we need to think about what that feeling of lying about yourself and your authentic identity must do to autistic children and young people, and how it plays into the sense of rejection that so many autistic adults describe.

There is one recent study which has looked at the links between lying, judgements of lying and reputation management among neurotypical children. This study asked 7–11-year-olds to agree or disagree with how accurately someone else had judged a classmate's ability, and found that children would agree with someone who falsely said that the classmate had done well – using and approving of lies to enhance other people's reputations, and their own by association (Ahn *et al.*, 2020). Although we have emphasized elsewhere that reputation management is not the same as masking, and we stand by this, exploring lies and reputation management is as close as any research has come to looking at the links between lying and masking to date. So, it is worth mentioning here as a tangentially related point, if not precisely answering the question!

Lying is hard work, cognitively. You have to create the lie, make it believable, remember it, keep track of who you have told what; there is the fear and anxiety around potentially getting caught and ending up in trouble...all kinds of things to think about.

It has been shown that neurotypical people find it easier to lie the more they practise doing it. This is not that they find it morally or ethically less challenging – practising lying makes it cognitively easier, with people who were 'trained' to lie making fewer errors, and those who were 'trained' to tell the truth making more errors (Van Bockstaele *et al.*, 2012). It isn't known whether the same effect is seen in autistic people, but we can speculate that the more people mask, the cognitively easier it is to fall back into that mask, and potentially the harder it is to drop the mask even when you want to because it is the way your brain is used to presenting yourself to other people. This will be an important area for future research, as understanding the ways in which autistic people learn to mask in terms of the underlying cognitive mechanisms might give us ideas as to how to make it easier for them to learn to unmask when they want to, and to connect with their authentic selves more consistently – something we know is associated with a better quality of life, wellbeing and mental health.

Helen commented:

> The biggest and most common lie I tell is simply saying, 'I'm fine', or 'No, that's okay, I don't mind' – if people just looked a little closer, they could probably see that it's a complete lie and I'm actually struggling or in pain, but it's easier for them to believe the lie because then they don't have to deal with the truth. Much of autistic masking is about avoiding standing out as different or creating conflict with

others, and so it hurts to recognize as an adult that the lies I told as a child were probably so flimsy and see-through, and yet everyone around me just accepted them because then they didn't have to try to understand what I was finding difficult. Lying may not seem like a logical thing for an autistic person to do, especially when we tend to crave honesty and clarity from others, and yet contextually it makes a lot of sense: people generally don't like being told that something they are doing is causing someone else distress, nor do people tend to like having to change something for 'just one person' – a lot of autistics who mask heavily learn young that requesting things be changed for us can result in scorn, frustration and even cruelty. When faced with those likelihoods it's no wonder we chose instead to start lying and hiding our real feelings and reactions.

In conclusion to this chapter...

We have discussed a whole range of ways in which autistic people can mask, some of the ways in which they might learn these strategies, and how they compare with the development of related skills in non-autistic people. And these things are skills! Any one of them involves observation of the people around you; working out what they expect from themselves, each other and you; finding a way to fit in with those expected behaviours, even when it goes against your instincts; and monitoring their reaction, so that you can adapt your behaviour and start all over again. All of this effort goes into trying to fit in and be accepted by those same people who have no idea how hard you are working at it, and who often focus instead on the times you get it 'wrong'. No wonder that long-term masking can be linked to difficulties with mental health, burnout, relationships and sense of identity – all discussed more in Chapter 4.

Other things to think about: Differences between neurotypical and autistic cultures

Masking has sometimes been described as a response to living in 'neurotypical culture' – that is, being part of a world where everyone else has a shared understanding of cultural (social) rules and norms that you don't understand. Some autistic people have said that they actually find life easier, and feel less pressure to mask, if they live in a culture different from the one they grew up in. In their 'native' culture, it's obvious when they miss social cues or don't communicate in the same way as everyone else, and others can get angry or frustrated at this. When they move to another country where the language or culture is different to their own, people can be more forgiving when they make mistakes. Not making eye contact in the same way most people do is much more acceptable if the reason is 'they're not from here', rather than 'they can't do that easily'.

This also reflects the observation that masking is a response to specific cultural norms. A lot of the masking behaviours we have described in this book apply to masking in British culture; some behaviours might sound ridiculous to people from other cultures, and there might be other essential aspects of masking for other cultures that we haven't described. As Nura Aabe, founder of Autism Independence, describes in Chapter 3, people who live in or have heritage across different cultures might find that there are specific cultural expectations that affect how and when people mask. Some cultures attach greater stigma to looking different (including looking autistic), and so there might be greater cultural expectation to mask autism and its impact in these cultures.

These differences in social norms or expectations across world cultures can be thought of as like the differences in social norms between autistic and neurotypical cultures. As autistic people become more connected through the Internet and social media, and autistic-led events become even more open and accessible, a sense of an 'autistic culture' is beginning to emerge. This culture is as varied as the people who contribute to it, and of course different autistic groups based in different parts of the world will develop their own cultures. However, some common social norms in neurotypical culture, such as needing to look at people when they are speaking, can be relaxed in autistic culture. Similarly, autistic culture might involve social norms that neurotypicals don't always follow; for example, using simple and direct language to say what you mean, or using sign language applause ('flapplause') rather than clapping for someone. As with any culture, these social rules will adapt and change over time, and are not always made explicitly clear. Although, as many autistic people prefer rules to be as explicit as possible, that in itself may be an autistic cultural norm!

As we discuss in Chapter 5, a supportive autistic culture can be one of the best ways to reduce masking for those who would like to. It can offer a safe place to be openly autistic, and to be accepted without needing to 'put the mask on'. However, by separating the world into autistic and neurotypical cultural spaces, there is a risk that this will lead to spaces where masking is explicitly discouraged, and spaces where it is explicitly encouraged. In addition to autistic cultural spaces that can allow autistic people to come together and be their authentic selves, it's also important to make traditionally neurotypical spaces more accepting and welcoming of people who don't obey all their cultural norms. A neurodiverse culture can be broad and welcoming, and so should be able to flexibly adapt to the needs of autistic people – as well as other neurodivergent people – within it.

CHAPTER 3

Why Do People Mask? And Where?

We know there are a whole range of ways in which people mask being autistic, from consciously stopping themselves engaging in certain behaviours to unconsciously adopting elements of the personalities around them.

But why do people do it?

There are probably as many reasons to mask as there are autistic people masking. It is one of those areas where the adage 'If you've met one autistic person, you've met one autistic person' really applies!

There are, however, some commonalities identified in research as to why people might engage in masking their autistic behaviours. Fitting in to avoid negative reactions of others, wanting to seem or even feel 'normal', actively being trained to mask through therapy or parental intervention, are all patterns that have been found in the research presented below, and in the accounts of autistic people throughout this book. We asked a range of autistic people why they mask, and, unsurprisingly, got a range of answers – but wanting to fit in, so that people are nicer to you, and therefore the world around you is a bit less hostile, was a common theme. For example:

I would want [a non-autistic person] to know that the autistic person is often trying unbelievably hard to do the right things and to fit in – but that it is usually to the detriment of the autistic person. (Helen, autistic woman, 54)

[Masking is] the fake you, the person you have to learn to be in order to survive the neurotypical world… I'm scared of the reactions of people if they were to see me stimming or not communicating verbally. (Isabella, autistic woman, 24)

I had thought of masking as an attempt to fit into mainstream society, often my learning to mimic neurotypical social behaviour…for me, masking is about what I don't do in public. It is about not letting my anxiety, fear, humiliation, shame and at times intense emotional pain show on the outside. (Wendy, autistic woman)

Is it just caring what people think of you? Reputation management

Short answer – no.

Longer answer – no, because although many autistic people do care what other people think of them, changing your behaviour because of what people think of you, known as reputation management, uses a different set of strategies to masking or camouflaging.

Reputation management is consciously acting a certain way in front of other people to try to influence them to think better of you in terms of your visible behaviour. In contrast, masking can be both conscious and unconscious, and is often used to try to make other people think better of you in terms of your identity and who you are as a person, as discussed in Chapter 1. It was first discussed in the 1950s by Goffman (Goffman, 1963), who described it as being similar to the idea of playing a role in a drama production, in that you may feel you are 'faking it', but your aim is for the audience to take the performance seriously. In daily living terms, it effectively means that you want other people to believe that you are the person you present yourself as, rather than seeing what you feel is your 'true' self. This can be complicated for autistic people who have masked most of their lives and who therefore may feel that they are unsure who or what their 'true' self is beneath years of trying to be who everyone else expected them to be.

Reputation management can be important because how people think of you changes how they behave towards you, and this can have an impact on things like your school or job opportunities, or your relationships. Therefore, most people of all neurotypes spend time and effort on presenting themselves in a favourable light, to access the benefits of being thought of positively (Bird & Smith, 2005). Reputation management was first investigated among non-autistic people, and so we will first look at that research before moving on to what we know about reputation management among autistic people.

There is a lot of evidence that non-autistic people engage in reputation management in a range of situations, from an early age. Research (and basic parenting) has shown that young children are more likely to behave well when they know they are being watched, for example. This active reputation management appears around 3 years old, expands significantly from the age of 5, and continues from there throughout the lifespan. The work with 3-year-olds found that when children had played a matching game either with images of eyes (a stand-in for being watched), or of flowers (the neutral condition), they were more prosocial and shared more stickers with a fictional other child who would be coming in next (Kelsey, Grossman and Vaish, 2018). In another study, 6- to 8-year-old children were fairer to other children when they knew that an adult was watching them, but when they could get away with 'seeming' fair to the adult, but actually give an unfair balance of rewards, they chose that option more often (Shaw et al., 2014). This shows that they wanted the adults to think they were 'good' children who would follow the rules and be fair to others. Similar effects have been seen in young children when they want to maintain a positive reputation among peers, as well as adults. By the age of 5, children who had been told that their classmates had informed the researcher that they had a positive reputation went on to cheat less in a guessing game than children who had not been told this (Fu *et al.*, 2016).

Of course, people do not just use reputation management to signal whether they are 'good' and 'fair', but also whether they are brave, intelligent, creative, wealthy, or any myriad of traits generally considered to be positive. Which traits individuals choose to highlight can be very personal, and partly a product of what is valued in their culture. For example, education research into why working-class boys are more likely to display poor behaviour in the classroom has found that appearing not to work hard and not to be invested in school is part of maintaining a strongly masculine image – an attitude that is specific to their cultural milieu (Connell, 2008). For all social contexts, however, the traits and characteristics people want to project tend to become more complex and nuanced as they move from childhood to adolescence to adulthood.

Interestingly, in adolescence research reputation management is more often called 'impression management', although this research describes very similar processes of consciously adapting behaviour and image to positively influence what others think of you. For adolescents, in contrast to children, the people they are often most worried about influencing the opinions of are their age-peers, rather than adults. This led initially to a wealth of research on how impression management may interact with socially desirable behaviours for adolescents to result in behaviours which are per-ceived as antisocial or potentially harmful by adults around them. For example, a large-scale study with nearly 500 teenagers found that a social identity where someone was perceived as 'non-conforming' was the strongest predictor of antisocial behaviours, along with an admiration for those behaviours, and that this was especially the case for girls (López-Romero & Romero, 2011). There is evidence of the well-known gendered double standard around antisocial or 'high-risk' behaviours among adolescents in terms of reputation management, in that engagement in sexual activity and the consumption of alcohol and drugs is detrimental to the reputation of girls, but improves the reputation of boys (Carroll, 2002). For girls who do engage in this activity, there can be a sense of bravado and 'flying in the face of social norms', which itself is a type of conscious reputation management as being non-conforming, rejecting stereotypes of passive femininity and potentially associating themselves with more masculine traits.

More recently, impression/reputation management research with adolescents has shifted focus to look at how teenagers and young adults interact with social media to manage their image among and relationships with their peers. A lot of this, as with much discussion around teenagers and the Internet, focuses on 'the dark side of social media': how greater social media use is linked to increased narcissism and attention seeking (Hawk *et al.*, 2019); how young people may consciously choose to be cyberbullies to create a tough, cool image and induce fear in others (Houghton, Nathan & Taylor, 2012); how increased social media use is associated with increased 'risky behaviours', especially 'risky sexual behaviours' (Vannucci *et al.*, 2020); the exponential increase in the posting of sexually suggestive images – and the gendered ways in which these are used and inter-preted, entrenching the male/female promiscuity double standard, where male reputations are enhanced but females risk losing their good reputation entirely for similar behaviour (Salter, 2016). These potential risks, and the permanent nature of the Internet (which means that teenagers' decisions can be brought up again years later, for example in job interviews – more on that later in this section), means that some schools now give guidance on how to manage your online presence – which essentially means your online image. Or to put it another way, some schools are actively teaching online repu-tation management to try to support their students in the long term.

On the other hand, it has been shown that this somewhat terri-fying narrative of a dysfunctional relationship between teenagers and social media is itself (at least partly) constructed, rather than being the whole picture. Traditional outlets, such as print journalism, tend to share the most eye-catching headlines, as we all know, and teenage social media use is no exception. What this means we miss is that social media can also be a positive influence in people's lives, including in terms of reputation management and identity-sharing. Of course, people can and do mask online, but it can also be an opportunity to be your 'true self' in a lower-risk environment. For example, many LGBTQIA+ teenagers seek information online before coming out to their friends or family, finding a community who make them feel accepted and enable them to make the next steps (Fox & Ralston, 2016). This is often also the case for people who have just realized that they are autistic, or who suspect they may be autistic, and the online community is a key element of many peoples' journeys. Among non-autistic people, social media is crucial for forming and maintaining friendships, and can be an active positive contributor to happiness (Manago & Vaughn, 2015). There is no reason to believe it is any different for autistic people.

The idea of reputation management has been tested in non-autistic adults as well as among children and teenagers. These reputation management studies often use a game in which people are asked to imagine they are giving money to charity, either with or without someone watching them, or use the 'dictator game' (we don't need to go into it in detail here – it involves deciding how much to share with someone else, with a risk of you both getting nothing, and all the variations on that). Consistently, research has found that people give more when they are observed than when they are not, and that they care more about what they are signalling 'socially' than about how giving the money makes them feels about themselves (Grossman, 2015). Similarly, people give more when they believe that other people also give more, because they want to conform to the socially normative level of donation – a phenomenon seen in real life as well as in slightly bizarre psychology experiments (Croson, Handy & Shang, 2009).

Reputation management is not just part of adult interpersonal interactions, but comes into business considerations as well – hence the existence of public relations professionals all over the world! When starting a new job, most people will do things to try to help them fit in and create a positive impression in their colleagues' minds – Felicity has a doctor friend who bakes for every new department she goes on in her rotations, for example. This is perfectly normal behaviour (the wanting to be liked, not the baking – that's a personal approach) and has been thoroughly researched. Through this work, different strategies have been identified, from 'self-promotion' to 'exemplification' and 'supplication' (though 'intimidation' is also in there, which establishes a particular kind of reputation) (Gwal, 2015). There have also been studies of how good workplace colleagues are at judging each other's reputation management behaviours, as being aware that someone is trying to seem a particular way can impact on things like team functioning (often because obvious attempts to project an image which doesn't match your actual output is seen as being fake, and is detrimental; Carlson, Carlson & Ferguson, 2011). One such study (Bourdage, Wiltshire & Lee, 2015) found that people are not good at knowing when people are trying to appear high in 'honesty-humility', but are reasonably good at identifying the Big Five personality traits of emotionality, extroversion, agreeableness, conscientiousness and neuroticism. This means that people are often good at spotting what someone is like in the majority of their interactions (their personality), which makes sense, but less good at knowing when they are 'putting on' the desirable traits of being humble and honest for their own benefit rather than because it is genuine. There is, however, a debate as to how much it matters in this particular instance – if someone is honest because it benefits them, they are still being honest, at least. It is potentially trickier if someone is consciously being nice for an ulterior motive, for example, because it may lead to hurt feelings later if that is seen as being a 'fake friend'.

As with many things, there is a gendered element to reputation management in the workplace (and elsewhere). In a study by Bolino and Turnley (2003), men who reported using 'intimidation' and 'favour doing' had higher salaries and better performance evaluation, but these tactics lowered female evaluations from their managers. Instead, women who used 'ingratiating' approaches, focused on being likeable, had better evaluations than those who did not. These tangible differences, both in approach to reputation management and in how it is received by peers and managers, are in line with social role theory (explained fully in the 2013 book by Alice Eagly, who created the theory), which states that the different roles assumed to be associated with men and women actually result in men and women acting differently. Those who fit with gendered expectations are often rewarded socially, whereas those who have traits counter to the social norm may face negative evaluations from those around them, and, in extreme cases, censorship or ostracization, known as 'the backlash effect' (Rudman & Glick, 1999). Generally, these social roles tend to code men as 'agentic' – active, assertive, leaders – and women as 'communal' – caring, calm, co-operative. Therefore, women who are assertive or use the 'intimidation' approach to reputation management may face a backlash of being seen as rude or bossy, and men who attempt 'opinion conformity' may be seen as pushovers. These perceptions in turn lead to worse performance evaluations than their peers who use reputation management tactics in line with their traditional social roles. A review of gender differences (Guadagno & Cialdini, 2007) in reputation management techniques in the workplace found that men more often use 'favour doing', 'self-promotion' and 'entitlement/acclaiming' (claiming a positive outcome for yourself), whereas women more often use 'modesty', 'opinion conformity' and 'flattery/compliments'. Other tactics, such as 'charm' and 'ingratiation', had more mixed results, with both genders using them to similar effect.

Employment-based reputation management does not just happen face to face, especially in the modern world. As with the teenagers discussed above, appearances on social media are more important today than previously, and this trend is likely to continue. For example, one study investigated how vets use Facebook in their personal lives, and how this reflects on their veterinary practice as a business. The researchers found that vets tended to disclose more information on Facebook than they would in a general conversation, and those who had higher need for popularity were most likely to engage in this disclosure (Weijs *et al.*, 2014). It is possible that, because people tend to reciprocate when someone tells them information about themselves, those who want to be popular are more likely to share online. Similarly, a post that reveals something significant (either positive or negative) tends to get more engagement from your social network, so it may be that this plays into their need to feel popular, because these posts are more likely to be acknowledged and responded to.

However, as has been seen in many high-profile cases recently, what is posted on the Internet is forever, and it is possible for someone to go back through years of your social media presence to find things to counteract your current position. This is essentially them using the things you used to previously manage a different 'reputational image' to undermine your current reputational image. One example of this was Paris Brown, a 17-year-old who was appointed to be the UK's first youth police and crime commissioner, but who lost the position just six days later because Twitter posts from when she was 14–16 were found to be racist and homophobic (BBC News, 2013). In this case, the timeline was fairly short, but it raised public awareness that employers can now search the social media profile history of candidates going back years, and that these may need to be justified or considered as grounds for both non-employment and losing a job. There are numerous other cases that you can easily find online, from Birmingham bankers who posted a fake beheading video, to prison officers who joked about violence in their institution in Maryland, in the United States. These incidents show how important reputation management has become – not just in person, so that the people around you think well of you, but also online so that anyone who searches your name finds evidence of whatever image you wish to project. In light of this, the value adolescents place on their online image discussed above makes sense, although what they post for peer approval may be different to what they wish they had posted for employer approval a few years later!

Reputation management in autism
It has historically been believed that autistic people would be either incapable, or at least less likely, to engage in reputation management

behaviours because of reduced social motivation. If you are less interested in social interaction, the argument went, you should also care less about what other people think about you, because you aren't driven by the thought of their approval. One early study of reputation management in autism asked children to rate hand-drawn pictures, both when they thought a random stranger had done it and when they thought the experimenter in front of them had done it (Chevallier *et al.*, 2012). Unlike non-autistic children, autistic children did not increase their ratings when they thought the experimenter in front of them had created the picture, which researchers interpreted as meaning that reduced social motivation resulted in less flattery and, by inference, this was a sign of less interest in reputation management. What the researchers also found, but failed to discuss fully in their paper, was that autistic children improved their rating of the picture if they liked the interviewer. Being nice about a picture because you care about the person liking you seems like the perfect description of flattery (and reputation management) in a lot of ways, but as it did not fit with the overarching theory, this was overlooked at the time.

Later research has shown that autistic people are very capable of engaging in reputation management behaviours – it is not just a thing among non-autistic people. Recent research on reputation management among autistic people found that they are just as capable of choosing to act in 'reputation-enhancing' ways (i.e. giving the other person more money when they want to appear more generous), but that they do this under different circumstances than non-autistic people. So autistic people gave more to the charity when they thought the other person was also giving money to charity, rather than giving more to the charity simply because someone was watching them. This suggests that autistic people are aware of what are considered 'reputation-enhancing' behaviours, but have different motivations for when they employ these (Cage *et al.*, 2013).

A follow-up study with autistic children by the same team also highlighted the different motivations that may be at play in reputation management from an early age. This study found that non-autistic children were motivated by social aspects (more socially motivated children did more reputation management), but autistic children were motivated by reciprocity (so if they expected the other person to share, they were more likely to share, just like the adults did) (Cage, Bird & Pellicano, 2016a). What this result, the finding about autistic children being nicer to researchers they liked and a commentary from the legendary psychology duo Uta and Chris Frith (2011) emphasize is that autistic people lack the hypocrisy that underlies much of non-autistic reputation management. Autistic people give their honest and genuine behavioural responses in reputation management research, but then this is interpreted somehow as being a bad thing, or a lack of social skills. Instead, it should be seen as a valuable strength, and modern research is much more likely to present it in this light.

When asked what kind of reputation they wanted to build for themselves, autistic adolescents said that they wanted to be known for being different – the opposite to what some people might expect, considering the amount of masking autistic people do explicitly because they want to fit in, as described by the contributors to this book:

> Masking means making myself smaller and more acceptable to the neurotypical world. Which then reminds me that my authentically autistic self is unacceptable to the neurotypical world. (Cassie, autistic woman, 34)

But what the autistic teenagers also said was that they wanted acceptance from their peers and the people around them. So, in wanting to have a reputation as being different, what they meant was to have a reputation for being themselves, and for that authentic self to be accepted and valued (Cage, Bird & Pellicano, 2016b). And that is perfectly in line with what our contributors wanted from non-autistic people:

> [when I told my non-autistic friend] I cringed, waiting for what could be said, but instead she was in awe, recognizing how much effort

it must take daily to accommodate everyone else. It was the nicest thing anyone non-autistic has ever said in response and I only wish everyone else understood. (Melissa, autistic woman, 26)

What all this research, and these quotes, emphasizes is that autistic people can and do engage in reputation management, and that this is separate to masking, although wanting to build a reputation to 'seem normal' (Bella, autistic girl, 15) blurs those lines for some people. Autistic people in experiments engage in less of the traditionally measured 'reputation management' behaviours than their non-autistic peers. How strongly this trend transfers into real-life situations is yet to be fully explored, but it may be that understanding masking – as we aim to in this book – starts on that journey.

The next section reflects in more detail on the why of masking, as we've now thought about the what, and how it differs from other psychological constructs such as reputation management.

Reasons for masking

So, to return to 'Why do people mask?' This seems like it should be a fairly simple question – most of the things people tell us can be summed up as wanting to fit in so that people are nicer to them. But to understand that reasoning fully, we need to understand some of the difficulties autistic people face when dealing with a majority non-autistic world.

There are sensory processing differences which autistic people are told they can't possibly be experiencing by people who have never heard the electricity running through the walls.

There are the incredulous looks when an autistic person says something they think is perfectly reasonable, but is taken as being very rude, such as a participant who said:

I don't bother seeing family at Christmas – I don't like most of them, and it's very boring. I'd rather stay home with my boyfriend and do our own thing. It's much less stressful and means that we enjoy our day, and they enjoy theirs more too, because I'm not there being what they call 'difficult'. (Anonymous)

This makes sense for this autistic woman and her partner, but if her family heard her talking about not liking them, or that she doesn't feel welcome among them, they would probably be offended and think she is being unpleasant.

Longer term, there are also the mental health issues that arise from living a life filled with these challenges. People can develop anxiety, such as about what each new room will feel like (sensory sensitivities are a major issue for autistic people, and have been specifically linked to anxiety levels in certain situations), or social anxiety about whether they are going to say the wrong thing in the next sentence, even though they made it through the last one, because they have spent years feeling as though they were 'getting it wrong'. We know from research that social anxiety is associated with communication difficulties for autistic people, such that social anxiety increases as people experience more challenges in communicating in a way that the people around them understand. This has the potential to form a negative feedback loop, where an anxious person is more likely to struggle to communicate, so they communicate ineffectively or are more difficult to understand, so the other person does not respond as they hoped, and so their anxiety increases about the next time they are in that situation.

It is also common for autistic people to develop depression (around 40 per cent of autistic adults meet clinical criteria at some point; Hollocks *et al.*, 2019). A lifetime of negative feedback from the people around you, being told that you aren't meeting your potential, or that you are useless at things that most non-autistic people do easily, is bound to have an impact. Potentially, autistic people can develop PTSD from a lifetime of repeated traumas from that rejection, or because someone decided their social naivety made them an easy target for manipulation and exploitation – a phe-nomenon called 'mate crime', which autistic people are especially likely to fall victim to (Forster & Pearson, 2020). Furthermore, recent research has shown that autistic people experience far more negative life events than non-autistic people – they have higher rates of unemployment, homelessness and sexual victimization, for example (Griffiths *et al.*, 2019). Considering this, developing depression seems like a reasonable psychological response, and is in line with work on the impact of negative experiences on rates of depression among non-autistic people. Autistic people may also be more likely to develop what is called 'complex PTSD', which arises from repeated traumatic experiences rather than a specific instance or situation, which also makes sense in light of the negative life experiences they are more likely to face. However, those with mental health issues, especially less well understood conditions such as PTSD, can face stigma if they disclose their diagnosis and difficulties. This leads to many people, both autistic and non-autistic, trying to hide the challenges they face around their mental health – something that has repeatedly been linked to lower rates of help-seeking and higher rates of suicide among non-autistic men (Möller-Leimkühler, 2002).

This all highlights how the world can be an especially difficult place for autistic people to exist in, and to navigate. In that light, developing a mask that helps you get through the day, helps you avoid stigmatizing responses from others, and potentially reduces your chances of ongoing negative experiences, makes a certain kind of sense, regardless of the long-term costs (discussed in Chapter 4).

Diagnostic bias

There are also groups of autistic people who, on top of these challenges, are often told that they *can't be* autistic. For them, developing a mask can be a form of survival strategy, as they often face much harsher social penalties for not meeting standard non-autistic expectations and do not benefit from the explanatory power of being able to tell people around them, 'I am autistic, and that is why I act this way'.

Women, non-binary people, trans people, people of colour and adults all face a harder road to getting a diagnosis than younger, whiter, men and boys. This is due to a historical bias in how we think about autism, from the very earliest studies which identified the condition. Kanner had a group of 11 children, 8 of whom were boys; Asperger, a group of 4 children with no girls at all. From the very beginning, autism was thought of as a male (and white, and childhood) condition, and this assumption coloured all autism research, diagnostics and support work for the next 70 years or so. Until recently, many studies excluded females entirely as being 'unrepresentative', or included small numbers and then failed to carry out gender-based analysis of difference, as there were too few females in the sample to explore gender differences with sufficient statistical power (Gould & Ashton-Smith, 2011).

MALE BIAS

There have been a range of critiques of the dominant approaches to diagnosing autism, often focusing on this male bias. Because the early conceptions of autism were male-focused, other forms of presentation (e.g. internalizing, where someone directs their anxiety and frustration towards themselves, rather than externalizing, where they display these emotions externally) were not accounted for in diagnostic criteria and tools. Internalizing is generally more common in non-male people, though this is not an absolute rule. Furthermore, prominent theories of the mechanisms underlying autism have relied upon presumed 'inherent' gender differences, especially the empathizing-systemizing theory and the extreme male brain theory (EMB) which arose from this idea of autism as a male phenomenon (Baron-Cohen, 2002, 2010). Baron-Cohen suggests that females are generally more empathetic (i.e. more focused on other people and their emotions), and males are generally more systemizing (i.e. more 'logical' and focused on mechanical or procedural processes). This was thought to be due to underlying neuroanatomical differences between men and women. The extreme male brain theory proposes that individuals on the autism spectrum display an extreme form of the more 'typically male' behaviour profile in relation to empathizing and systemizing, leading to aspects of autism such as a preference for sameness, difficulties with social relationships, and atypical behaviours in childhood (such as lining up toys) (American Psychiatric Association, 2013). This has then been linked to neuroanatomy, with functional magnetic resonance imaging (fMRI) studies arguing that autistic brains can be seen as being even 'more masculine' than those of neurotypical males in terms of structure and neural function (Baron-Cohen, Knickmeyer & Belmonte, 2005). This research can be contested, however, as the numbers involved are small and do not represent the range of variation across a whole population. Further, there are men and women who display the 'typical brain' of the other gender, which suggests that these are not absolute categories or findings, and so such gender-based essentialism cannot be the answer to what autism is or how it presents. More recent MRI research has also shown that autistic and non-autistic women activate similar parts of their brains when taking part in an activity related to camouflaging, areas that are distinct from those that activate when men take part in the same task (Lai *et al.*, 2019).

In fact, much research in the past 10 years or so has shown the ways in which autism may present differently in girls to boys, and these differences contribute to girls not being picked up as quickly – or at all – in the diagnostic process. Autistic girls may be more likely to have apparently typical social development (Bauminger, Solomon & Rogers, 2010) because they may be more skilled at imitating the social behaviours of their peers, such as engaging in co-operative and pretend play (Kopp & Gillberg, 2011). Autistic girls have been found to have higher levels of social reciprocity than autistic boys (Backer van Ommeren *et al.*, 2017). Further, autistic girls may have superior social skills to autistic boys, such as being capable of more complex imitation in make-believe and other games, which is crucial to being 'part of the action', and being more socially co-operative (Mandy *et al.*, 2012). However, these skills also mean that the social isolation of girls is less obvious, being more akin to neglect than active rejection – think being ignored on the playground rather than people running away from you (Dean *et al.*, 2014).

Outside of social differences, autistic girls appear to develop intense interests (called restricted repetitive behaviours and interests, or RRBI, in most of the research) in areas which are considered typical for their age and gender, such as a focus on soft toys, fiction, or make-up tutorials, and to have lower levels of RRBIs generally (Lai & Szatmari, 2020). Indeed, these core differences in the rates and types of RRBI have recently been suggested to be the key difference in how autism presents in boys and girls (though this is a somewhat controversial position), with a call to make gender-specific RRBI norms a feature of diagnostic approaches, along with sensory profiles and a call for more brain imaging research (McFayden *et al.*, 2020). This does make sense in part – it has been shown that the RRBI portion of the current diagnostic tool is significantly better (has more 'sensitivity') at spotting autistic boys than girls, and that this is – for boys – the most useful part of the diagnostic tool overall. In contrast, for autistic girls in the same study, focusing on reports of compulsive behaviours, insistence on sameness and the presence of self-injurious behaviours were the most accurate predictors of someone being autistic (Antezana *et al.*, 2019).

In summary, findings around gender differences in autism suggest that, from a young age, autistic girls might be less likely to be referred for diagnosis, as their social skills and special interests may not trigger enough of the traditional flags to warrant referral for an autism diagnosis.

This set of circumstances, where autistic girls tend to be less disruptive and therefore seen as in less need of a diagnosis or access to support and services, is typified by the differences in internalizing and externalizing behaviours that have been found. Girls on the autism spectrum are more likely to internalize their problems, resulting in high levels of anxiety and depression (Sedgewick, Leppanen & Tchanturia, 2020) relative to non-autistic girls and boys, and even relative to boys on the spectrum. This may mean that they also have fewer externalizing behaviours than autistic boys, such as anger issues or disruptive behaviours, although research has found similar levels of emotional and behavioural problems on parent-rated measures (Pisula *et al.*, 2017). This makes autistic girls less visible, especially in the classroom (and school endorsement is often essential for involving educational psychologists or supporting diagnostic referrals). And sadly, too often, less visibility results in getting less help, meaning that the long-term impact of trying to cope with the world unsupported and unrecognized is often compounded by being told by those around you that nothing is wrong anyway.

This has led to many women, non-binary and trans folks, as well as some men, being told that they 'don't look/seem autistic', often because they do not meet common cultural stereotypes about autism which are reinforced in the diagnostic criteria. There is growing work showing that parents seeking autism diagnoses for their children report facing these difficulties, such as:

She had her down with having anxiety, and she diagnosed dysgraphia...ADHD, everything bar the word autism... You get answers, but they're not the right ones. (Quoted in Fowler & O'Connor, 2021)

This shows how thoroughly conceptions of autism are based on a male model, as even girls who display behaviours which would automatically flag them as autistic if they were a boy are often missed. Not only is this a problem at the first stage of the process, where family, teachers and medical professionals need to simply consider autism a possibility, but it is also endemic in the later and more formal stages. For example, one of the most widely (and freely) available screening tools, the Autism Quotient (AQ; Baron-Cohen *et al.*, 2001), is a 50-item questionnaire, where someone rates statements from 'Strongly Agree' to 'Strongly Disagree', getting a score out of 50, with anything 32 or above suggesting they are likely to be on the autism spectrum. This measure has been cited in over 4000 papers at the time of writing, often used as a tool to verify the autistic status of participants, or as a measure of the number of autistic traits they endorse, in order to establish whether there is a link between this and other factors investigated in the study. Despite how frequently this measure is used, however, it has been pointed out that it has a strong bias towards stereotypically male elements of autism presentation, such as items which ask, 'I like collecting information about categories of things, e.g. trains, cars' – whereas girls have been shown to have more age- and gender-typical special interests which might not flag up on this question (Mandy *et al.*, 2012). It also asks someone to rate whether they 'prefer to do things with others than on my own' (the question is reverse scored, so saying yes means you are less likely to be autistic and saying no means you are more likely to be autistic). This reflects an old assumption about autism predicated on the idea that autistic people have low levels of social motivation (Chevallier *et al.*, 2012) and do not want friends, whereas more recent work has emphasized that this is very much a myth (Sosnowy *et al.*, 2019).

As another example of the male bias in who is recognized as, and therefore given allowances for, being autistic, the Autism Diagnostic Observation Schedule (ADOS), considered the 'gold standard' diagnostic tool for autism, was developed with an 87 per cent male sample (Lord *et al.*, 2012). This means that it is very good at picking up stereotypically externalizing (read: male) behaviours like outwardly visible or unusual stims and repetitive behaviours – for example, obvious lack of eye contact, or talking about not having any friends. What it is not as good at is recognizing when someone has a stereotypically internalizing (read: not-male) behaviour profile – playing with their hair rather than flapping their hands, or looking at a spot between your eyes rather than avoiding eye contact completely. Autistic girls therefore have to display a higher number of external, visible, 'challenging' behaviours in order to be given the same score on the measure as their male peers. This disparity means that many autistic girls – and boys – who have a more internalizing behaviour profile are often missed by the algorithm, unless interviewed by a clinician experienced in atypical presentation.

YOUTH BIAS

Girls and those with atypical presentation are not the only ones who can face difficulties in getting an autism diagnosis and the understanding that comes with the recognition of an aspect of your identity that was previously unclear. Many studies on the diagnosis experiences of autistic adults have outlined similar challenges, despite having participants from a variety of settings, age ranges and genders. There is evidence that adults find it harder to get a referral for diagnosis than children, a phenomenon explored in several pieces of research. For example, initial resistance from healthcare professionals is common, with attitudes either being that an adult cannot be autistic because they do not appear to meet stereotypical criteria, or that even if the doctor agrees that they are autistic, there is no point in getting a diagnosis 'this late in life' because they have 'coped this far'. One adult said, when describing how they struggled to get an initial referral from a general practitioner (GP):

> I felt completely at the mercy of whether they believed me or not… whether they agreed with my assessment of myself…I was really very worried. (Quoted in Crane *et al.*, 2018, p. 3766)

From another study on the experiences of autistic women, there are quotes that really emphasize this narrative of having masked when younger, just about coped and then had those lived difficulties questioned precisely because they have done 'well enough' on some metrics:

> I had a hell of a time getting diagnosed for the ASC [autism spectrum condition] because I had any number of clinicians go, 'Oh, look, you're a parent, and you got married, and you have a job – hey! Let's not even go down that path…you can't be autistic.' (Quoted in Seers & Hogg, 2021)

> She [general practitioner] dismissed me with 'I think if you finished university, you can't have Asperger's.' (Quoted in Seers & Hogg, 2021)

Adults of all genders are likely to find the diagnostic process challenging, from recognizing traits in themselves and the challenge these may present to their sense of self, to presenting 'atypically', so that they do not appear to meet the criteria for the simpler screening tools (which themselves have issues, such as a negative interpretation bias which means that autistic people are likely to think the question means something different than non-autistic people do), or even simply do not fit with clinicians' stereotypes about autistic people – such as being in a long-term relationship, or living independently, or being in employment, all reasons for clinician reluctance that have been shared regularly in the autism community.

Similarly, one woman recently shared her story online – when asked if she liked to collect things (as in the child version of the ADOS, and in other assessments), she responded that she knew the choreographers of all Broadway shows for the last couple of decades. Most people would consider that to be a clear special and intense interest which should meet the criteria, but the clinician she was speaking to decided that it was 'different' because that is information rather than a physical collection. Hopefully, this is an increasingly rare situation, but it highlights the extent to which diagnostic criteria can be interpreted in ways which are biased against those who have anything other than a stereotypical presentation, especially beyond childhood.

Of course, what these assumptions and statements do not account for is that often, the autistic adult does not meet standard criteria because they have learned to mask many behaviours that have had negative responses over their lifetime. Also, adults often reach the point of approaching their doctor because they are in a crisis of some kind and have realized that they need the formal diagnosis in order to qualify for reasonable adjustments and supports in their lives.

While it must be acknowledged that the information and guidance available for autistic adults through official channels in a given local area is currently patchy at best, and often minimal to non-existent, there are growing networks of support run by and for autistic adults. One of these was recently evaluated in a piece of co-produced research, which found that people signed up to take part in the programme because they wanted to know more about autism than the basic information they had often been given, that they wanted to feel empowered in their autistic identity and that they wanted to learn about coping strategies from other autistic people with first-hand experience (Crane *et al.*, 2020). Pleasingly, participants felt that they had met these objectives, and talked about how they especially appreciated that it was run by other autistic people, that they got to meet a range of autistic people, and that it helped them to develop a much more positive understanding of themselves and of being autistic.

The power of having a better understanding of yourself cannot be understated. It is a theme that comes up not only in work specifically focused on diagnostic experiences, but also in other work about life as an autistic adult.

For example, in a piece of research about autistic women's friendships and romantic relationships, one unexpected theme raised by nearly all participants was the impact of getting an autism diagnosis. Alongside discussions of what made a good friend or partner, difficulties with making friends or being bullied and how to manage disagreements in relationships, women talked about how receiving their formal autism diagnosis changed how they interacted with other people. Knowing and understanding that they were autistic, and that things like socializing in large groups or 'reading between the lines' were difficult for a reason, significantly helped their self-esteem and their ability to advocate for themselves. One woman said that after her diagnosis, she felt newly empowered to tell people:

> I don't need your neurotypical drama. (Quoted in Sedgewick *et al.*, 2018)

Another participant talked explicitly about how she no longer felt she needed to mask her autistic traits and her need for certain things (like no music in a restaurant) around those she trusted, because everyone in the situation knew she was autistic, and that this increased acceptance had improved her relationships in turn:

> ...now I actually have an understanding of what I'd like out of a friendship. (Quoted in Sedgewick *et al.*, 2018)

RACE BIAS

The difficulties in getting an autism diagnosis – central both to under-standing yourself better, and to others understanding your needs and making space for them, so that you can drop the mask – do not just apply to women versus men. Along with gender biases, there are often issues around access to diagnosis and post-diagnostic support for those from non-white backgrounds. This issue is wider than just autism, as shown by the increasing recognition of institutionalized racism across all areas of society, from justice systems to medical treatment. Those from black, Asian and minority ethnic (BAME) and immigrant communities often find that their children are dismissed as naughty, or indeed that their families are labelled 'problem fam-ilies' with 'poor parenting'. However, it is worth acknowledging and recognizing the work that has been done to date around the question of autism and race, both in the West and the emerging work from the Global South.

It is also worth noting that the majority of work on racial dispari-ties in autism diagnoses and access to support has been carried out in the United States, where race relations work is often more prominent than in other countries. This work has found that non-white autistic children face delays in being recognized as autistic, and are less likely to be diagnosed as autistic overall (Mandell *et al.*, 2009). There has been some research examining racial/ethnic bias in diagnostic tools, finding that three items on the ADOS have significant biases – unusual eye contact, stereotyped/idiosyncratic use of words or phrases and immediate echolalia (Harrison *et al.*, 2017).

Beyond potentially biased diagnostic tools, it is common for non-white autistic people to be misdiagnosed with other conditions. For example, black American boys are more likely to have a prior diagnosis of behavioural and conduct disorders, or anger manage-ment problems, whereas autistic Hispanic and Latino American children are often misdiagnosed as having speech, language and communication needs (Mandell *et al.*, 2007). Once these children have been more correctly identified as being autistic, there is often an assumption that English is an additional language for them, rather than the primary language at home, and a recommendation that they will have better outcomes in a monolingual environment. This recommendation assumes that because autistic children often struggle with language development, having a delay compared to non-autistic children, or using idiosyncratic grammar and pronouns, it will be easier for them to learn in just one language rather than trying to use two languages with potentially different structures as well as different words – an assumption that can come from parents as much as from professionals (Hampton *et al.*, 2017).

There is growing evidence that this may not be the case. There have been suggestions since the 2010s that bilingualism may not be detrimental, and may even be an advantage, for autistic people – one review found that bilingual autistic people score better on non-verbal intelligence testing than monolinguistic autistic people, and many studies have shown that monolingual and bilingual autistic children score very similarly on a range of developmental measures (Wang *et al.*, 2018). Recently published research from a team in Edinburgh studied autistic adults who had either been brought up bilingual or had learned additional languages later in life. For these adults, they found that the more languages spoken predicted better social quality of life (Digard *et al.*, 2020). Overall, these studies combine to suggest that hearing and learning multiple languages is not automatically or inherently going to have a negative impact on the development of and outcomes for an autistic person, but instead may be beneficial on some standard measures, and indeed for their quality of life if it gives them access to a special interest or to more people to make friends with.

Some black autistic people have been open in discussing their lives at the intersection of black and autistic identities, often under the Twitter hashtag #AutisticWhileBlack (which is highly informative and worth a look for those who do not have these lived experiences and want to learn). Along with increased chances of negative interactions with police and other professionals, especially in the United States, the conversations about *code-switching* are pertinent to thinking about masking.

Code-switching is a term that was initially created in the field of linguistics to refer to people who switch between two or more languages within a single conversation. But it has gained a wider cultural meaning – it is now generally used to describe a process of changing how a non-white person presents themselves around those of their own and of other races (this is sometimes true for class-based code-switching as well, but is most commonly discussed in terms of race). George B. Ray described it as 'a skill that holds benefits in relation to the way success is often measured in institutional and professional settings' (Ray, 2009, p. 72). It involves being aware of how others are likely to perceive you because of the colour of your skin, and then consciously (or unconsciously) acting in such a way as to counteract potential negative stereotypes. This can mean adjustments to the way you speak, the way you dress or present yourself, the way you behave, and even to your facial expressions and body language. Code-switching is a result of the systemic racism non-white people face when interacting with the world, and has been described by some as a survival mechanism enabling them to exist in otherwise hostile environments – those who do it have been found to be judged more positively both at school and in the workplace, for example. However, code-switching can carry a psychological toll. Constantly being aware of stereotypes others hold about you and how they can negatively impact you (called 'stereotype threat' in psychology research) is cognitively and emotionally exhausting, has been shown to reduce performance in the workplace, and can undermine relationships with peers and colleagues if someone is thought to be inauthentic – exactly what people are trying to avoid (Walton, Murphy & Ryan, 2015; West, Muise & Sasaki, 2020). Furthermore, high levels of code-switching are linked to experiencing more, and earlier, burnout and breakdown.

The parallels of this to autistic masking are clear, but the process is that much more complicated for non-white autistic people who are trying to concurrently manage how they are perceived due to their skin colour at the same time as trying to mask or suppress autistic traits. Inappropriate use of restraint, difficulties with communication and differences in understanding social expectations can all lead to autistic people being at risk in police or other official interactions, something that one contributor said she was acutely aware of:

> I was in meltdown, crying hysterically and trying to cover my ears. I grew more nervous when I saw the police passing through the station, knowing the stories of arrests or questioning that autistic people are often met with during meltdown. (Melissa, autistic woman, 26)

There are sadly too many cases, again mostly from the United States, of autistic non-white people in meltdown being interpreted as dangerous by armed police, and being shot or harmed because of this lack of general knowledge and understanding of autistic people, and particularly of non-white autistic people.

Bearing in mind the difficulties outlined here, is unsurprising that global majority ethnic people (those who are not defined as white and Western) can struggle with the diagnostic processes in Western cultures, as racial stereotypes interact with autism stereotypes in the minds of those professionals and clinicians who are the gatekeepers of the 'label'. And, through being gatekeepers of who is designated as autistic, these people also act as gatekeepers for who can access support, as in most educational and health systems it is necessary to have a formal diagnosis to be able to make claims for additional resources or reasonable adjustments.

Below, we have a piece written for the book by Nura Aabe, about her experiences of raising her autistic son and the challenges she faced within her own Somali community, alongside the diagnostic processes and navigating how to best support him, which discusses some of the ideas we've raised here.

Personal piece: Nura Aabe, founder of Autism Independence, on how autism is perceived by members of the Somali community, masking, not masking, and saving 'face'

Strikingly, both the Somali and Western communities do not yet know autism rates among Somali migrant children living in Western countries. Somalis call the condition 'a Western disease'.

As a Somali British mother with a child with autism, dealing with this unknown condition has been a challenge, and stigmatizing, with no written literature from a personal and most importantly from a Somali perspective to relate to.

Here I share my journey with my beautiful son's diagnosis of autism, the unknown condition that led me to do the unexpected as a Somali Muslim woman and search for comfort in accepting and loving my baby for who he is by speaking about his autism publicly.

When Zak was diagnosed with autism, I never thought family reputation and reaction would be one of the greater challenges I would face. I remember leaving the multiagency meeting Zak was diagnosed at, the word 'autism' spinning around my head. I had never heard the word before, nor can I think of a word that describes autism in the Somali language. Being different comes with stigma and negative connotations in the Somali culture. Because there is no concept of autism in the Somali culture, mental illness is the closest interpretation of autism.

There is no direct translation for the words 'mental illness' in Somali language. Instead, people use 'wali', meaning 'crazy', or 'gini', referring to threatening external forces causing mental illness. This is negative but also has spiritual connotations. These beliefs about what mental illness is are generally perceived as spiritual or metaphysical by the Somali culture, meaning that mental illness comes from God or evil spirits. Therefore, mental illness comes with stigma in Somali culture as it is often perceived negatively, and this results in social exclusion.

Family events have always been difficult to take part in, as there is the assumption that it will affect family reputation (called 'face'). Therefore, hiding Zak and keeping him at home is generally expected. Family face is very important in the Somali culture, painting a particular picture to maintain respect. You are often labelled by your child's disability, which affects a family's reputation, and therefore people think the best way of dealing with difference is to hide any illness. My family feared people would label us and link us to undesirable characteristics (in our case, Zak's autism). So, a rationale is constructed for rejecting, devaluing and excluding 'different' people from the community.

Missing festive celebration events became normal as it was easier to avoid whispering and opportunities for people to look down on you. I remember how difficult making these decisions had been, especially for my other children to understand why we were not taking part in family or community gatherings. For years, I saw very little of my community. Sad, but I had to make the choice to help Zak, and that meant I had to surround myself with people who accepted Zak with his autism, and who believed that he could make progress. Not seeing much of my community meant I didn't have to be reminded of the empty feeling that Zak is mentally ill, and that he cannot lead a normal life. Goffman (1963) describes the feelings of the stigmatized person as being conscious of the attitudes of others towards them, and for us as parents describes the experience of being stigmatized because of our links to our autistic child.

The segregation Zak and I experienced encouraged me to set up Autism Independence, using my personal and my professional experience. I want to change the behaviour of hiding and the cultural focus on 'face', by sharing Zak's autism and what truly comes with the condition. I could see that acceptance was possible among non-Somali people and institutions, but it was impossible in the eyes of my family and social group, as Zak's autism hurt the family face. This meant that I had to make the decision to make a shift for myself and Zak in relation to who we surround ourselves with. This was like an identity crisis, finding out who I am, alongside finding a way to help Zak. I started feeling accepted by new surroundings of Western people, both in the professional field and other parents. They also believed in the idea that someone with autism can learn and talk and can lead a normal life. It felt good and empowering to believe Zak is not mentally ill, that autism is not a mental illness, and it has nothing to do with spiritual acts.

For years, I was named and shamed for using my son's condition to benefit me and to advance my career, hence why I am discussing publicly my son's autism and breaking cultural norms doing it. Autism Independence has been a public platform and an opportunity to help Zak and me be accepted by my community, but also to encourage other parents to speak up and seek help and support early on.

Over the years of my journey setting up Autism Independence, I have learned to build a thick skin and challenge the cultural ignorance around autism. This has led to 100 families coming forward and seeking help under Autism Independence. Regarding my role in the community, I am respected to certain extent, and I continue to be contacted by mothers around the world. I will never forget, though, the day I received a call from a desperate mother, begging me to not tell anyone she rang me about her concerns about her child.

Zak and I continue to publicly enjoy accessing a variety of activities, including family and community gatherings. I only worry about comforting him and ensuring he is comfortable by giving him anything that supports his anxiety, such as fiddles.

No doubt there is a long way to go in challenging masking and hiding autism, because the cultural sensitivity still very present in the Somali community, but I have been fortunate enough to offer some consolation and to use my experience to support others – but most of all to watch how much my son is now thriving.

Being forced to mask

Having the choice to mask, and consenting to mask, are different in feel and outcome to feeling forced to mask by the people or situation around you. Having autonomy is associated with better engagement (say, at school) and better outcomes (such as greater quality of life and wellbeing).

All children learn that they are able to make choices fairly early on in life – toddlers say 'no' to foods they do not want to eat, for example – and it has been shown that having your choices consistently over-ridden or ignored leads to difficulties later on. One example of this is around authoritarian parenting, where the parent feels as though they have the right to make all decisions and control the behaviour of their child, and enforce this through punishment. While this can result in very obedient children (though not always), those children are also more likely to have emotional and mental health difficulties as they grow up (Thompson, Hollis & Richards, 2003).

What can also be important is learning which adults to listen to, and who you should be more cautious about trusting and taking direction from. This can be complicated for many children, but especially autistic children, because the rules are not always clear. First, there are differences between the adults you meet – your mum can make you wear a coat to the park because she can ground you if you don't, but your postman can't (and probably wouldn't care to try!). Second, the rules change as you grow up – when you are 4 your mum simply puts the coat on you, and when you are 14 she has to threaten you with being grounded. Third, there are some situations that cover both of these bases. When you are young, it is common for people to pick you up, touch you and even kiss you without checking whether you want them to, and you are the one who is considered to be 'in the wrong' if you loudly announce that you don't want to hug Granny.

As you get older, other people may touch you without your consent, but most non-autistic people learn how to assert their boundaries and respond if those lines are crossed. For autistic people, learning this can be more difficult, because it is harder for them to change the 'rules' they are operating under. Instead, they may fall back on their mask to get them through the situation, but this is very much being forced to mask rather than choosing it. We will discuss some of the obvious risks this has in Chapter 4.

When talking about autistic people being forced to mask, it is worth mentioning applied behavioural analysis (ABA). ABA was described in more detail in Chapter 2, but it is a training approach that is popular with some parents and professionals while being deeply unpopular with many autistic adults. It aims to alter behaviours, and often the goal of the intervention is to make the child appear less 'obviously autistic', for example by reducing repetitive behaviours, making them make eye contact and increasing verbal communication over other forms. ABA therapists respond that they also help to reduce self-harming behaviours and can teach things like pictorial communication for non-verbal children, which are positive for the child. The problem comes in around the methods used, which are often described as having been traumatic by autistic adults, and in the fact that ABA undermines autistic children's sense of self-esteem by telling them that their natural reactions are in some way wrong. In this way, it can be seen as forcing children to mask, from a very young age (early intensive intervention can start as young as 18 months), and it takes little account of their consent or autonomy in doing so.

Choosing when to mask
Most of the time the reason autistic people choose to mask is because of a fear of other people's reactions:

> restricting my outward emotions and what I say and do so that others don't find me odd. (Mark, autistic man)

> I have a huge fear of losing control of my emotions at work, so this is a constant worry. (Olivia, autistic woman)

> When I go out, I can feel those pressures return immediately. It's like autopilot now after 24 years. It's a sort of survival instinct because

I'm scared of the reactions of people if they were to see me stimming or not communicating verbally. They might not understand. When I'm out in public I'm anxious, stressed and on high alert constantly. It's exhausting. It doesn't get easier despite how long you've been experiencing it. (Isabella, autistic woman)

This is not the only reason to mask, though, as we have seen elsewhere in this chapter. Sometimes, autistic people can also make a positive choice to mask – deciding to use the mask to help them do something that they know they want to, even if it will be challenging. Helen (one of the authors) likens it to wearing high heel shoes:

You know they're going to make your feet hurt but you want the extra few inches, and they go so wonderfully with your outfit that you're willing to risk the pain, all the time praying that you can have at least a few hours of dancing before it becomes unbearable!

In this type of situation, an autistic person has a choice over whether to mask, what elements of a mask to use and for how long, in full knowledge as to why they are masking and what they will get out of it. Psychologically, this is very different to masking either because you feel it is your only choice, or without even realizing because it has become so ingrained. It can loosely be compared to the concept of learned helplessness – those who feel they have no control over their situation are more likely to experience hopelessness and despair, and to do nothing to avoid painful experiences. Those who feel they do have control, even if it is in a small way, tend to have better mental health, retain hope about improving things and will be more proactive in going for what they want (Maier & Seligman, 2016).

Being able to choose when not to mask is therefore essential to good mental health for autistic people, and learning to recognize your masking, recognizing safe spaces and having techniques for taking the mask off are central to this.

So, to sum up this section...

This was all a very long way of saying that to the best of our knowledge, any autistic person can and does mask, to some extent, at least some of the time. But for a lot of people, dropping that mask can come with additional risks of social or even criminal judgement, meaning that it becomes more of a habit and harder to put down, which, in turn, can lead to difficulties being identified as autistic, because clinicians expect to see a certain set of behaviours in order to grant a diagnosis. There can be complex decisions weighing up pros and cons in masking and not masking, beyond the reasons described elsewhere that people give for why they mask.

So, where do people mask?

Frankly? Everywhere. Are there other people (especially non-autistic people)? Then chances are, an autistic person uses their mask to get through that situation at some point. As we've discussed so far, autistic people mask for a huge variety of reasons, and in a real range of ways, so it makes sense that these would cover a wide range of situations.

Masking at school

Autistic children at school are often classified as having special educational needs and disability (SEND), which comes with an individualized plan for their support needs. Regardless of what is in this plan, many autistic children will find themselves in a range of situations at school where they feel the need to mask. We are going to discuss some of these situations, and the research into them, below.

Masking with peers
As children and teenagers, most social events are mediated through parents or carers – they are who you have to ask for permission to go

to something, who take you there and pick you up, and who you are most likely to tell how it was on the way home, or once everyone has left your house. Some children who find these events difficult may try to mask this fact from their carers and pretend that they have really enjoyed the event, so that they are supported in going again in the future. Taking part in informal social events like play dates or sleepovers is crucial to making and maintaining friendships in childhood and adolescence, as this involvement helps to keep a place in the social networks at school. In turn, having friends, or even just one best friend, acts as a protective buffer against things like being bullied. This association is true for autistic children just as it is for non-autistic children, and for autistic girls as much as autistic boys. For autistic children, who are among the most bullied groups of all young people in school, finding ways to be more accepted can feel even more important than for their non-autistic peers.

This can lead to masking in friendships, as autistic children and young people are keen to keep the friends who both help them avoid bad experiences like being bullied and make life in school so much more fun – as well, of course, as having all the same reasons for wanting and choosing friends as anyone else! This was shown in a recent paper, where they found that autistic children chose friends who were similar to them socially, in terms of how they did in class, who had similar likes and interests, and who wanted to socialize in similar ways and at similar levels (Bennett *et al.*, 2018). This pattern of homophily (liking things that are similar) is also seen in both autistic and non-autistic adults when choosing friends and partners. Therefore, to appear more like their peers, autistic boys and girls may mask some of their natural behaviours to try to increase how accepted and liked they are by their peers.

Being bullied is a distressingly common occurrence for autistic children and young people – they report being victimized at least twice as much as non-autistic young people, and more than those with other disabilities such as being hard of hearing. Decades of research have shown how negatively being bullied affects people – it can worsen mental health, reduce self-esteem, and mean that people struggle to engage with school and learning, which potentially has lifelong knock-on impacts on employability. This is just as true of cyberbullying as it is in-person bullying, something which is increasingly important in our ever-more-online lives.

Research has shown that autistic children who have greater social communication difficulties and emotion regulation difficulties, and who score lower on traditional theory of mind tests, are more likely to be bullied (see Sreckovic, Brunsting & Able, 2014, for a review). These are all the kinds of things that masking may seek to hide from peers – trying to copy the communication styles of popular peers, for example, or trying to hide their emotions when they feel overwhelmed so that other people don't pick on them for being 'sensitive'. One of the people who wrote to us talked about masking for exactly that reason:

> Unfortunately, it is not difficult to trigger quite an extreme emotional meltdown in me... It can be triggered by any kind of perceived criticism, due to the humiliation I feel... [This] might well be a source of amusement or annoyance to others. So a lot of effort needs to go into trying to appear unruffled on the outside and not letting my true feelings, especially uncomfortable emotions such as fear, shame and humiliation, show. (Wendy, autistic woman)

On the other hand, it has also been suggested that autistic children who have higher levels of social skills may also be more likely to be bullied than those with an 'average' or 'middling' level of social skills (Rowley *et al.*, 2012). This is possibly because having fewer or less obvious social difficulties leads to the people around them having higher expectations of what they can do, or how they will interact. If an autistic child doesn't live up to these higher expectations, their peers can then almost 'punish' them for being different or 'failing'. Children and young people (both non-autistic and autistic) who display internalizing behaviours (such as being quiet or anxious) are also more likely to be bullied than those who display externalizing behaviours (such as difficulties with anger management) (Zablotsky *et al.*, 2014).

Considering the high levels of anxiety and social anxiety among autistic people of all ages, this may be another factor that makes autistic children stand out as 'easy targets' to bullies. This may be especially the case for autistic girls and women, who tend to experience more anxiety than autistic boys and men, and who are facing more complex and subtle social expectations due to the gendered nature of social behaviours. Of course, if the expectations are more complex and subtle, it is also easier to get something 'wrong' and can be more difficult to interpret or understand when someone is being mean. There are differences in how bullying is carried out by gender – boys are more likely to do what is called 'overt' aggression (hitting, chasing, taking someone's lunch), whereas girls are more likely to use 'relational' or 'social' aggression (gossiping, stealing friends, rolling their eyes every time someone tries to talk or join in). This means that autistic girls may be particularly vulnerable to being bullied by their non-autistic female peers, because these are the kinds of behaviours that it can be difficult to concretely describe, especially to an adult or teacher who may not 'see' them and so doesn't step in to help. It has also been suggested that (non-autistic) girls are more deeply impacted by this kind of bullying than boys are by their more overt bullying (Paquette & Underwood, 1999). Recent research on the gendered impacts of bullying among autistic young people has found something similar, with bullied autistic girls having higher rates of anxiety and depression than boys, especially if their bully was using the social and relational tactics described above (Greenlee, Winter & Marcovici, 2020).

Using masking behaviours to avoid bullying was discussed in work by Sedgewick and colleagues on the friendships of autistic boys and girls in both special education (2016) and mainstream settings (2018). In both these studies, the researchers interviewed autistic young people aged between 11 and 18 about their views on friendships, good times they had with friends and bad times they had with friends. Alongside lots of positives, like 'having someone to listen to me', 'feeling part of the group' and 'having people I trust and share things with', some participants talked about the links between being seen as different and being bullied or being excluded socially. One 18-year-old autistic girl reflected on how, at her previous school, she had:

> deliberately stopped people from [her] primary school being [her] friend when they came to [her] secondary school [a year later], so they wouldn't end up being associated with [her] and treated the same.

This came after she had been bullied and socially excluded by everyone else in her year for 'being weird'. In her case, this meant having been open about and monologuing on her special interests, and not suppressing her visible stims and other typically autistic behaviours when she first joined the school. The other students picked up on these things as making her 'odd', and sadly this made her a target. After leaving that school because of the bullying, she had started off masking at the next one in order to try to fit in and make friends, which had worked, and then as she became more comfortable in the relationships she had masked less and less around these trusted people. She described her current friendships as genuine and how she 'can be herself' with them, and that these people accept her for who she is, including the fact that she is autistic and the ways this means she behaves at times.

Many of the participants in these two studies talked about being bullied for being different to their peers in some way, and this was also something people who wrote to us for this book mentioned happening into adulthood:

> If I'm authentically me, then I know I'm vulnerable, an easy target. (Melissa, autistic woman, 26)

> Growing up, I was called shy and sneaky. I realized years later that I was just afraid to be myself because people would bully me or take advantage of me. (Cheyenne, autistic woman, 29)

If I last long enough in a social/work environment, people will gradually grasp that whilst I'm acerbic and 'abrasive', my solutions will work and everyone will be considered fairly. Then I seem to get a kind of acceptance...[until] some new NT will join and start bullying until I run away. (Paula, non-binary autistic person, 64)

Interestingly, one paper that looked at masking behaviours in both autistic and non-autistic children and young people showed that while autistic participants endorsed more masking behaviours overall, non-autistic participants (especially girls) also said that they engaged in many of the same behaviours (Jorgenson *et al.*, 2020). Where there was a significant difference between the two groups was that non-autistic girls in particular said that they did more assimilation behaviours, meaning that they watched the people around them for cues as to how to behave in order to fit in, especially after the age of 14.

This fits with what we know about how much more important it becomes to be socially accepted as children enter adolescence, as puberty and high school and all sorts of other factors combine to create a major change in the social lives of teenagers. Relationships become more complex, opposite-gender relationships increase in number and romantic relationships start to emerge, and there is a shift from a focus on doing things or playing together to emotional sharing and bonding. The findings of this research also agree with qualitative work with teenagers where both autistic and non-autistic teenagers, particularly girls, talked about changing their behaviour to fit in with their peers and be accepted (Sedgewick *et al.*, 2018). It should be noted, however, that there are some issues with the Jorgenson paper – the overall sample size was very small for the type of statistical analysis carried out, meaning that the results may not be reliable, and further research is needed to understand the impact of adolescence on masking.

Masking at university

Going to university is a big rite of passage for many young people, including many autistic young people. It is one of the biggest transitions most young people will face in their lives to that point, and carries a huge range of opportunities – but it can also be intimidating and have its challenges. Going to, and being at, university is known to be a challenging time for any young person, regardless of whether they are autistic or not. It is a time of transition, with increasing independence and new academic demands, all at the same time as trying to make new friends, learn how to get on with new lecturers, figure out what societies you want to join and find your place in the wider university organization.

Even among non-autistic university students, mental health is known to be poor, with anxiety and depression being the most common issues (Ibrahim *et al.*, 2015; Storrie, Ahern & Tuckett, 2010). These can arise from those same opportunities mentioned above, which can feel overwhelming for anyone when faced with all of it at once. What we do know, though, is that for many non-autistic students their mental health improves across the academic year as they settle into their living arrangements, make friends and get used to the demands of their course. There are predictable spikes (particularly of anxiety) around exam periods, and third years tend to have more difficulties due to the pressures of final assessments, but overall mental health gets better over time (Bewick *et al.*, 2010).

For autistic students, the challenging parts of university can feel that much more challenging. We know that transitions can be difficult for autistic people of any age, and university is a huge transition. Making friends can be tricky at the best of times, so it is natural that meeting lots of new people, as you move into the totally new environment of university halls, is understandably something a lot of autistic students worry about (Lei *et al.*, 2020). University has a lot less structure than school does – you are given a timetable, but this tends not to cover 9 a.m. to 4 p.m., five days a week (depending on your course, obviously). This means that for autistic students who have been used to a lot of direction and structure previously, the change to being self-directed can be difficult and cause them anxiety, or lead to them feeling overwhelmed with all the choices of what to do with their day (though it is worth noting that this does not only happen to autistic students, and there are whole departments at every university for teaching study skills like time management!).

On top of these practical elements of university life, which are faced by all students though perhaps more intensely by autistic students, being autistic itself does not change or go away with the move to university. Autistic students often still feel different to their non-autistic peers, as they did at school, and often face a lack of autism knowledge and understanding among the academic and pastoral staff. This can lead to stigmatizing attitudes from those staff, and from some other students (Lipson *et al.*, 2020). As for any minority or stigmatized group, encountering and having to deal with these attitudes can contribute to worse long-term outcomes and mental health for autistic students, leading to many feeling that dropping out is their only option regardless of how academically capable they are (Cage & Howes, 2020; Vincent, 2020). Many autistic students report feeling isolated, stressed, anxious and depressed. If they go to university support services, some report finding these difficult to navigate or lacking in specialist autism knowledge, which can mean that the suggestions they make and the support they offer are ineffective (Anderson, Stephenson & Carter, 2020).

Outside formal support structures, making friends or establishing romantic relationships have been shown to be two of the best ways to improve autistic student mental health and wellbeing (just as friendships are known to be key in preventing or minimizing being bullied in school). Autistic students who have this informal support network report feeling happier both personally and academically, especially if those friends are made through a shared interest or being part of a society:

That's pretty much where I've made all my friends, is through cheer...

That's really helped me a lot with my confidence. (Quoted in Scott & Sedgewick, 2021, p. 5)

Knowledge about autism appears to be increasing among students and staff, with correspondingly lower levels of stigma (Stronach, Wiegand & Mentz, 2019; White *et al.*, 2019). On a hopeful note, recent research suggests that if students are made aware of someone's autism diagnosis, they rate that autistic peer more positively and this increases acceptance of that student. It has also been highlighted that finding staff who know about autism can have a significant positive impact on their time in higher education, so we can predict that as knowledge continues to increase, autistic students will have more experiences like this student quoted by Scott and Sedgewick, helping them to have a more positive university experience:

They said 'we can give you a tutor who knows autism' and I was like 'great, go for it', and that helped cos she knew what to do to work with me. (Quoted in Scott & Sedgewick, 2021, p. 6)

Students are as likely to mask as any other autistic person, especially in the early days of their first year when they are trying to make friends and may push themselves to do uncomfortable things so that they are included:

I think where the autism was so hidden, I've always been very good at being sociable and being outgoing...[from that] my mental health has suffered.

I just felt like I couldn't enjoy a lot of social situations in first year without being drunk, 'cause they were so fucking loud, or stressful. That was something that made me quite depressed: I'd come away from hanging out with new people or going on a night out or something being like 'oh my god I'm never gonna like fit in'. (Quoted in Scott & Sedgewick, 2021, p. 5)

These quotes highlight the direct links between masking, social expectations and mental health for autistic students. This fits with what we know about camouflaging and mental health in general – that doing more camouflaging is linked to more anxiety and depression – and is further evidence of how that relationship holds true in a range of groups of autistic people. The same study tracked the mental health of autistic students across an academic year, looking to see if and what might change in that time. What they found was that, unsurprisingly, autistic students arrived at the start of the year with high levels of anxiety, social anxiety, ADHD and OCD; moderate levels of depression and eating disorders; and low levels of drinking and drug use (despite the first round of data being collected in and around Freshers Week!). These levels then stayed generally stable across the academic year, although alcohol use went down (this may be partly due to the COVID-19 pandemic though, as there were fewer places to drink and people to drink with in the latter stages of data collection due to the lockdowns). Interestingly, their mental health did not get significantly worse during the pandemic, with most levels staying pretty much the same – and social anxiety actually went down for some participants, probably because they were spending less time socializing or in spaces that might make them feel anxious. The findings on mental health from this study suggest that autistic university students face significant mental health challenges across their time at university, and that current formal support systems might not be helping them well enough currently.

This study also explored the coping styles of autistic university students, getting them to say what their preferred methods of coping with difficulties were at three time points across the year. Considering the relatively poor mental health students were reporting, understanding their coping styles might be a clue for universities as to how to support students better. This portion of the study found that autistic students were slightly more likely to say they used what are called approach strategies (things like positive reframing of a situation, asking someone for emotional or practical help, or planning how to change things for the better) than they were to use avoidant strategies (such as denial, substance use, or refusing to engage with what is happening). These two types of strategy were much more equally used than in non-autistic people though, who tend to have a strong bias towards approach coping styles. When the researchers looked at how mental health and coping styles related across the year, they found that anxiety and depression were consistently linked to avoidant coping. This means that the people who were more likely to use avoidant coping strategies were more likely to report high levels of anxiety and depression at each point in the year than people who used approach strategies. This is the same as we see in non-autistic people, where avoidant strategies are also associated with worse mental health, and it has been suggested that this might be because chronic anxiety and depression decrease people's energy and ability to seek out help with those same conditions. It might be that making it easier to access help and support, especially support which is tailored to autistic people, could have a significant positive impact on the mental health of autistic students at all universities.

Halls

One of the key settings for university life – and usually the first one someone arrives at – is halls of residence. At most British universities, first year students are offered accommodation run by the university, where they are put into flats or corridors of bedrooms (in modern blocks these are usually en suite, in older buildings there will be shared bathrooms) with a communal kitchen/socializing space. People normally don't know who will be in the flat before they go, though sometimes people will set up something like a Facebook group for those who are going to live in the same building before everyone arrives.

This process can involve a lot of anxiety for anyone, autistic or non-autistic. There is the physical move, which involves packing and planning what to take, the travel and the unpacking in a new space which is probably very different to home. There are the emotions around moving – the sense of growing up, the potential sadness of leaving home (even knowing they will go home for the holidays), the excitement of getting to start university... A lot is going on, especially coming hot on the heels of all the stress and anxiety about exam results! And there is also the social side of it all – meeting new people, wondering what everyone thinks of each other (everyone does this, and everyone is worried, no matter how relaxed and confident they seem, honestly), trying to guess who will be friends (or not), trying to work out what people might be like – again, there is a lot going on. All those things are going on for everyone, but new autistic students might feel them more intensely and find it harder to express what they are feeling. This can make the transition to halls more difficult, and when a lot of friendships are formed in the first couple of weeks, people can feel anxious that they aren't doing 'well enough' or getting the 'right' university experience. Most young people have clear expectations of what going to university will be like, whether that comes from TV, films, or knowing older siblings and friends who have already gone. If their experiences don't match up to these expectations it can be upsetting, and this in turn makes it harder to access the things that are part of those expectations, like big social events or university societies.

What is important to remember is that everyone has very different experiences at university, and the ones in the media are not the norm at all. Some people don't make their best friends for life in Freshers Week, but in a second year seminar, or at a third year guest lecture. Some people find the society that will be their passion at Freshers Week fair, and that will structure all their free time for three years, and others will come across it by chance two weeks before the end of the second term – and most people join two or three things that they are interested in, and do each of them a bit more casually around the rest of what they enjoy spending time on. All of these are perfectly valid ways of 'doing' university, and what is most important is finding something that works for the autistic student as an individual rather than worrying about what university is 'meant' to be like.

Where this can be difficult is if a student does not get on with the people they live with, for example. Again, this is more common than lots of people want to admit. The nice thing is that everyone gets to choose who they live with after the first year, and can choose to live alone (finances allowing, of course), if that works better for them.

Helen commented about her experience:

> I definitely rushed my choices when it came to sorting out where to live in my second year. Everyone was panicking me by saying if you didn't have a house sorted by February then all the good ones would be gone! Four months into university and I'd already committed to a tenancy with two relatively new friends I'd met through my course, before I could really say I knew them properly. As it turned out I didn't get on well with my course, and living with a classmate was one of the worst things I could have done. Not have a great living arrangement made the year really hard, as home didn't feel like my safe place any more.

Every university has a housing office that can help with finding secure private accommodation, and support students in dealing with difficulties around housing of all kinds. Most halls of residence also have a team of staff who look after the buildings and the students, so if someone is having major issues it is worth talking to them and to whoever is responsible for their pastoral support (these have different titles in different universities, but are generally called personal tutors). The key message for an autistic student is to talk to someone if they are finding halls or housing difficult, not to just try to put up with it or struggle through – there are mechanisms out there to help.

Lectures, seminars and lab work

Other aspects of university life that may involve masking by an autistic person are lectures, seminars and labs (depending on the degree they are taking, some people will have some, or all, of these activities on their timetable, in different proportions). The details for specific courses will all be in the course handbook, which is normally made available before the start of each term.

Lectures tend to be one or two hours long, and involve sitting and listening to the lecturer talking about a specific topic, sometimes with activities or small group discussions built in. They will be open to everyone on the course or unit/module, so there can be a lot of people in the room depending on how many people are signed up. Traditionally lectures took place in official lecture halls, which tend to be tiered seating like a theatre, but in modern universities smaller groups especially may be in smaller rooms and seated around tables in groups, more like a school classroom. Most universities now ask lecturers to post the lecture slides online for students a week in advance of the live session, so students will have an idea of what is going to be talked about. This can help to reduce anxiety for autistic students, which makes it easier to focus in the class itself. Many lectures, especially those with a lot of students, tend to be based more around listening than interacting, and taking in information that way can feel very reassuring for autistic students.

Seminars tend to be smaller than lectures, with students either being split into seminar groups who go at different times, or, on a small course, all attending at the same time but working in groups. These are more based around interaction, group activities and discussion, rather than listening to the lecturer giving the information. Sometimes the task will be set before the session for students to think about in advance before discussing their answers/solutions/ ideas in a group. Seminars might feel intimidating at first, but can be incredibly valuable because they share different opinions and useful readings without each student having to do all the work themselves, and give practice at things like presentations which are often part of work after university, but in a safe and supportive environment.

Labs are more relevant for science-based subjects such as medicine, chemistry and physics than they are for subjects like law, English or history. These will vary significantly by discipline, but are usually at a set time and place (due to equipment requirements) and involve carrying out experiments, both short and longer term (e.g. some experiments can be completed in one session, and some will take several weeks). These normally involve working in groups of two or three, and it is up to the individual course leader whether people choose their own groups or the teacher organizes them. The point of labs is often to learn about the scientific process – how to plan an experiment, set up equipment, collect data, analyse it and write everything up to a high standard. It can be very methodical and ordered, which can suit autistic people – but also, things can go wrong unexpectedly, and sometimes for no obvious reason, so it is important to be aware of this and for autistic students to be supported with the upset they may feel (as do non-autistic students!). University students are not expected to be perfect scientists or brilliant at every aspect of their course, because the whole point is that they are there to learn. Lecturers know that accidents happen, and are unlikely to be angry or disappointed when they do – they have experience with this and are more likely to suggest solutions than anything else.

Important to know: Every university has a disability support service. These are the people students can go to in order to get help with anything related to being disabled, including being autistic – they write what is called a disability support statement, which tells lecturers and other university staff what accommodations they should make to support any autistic student. This can include things like being exempted from group presentations, extra time in exams, or even getting a room in a quieter accommodation block. But they can only do this if they know someone is autistic, so even if it feels scary to disclose, it can be worth doing.

Masking at work

After university, most people go into work of some description – whether this is related to their degree or not. Lots of people also go into work straight after school, without getting a degree – either route is fine. Regardless of their level of education, autistic people often find themselves masking at work, for a variety of reasons.

To disclose or not to disclose?
One of the first questions many autistic people face is whether or not to tell the people they work with (or are applying for a job with)

that they are, in fact, autistic. Many autistic people do not disclose, because they fear stigmatizing attitudes from the people they tell, or because they worry that it will prevent them getting the job if the interviewer holds negative stereotypes about autism (Romualdez *et al.*, 2021). This same study found that only a third of autistic adults disclose that they are autistic to everyone in the workplace, most disclosed either in the paper application or once in work (but rarely at interview), and that a third had only disclosed after having problems at work when they were seeking reasonable adjustments. Those who did disclose that they were autistic at work did so in the hope that people would be more understanding of their differences and would treat them better because of this knowledge. This is a reasonable assumption – research has shown that the first impressions people form of an autistic person improve if they know that person is autistic in advance (Sasson & Morrison, 2019).

By law, you do not have to disclose any disability, and at the recruitment and interview stages, employers can only ask what reasonable adjustments someone needs for the recruitment process, and to check that they are able to carry out all functions of the role if reasonable adjustments are in place – for example, they can ask a wheelchair user applying for a shelf-stacking role whether they need a ramp to enter the interview building and whether they are capable of putting products on the top shelf. Once someone has been offered a job, an employer should further ask what adjustments someone may need to be able to do the job to the best of their abilities – such as support, training, shift patterns that fit around regular medical appointments, etc. It is worth knowing that there can be times when confidentiality about a disclosure cannot be total – for example, a disabled employee might need support from their colleagues, so those colleagues need to know that, or there might be health and safety reasons for other people to be aware of something that has been disclosed.

'Reasonable adjustments' is a phrase that has come up several times in this section. These are, in effect, changes an employer or people around you make that mean you are more able to function.

'Reasonable' is a nebulous term, and each situation is assessed individually rather than there being a set of rules for what is and is not considered a reasonable adjustment. Usually though, the assessment involves things like whether the adjustments are practical for the employer to make, whether they can afford them, how well they are likely to overcome difficulties and whether they will have a negative impact on other people in the workplace. 'Reasonable' is also an assessment of how quickly the adjustments can be made: if an autistic person starts a new job but doesn't tell anyone at the organization that they are autistic until their first day, then it would not be reasonable to expect adjustments to be put in place by the end of the day. However, if they had disclosed early in the recruitment process then there should have been an ongoing dialogue between the autistic person and the organization in advance of their first day to discuss what reasonable adjustments might need to be put in place for the start of their employment.

Is it also worth thinking about exactly what you want to disclose when you are making a disclosure decision. For example, deciding to disclose that you are autistic, or that you have a mental or physical health condition, does not mean that you have to share every aspect of your disability or medical history. There may be things that you feel are not relevant to your job, and it is your right to keep those private. Equally, there may be things that you know are highly likely to impact your work day to day, so those are what it is most important to share. This way you can also build in suggestions for the things that help you, and the things that are particularly difficult for you, so that people who know are best placed to work with you successfully. You also do not have to tell everyone in your company or who you come into contact with (such as customers, clients, corporate associates) – it might be relevant to the team you work with every day, but not to each customer you speak to, for example. It can also be useful to think in advance about how you want to tell people – would you rather do it in writing, or in person? In a group all at once, or one to one in your own time? Planning exactly what you want to say in advance can be helpful and means that you are sharing what you want to, with who you want to, giving you more control over the process.

Disclosure is a significant, complex and highly individual decision. It is specific to each person's situation and experiences, and there is no right or wrong answer on whether or when to disclose at work. A recent review of the papers looking at disclosure experiences of autistic people at work found that others (such as parents) generally expected the outcomes of disclosure to be positive, whereas autistic people themselves were often more worried about negative reactions and stigma (Thompson-Hodgetts *et al.*, 2020).

> Once someone knows you are autistic they start to make assumptions about what you can and can't do. I had to bite my tongue so much to stop myself having a go at one manager who persisted in treating me like a child after being told that I'm autistic. (Anonymous)

Indeed, other studies have shown that there are a range of reactions people face when they disclose, from supportive adaptations to their job through to stigmatizing assumptions about their abilities, regardless of previous performance.

The factors that we know affect disclosure are age at diagnosis (earlier diagnosis was linked to greater likelihood to disclose, due to higher self-esteem and perceived lower discrimination), the social demands of the position (the more social demands involved, the more likely to disclose and ask for reasonable adjustments) and workplace policies (so people working in a company with explicit policies to support autistic people were more likely to disclose) (Lindsay *et al.*, 2021). As more autistic people with early diagnoses enter the workplace, such as the current generation, who are more likely to have known for most of their lives that they are autistic, it is to be hoped that the supportive reactions of those they tell become more common as employers and colleagues are more familiar with autism. This should lead to a more accepting and positive working environment for all neurodiverse people, not just those on the spectrum.

Interviews

One of the major stages of getting a job is often the interview – most positions will require some kind of phone or in-person interview (or Zoom interview during COVID-19 times, and these are likely to stay an option for interviews at a distance). Interviews do not necessarily naturally play to autistic people's strengths – they require intense social interaction, with specific norms and expectations which are not made clear to the interviewee, and may actually be very different to the day-to-day job (think being interviewed for a job in a warehouse or as a computer programmer, neither of which are social-skills heavy in contrast to an interview!). These factors can put autistic people at a disadvantage, and mean that they do not present themselves to the best of their ability or demonstrate their ability to do the job they are being interviewed for.

If someone is masking their way through the social element of the interview, for example worrying about who to make eye contact with, for how long and how frequently; or putting on their best 'enthusiastic but normal' facial expressions; or working out how to pitch their voice so that they sound like the type of person the interviewer wants to work with, they will have less brain capacity to focus on the actual answers they give, or to listen out for hints from the interviewer about something they've missed (interviewers often do this, to give candidates a chance to go back to a point they are specifically looking for). Masking not only takes a lot of cognitive effort, which is not ideal in an interview situation, but it means that the interviewers are not seeing the 'real' autistic person, and so may be surprised when they actually start work if they behave differently – it can feel to the autistic person that they are setting themselves up to have to mask for the rest of their time at that job. Which, considering how much time we all spend at work, can be exhausting and intimidating. Helen commented:

> I went for an interview at one place that was so visually overwhelming that from the minute I walked in I knew there was no way I could work there. By the time I got to the room I was being interviewed

in my mask was already straining under the pressure of a sensory overload; no way would I be able to keep up the charade working full time in that environment!

There is some research about autistic people and interviews, though none of it specifically addresses masking in interviews. Most of the early work focuses on teaching autistic people how to 'do better' at interview – and there is now lots of video modelling, virtual reality training and role-play intervention work out there (Hayes *et al.*, 2015; Rosales & Whitlow, 2019; Smith *et al.*, 2014). Recently, however, research has shifted focus to how employers can make interviews more appropriate for autistic candidates, and encourages them to think about whether the role even requires an interview at all. A new study from Katie Maras and her team showed that adapting interview questions (to being more clearly defined) improved how everyone performed, but that the improvement was bigger for autistic than non-autistic participants (Maras *et al.*, 2020). This shows that simple changes to things like the interview questions can create a much more level playing field for autistic people entering the workplace. Equally, being clear as to what skills the position actually requires, rather than putting down standard phrases on a job advert (especially things like 'good communication skills' or 'good team player') can improve autistic people's likelihood of applying for jobs that they are a good fit for – something called 'job match' in research on factors enabling employment (Dreaver *et al.*, 2020). If a job does not actually require lots of time spent working in teams, making this clear could appeal to autistic people in the sector who prefer to work independently, rather than them being put off from the outset.

Masking once in employment

Once in the job and doing it day in, day out, there are a whole raft of new ways in which masking is likely to come into play for an autistic person. New recruits normally don't know their colleagues very well, so are unlikely to feel comfortable enough with them to be their true selves. This isn't just an autistic thing – most people put on their 'best face' when they start a new job, or their 'professional face' while they are at work in general, and this tends to be different to how they would act and behave when they are feeling totally relaxed, for example. But as we have said before – masking is not the same thing as acting a certain way in a certain context. Have a look at the section 'Case study: A comparison of a day presenting at a conference' in Chapter 4, where Laura and Helen describe their different days at a conference to see how this can differ for autistic and non-autistic people in a professional setting! An autistic person masking with colleagues is a facet of trying to convince them that they are not autistic, or are less autistic than they really feel, and suppressing natural behaviours or reactions which might mark them out as different. This can be anything from forcing themselves to take part in small talk in the office or putting up with people interrupting their hyper-focus flow 'just for a chat', to hiding the fact that the office lighting is causing them pain or that every after-work drink event causes them to panic for an hour before they get to the venue.

It is not just direct colleagues with whom autistic people are likely to mask at work. Most of us also have to interact with our managers or people higher up in the organizational hierarchy, who have more power and are seen as more important than us. The unwritten social rules for talking to, emailing and working with these people are different than they are for people at the same level as you. Everyone is expected to show them more respect (however that is displayed in that setting), to listen to their thoughts (regardless of what you think of them) and to only contact them for certain things (they are not the person you go to if you don't know how to work the printer!). Interacting with seniors at work can require a different mask to the one autistic people use with their colleagues. Switching between masks can be even more difficult than maintaining just one mask while at work, as this is an extra cognitive task and another set of things to remember to do and say, or not do and not say.

Both direct colleagues and managers can be part of something that autistic people have told researchers they find particularly difficult – *office politics*. This is the name for when people use the

WHY DO PEOPLE MASK? AND WHERE?

relationships within the company or organization for their own ends, rather than purely focusing on the tasks of work. Things like gossiping about other workers, only inviting certain people to go and get lunch together, or who gets included in different projects can all be part of office politics. Because this is essentially based on the same principles as the relational aggression we described in the section earlier in this chapter on masking at school, it can be just as confusing and difficult to navigate for autistic people as it was in high school. Helen commented on her experience of office politics:

> It was just like being back at school with the whispering behind my back and being left out of things. Every Sunday night caused a panic attack as I got so anxious about what it would be like on Monday morning when everyone did the 'what did you get up to at the weekend' chit chat round the kettle.

And struggling to recognize or react to relational tactics can lead to further difficulties in the workplace – being isolated or ostracized, feeling picked on, being excluded from opportunities, or even being overlooked for promotion or being seen as the easy first person to fire because an autistic person is not 'part of the group' in the same way.

> It chips away at my confidence; I am made to feel like a lesser being because my views or feelings are deemed insignificant. (Maria)

These are all things described in an Australian paper that looked at autistic people's experiences in employment, which found that autistic women were especially subject to these challenges (Baldwin & Costley, 2016; Baldwin, Costley & Warren, 2014). Getting through office politics, once you know that this is what is happening around you, can again require adapting your 'work mask' to account for the interpersonal relationships around you and the ways they are being used by other people. This can play into the hierarchies of being at work in general, and the ways in which these function can feel very opaque to autistic people who are used to thinking of things in more straightforward ways, as discussed by one of our contributors:

> I've never mastered social hierarchies properly; I can never understand why credit for my work should be given to someone else, for example, or why I can't implement a sensible solution to a problem because my boss doesn't understand it. (Paula, autistic person, 64)

The same contributor talked about the impact that masking, and the difficulties of masking, had on their career over time:

> [it] cost me a steady career, recognition, financial stability, and has had a serious negative impact on my health as well as my self-esteem. It's not only masking but more importantly the limitations of my ability to mask successfully over longer periods because of how exhausting it is... It's been extremely stressful and a constant exhausting balancing act to keep financially afloat and mentally healthy at the same time.

While not all autistic people find being at work, and masking at work, to be distressing and impactful to this degree, it is true that it can have this effect on some people. Especially as society becomes more knowledgeable and accepting of autistic people and their needs generally, the picture in employment should improve, and this will lead to greater inclusion and a focus on the skills autistic people can bring to a workplace, something Paula also highlighted in their comments:

> We're conscientious, need minimal management, often have really strong and rare skills, and we work hard to deliver to high standards on time.

Autistic women and female-presenting people can also face the additional challenge of thinking about personal relationships and safety at work. While this is not an issue exclusive to women and female-presenting people, as men can also experience difficulties in this area, it is much more common for women and those who present as female. Autistic women and female-presenting people who use their mask to be polite and sociable are more likely to be misinterpreted as flirting, for example, and need to be prepared for this – 'polite flirting' is actually a recognized flirting style, so this misunderstanding can happen a lot (Hall & Xing, 2015). Difficulties interpreting facial expressions, tone of voice or 'hidden meanings' in what people say, as well as an increased chance of being misinterpreted themselves, can mean that autistic women are more likely to experience unwanted attention. This does not have to be romantic or sexual – it can also be someone who wants more of your time than you want to give them because they want to be your friend. It can be very important to be clear in your own mind about your boundaries and what you want from a working relationship, as this helps you make it clear to other people if they have overstepped your preferences. Remember, though, that just because you know someone from work doesn't mean that they can't become a friend! Helen and Felicity first knew each other in a work context, but have become friends over a shared love of rugby.

This section is only a brief overview of how masking can impact autistic people in employment. It does not cover every job, or every situation one might meet in a job. Instead, it is a general discussion of some of the issues people might face, and of what insights autism research and autistic people can give us into these challenges. There is also another side to it all – what happens if masking goes wrong at work? This is discussed in more detail in Chapter 4, in the section 'Burnout'.

Masking at social events

The term *social events* in itself covers a plethora of situations – from family weddings to football matches to the pub on a Friday night. Each one of these has different rules and expectations, and so needs a slightly different mask, or different aspects of the mask an autistic person has built for themselves. No single book can fully cover every situation where an autistic person might mask, obviously. But there are some key events outlined below, working from smaller to bigger numbers of people (probably).

Family events

Family events, as with social events, cover a wide range of situations. Weddings, funerals and birthday parties are often all family events, but have very different behaviours. For example, although people tend to cry at weddings and at funerals, it is for different reasons – we hope!

There are also different 'categories' of family member – your immediate family are usually the people you have grown up living with and who know you really well (think parents and siblings, sometimes grandparents), whereas you may have spent less time with your extended family and know them less well (Felicity has cousins she has met only twice in her lifetime, for example). These factors – type of event and type of family present – mean that people may mask differently at different family events.

Birthday parties

At their own birthday party, with just the people they have chosen to have with them and who they feel comfortable being with, autistic people may mask very little. Someone would hopefully feel comfortable to stim with joy or excitement at receiving a present they love, or asking everyone not to sing 'Happy Birthday' because it triggers their sensory sensitivities.

These kinds of changes are easier for adults to request than for children, though, and especially for children pre-diagnosis, parents might be confused as to why they seem to hate their birthday parties. Think about a stereotypical children's birthday party for a moment... the whole class invited, normally doing some kind of loud or energetic activity, music playing, maybe finger food options, balloons out... There is the potential for a lot of this to be difficult for an autistic child! One mother who talked about her experiences around her daughter's birthday party has told us how 'she didn't recognize any of her friends, because she had only seen them in school uniform and so she couldn't work out who they were in other clothes' (anonymous), and so her daughter was anxious because she thought there were lots of strangers at her party. Once her daughter had explained this, the solution was to get all the children to wear name badges so she knew who was who – under the excuse that the magician or the balloon man, or whoever, needed it so they could talk to the kids by name during the act. Up until that point, though, her daughter had been in full-on masking mode to be polite and 'normal' with all these strangers. Once she knew that these were her friends, she could relax that mask, be more herself and enjoy the party a lot more.

Birthday parties do not stop with childhood, though, and autistic adults can have difficulties with their celebrations too. 'Big birthdays' like 18, 21 and 30, can bring their own pressures and expectations, and this can lead to autistic people masking heavily through an event that is supposed to be about making them happy. There can be an expectation from other people that they will have a 'blow-out' with lots of alcohol (and people), often involving going out to bars or clubs, or some sort of large organized event – all things that autistic people can find difficult, or just not to their taste. As you get older – the big birthdays of 40, 50, 60 and so on – celebrations tend to be more family oriented. This can mean less alcohol (though not always), but in its place there can be children running around and making noise, unfamiliar people in the form of partners and other sensory difficulties which also lead to masking.

It is possible, of course, to have an adult birthday party where an autistic person feels they need to mask very little. Usually, the way to do this is forward planning, and forward planning that actively involves the autistic person, is open to their preferences and does not involve judgement for those preferences. Helen commented about her birthday meal:

My 18th birthday meal with my family ended up being a really nice event that I didn't need to mask much for. But this was only because

I had the confidence to put a personal demand in place early in the planning stages – no plus ones or partners if I didn't know them well enough; every single person who came on the day was explicitly invited by name, and therefore everyone around the table was a safe, known person. And no one was spending their time 'looking after' someone who didn't know anyone else there.

Even if you know someone very well, planning a surprise party carries risks – autistic or not. It is possible to invite/not invite someone who should have not been invited/been invited, or choose food they don't like, or they may simply not be surprise party people. The same goes for autistic people, but the surprise may be especially unwelcome. Autistic people tend to like to have a clear plan and to be able to predict what is going to happen, and uncertainty and change are linked to experiencing anxiety (Hwang *et al.*, 2020). Even with the best of intentions, a surprise party is definitely a change to someone's day! There is, for anyone given a surprise party, the initial shock, but an autistic person may not be able to get away to recover from this, and it could trigger a meltdown. Many autistic people would try to get through this by masking, but they may also feel betrayed because people have lied to them to set the party up. Again, despite there being good intentions behind those lies, this can be difficult for an autistic person to separate from the fact of lying (Margoni & Surian, 2016). It can also be that autistic people feel 'robbed' of the joy of planning the party and being involved in that group activity, which can be upsetting.

Funerals

Funerals are usually a very different type of family event to a birthday party. However, there are some thematic similarities – often large numbers of family who you haven't seen for a long time or don't know very well, a set of expected emotional responses and all kinds of organization challenges that you may be involved in to different degrees depending on who has died. These things are even harder to process and manage when you are also grieving, a process which is emotionally intense and very difficult. There are often fewer instruc-tions given prior to a funeral than for a wedding (e.g. what to wear, whether to bring flowers or not, whether plus ones are welcome), meaning anxiety can be heightened on top of all the other emotions people are feeling, especially as funerals have far less prior warning to them than other major family events, particularly in the case of an unexpected death. When people are experiencing emotional distress, they are more irritable and have less tolerance for others. Knowing this, an autistic person may feel increased pressure to mask and behave 'normally' in order to avoid annoying or upsetting the people around them. Sadly, this can mean that the autistic person them-selves has less opportunity to work through their own grief. There is a possible silver lining though, in that grief is widely culturally acknowledged to be a more individual process than joy is expected to be, and so people are more likely to accept it if an autistic person is grieving in a way that is different to themselves.

Personal piece: Helen and Laura's perspectives on a funeral

Helen's experience of a family funeral

My paternal grandfather died when I was away at university, his funeral taking place amid my end-of-year exams. I had been aware that he was having serious health problems and that dialysis was being discussed, but hadn't been prepared for death being an imminent thing, so when the phone call came from my father at 6 a.m. one miserable Wednesday it felt like a sucker punch to my gut. The feeling of disorientation and mental fog lasted until the day of the funeral; looking back I think I was unable to process what had happened until I could physically see my family and 'see' the hole my grandad had left.

The day of the funeral was tough. My mum had come with me and my brother, as she had kept a good relationship with her former in-laws even after my dad remarried when I was 8, but it did give me an odd sense of awkwardness sandwiched between the comfort of having her there to support me and the relief at not having to figure out how to get to the funeral as a non-driver. I was okay initially, grief wasn't a new emotion for me to be processing and I took a lot of comfort from knowing my nanny's Catholic faith was guiding her through her widowhood, but as we arrived at the crematorium my sensory triggers started to kick in as I was overwhelmed by the heady mixture of multiple perfumes, aftershaves, flowers and a strange scent I later identified as 'wet tissue'. But I couldn't wrinkle up my nose and pull a face at the smells, or groan and hold my head at the impending spike of pain through my temples – to do so would potentially cause an issue with the family members who were unaware of my autism (yet to be formally diagnosed at this point) and would feel distasteful given where we were.

My mask at this point was fixed, and I had an odd sense of security in it that I wouldn't normally have in any other situation, but I knew that as the funeral went on a 'crack' in my coping wouldn't seem out of place as everyone was struggling and sobbing. The hardest part of the day for me came afterwards, when various family members were embracing each other and giving comfort through hugs. The last thing I wanted at this point was to be physically touched; internally I was in near-overload and desperate to reach a safe haven where I could stim without it looking like I was fidgeting and being rude. My mum asked me if I wanted a hug. I knew she wanted one, but she also understood me well enough by then to know to ask first. But because others in my family didn't know about my autistic needs back then I had to force myself to accept their hugs like they expected me to so as not to upset them by 'rejecting' their offer or 'being difficult'. All I wanted to do was say no, say I couldn't cope with the touch or the close encounters with more smells from shampoo/make-up, and so on, but my internal voice was screaming to 'be normal, do what everyone else is doing, don't cause a scene' so I had to squash down my authentic reaction and act the way I perceived

I should for that situation, no matter how much it caused me additional pain.

Laura's experience of a funeral

When I was at university I attended the funeral of a friend from school. Although we had been close in previous years, I had lost touch with her after going to university. I attended the funeral with a small group of school friends, but I didn't know most of the other attendees – they were her extended family and neighbours. As a result, I felt more pressure to behave in the 'right' way at this funeral, rather than being more genuine in my emotional expressions. I was very much aware that other people at the funeral had different memories and relationships with my friend, and I didn't want to 'take over' any part of the ceremony or reception with my grief. I tried to keep my sadness contained, trying not to cry too loudly and to smile and greet her parents at the reception. This was particularly tricky at one point in the ceremony, when a song that we had listened to together was played; it made the moment feel much more personal to me and I had to hold back sobs. However, that was the only point during the funeral that I felt I really had to mask or control my emotional response. The rest of the time, I felt that my genuine level of emotion (sadness, but not overwhelming) was appropriate for the situation. I even felt comfortable at the reception laughing and joking a little with my friends, as we shared funny memories of our friend with her parents. I was aware of monitoring myself, to make sure that the stories I told would bring good memories to those around me, but beyond that I was able to relax more despite the noisiness and emotions across the reception. I felt that the way I was responding to the situation was appropriate and that I was expressing my emotions in the same way as other people around me, so I didn't need to change anything about what I was doing.

Reflections on the two sets of experiences

When considering masking in a recognized difficult setting like a funeral, it's clear that the additional sensory demands of being autistic can make dealing with complicated emotions even harder. This creates greater pressure to mask those sensory demands, as well as more difficulty in keeping up an appropriate social mask, as Helen describes when having to hug people at the funeral. Laura describes one point where she needed to mask her grief, since she didn't want to take attention away from others at the funeral. However, she was able to do this without too much effort – possibly because she wasn't trying to cope with sensory issues on top of her emotions. Laura also expressed her grief in ways which were generally acceptable to others at the funeral, and so was able to meet the social expectations of the situation – talking to her friend's bereaved parents – while still experiencing her genuine emotions. In contrast, Helen felt like she had to hold back her need to stim at the funeral in order to not upset other people, which made it even harder to go along with what other people were doing. This demonstrates how masking is often hardest in the situations where there might be the greatest expectation to mask. Emotional events such as funerals, which often involve interacting with people who don't know you very well, come with many different social expectations. Different people are 'allowed' to express grief in different ways, and there is an expectation that the needs of the immediate family of the deceased will come first. However, if those needs conflict with other family members' needs (such as wanting hugs versus needing to avoid contact), it can create problems! Masks can be useful for all people, autistic or not, in settings such as funerals in order to get through and avoid disrupting an already very difficult day. A non-autistic person might only need to mask for a short amount of time, however, whereas an autistic person's mask might get harder and harder to maintain as the event continues.

Weddings and associated events

Something like a wedding is a very different family event again. People are celebrating rather than grieving, and there are many more social norms involved, both about what happens on the day and how you are expected to behave. Add to that the emotional weight people attach to having 'the perfect day' and it is understandable that autistic people might feel a lot of pressure to mask and play their part in making everything go smoothly.

From the perspective of a wedding guest, the pressures of a wedding start long before the day. If you are close to one of the people getting married, you might be invited to the stag or hen do, often events associated with going to an unfamiliar place, with at least a couple of people you might not know as well as the person getting married, and potentially new activities or a lot of alcohol involved, and often an explicitly sexual tone to games, for example. In this kind of situation, people are often expected to be excited, happy, 'up for it' and to get involved in what is going on regardless of how they feel. So, it is understandable that an autistic person would utilize their mask to get through elements they don't enjoy, or to socialize with people they don't know, so that they don't 'spoil' the experience for their friend getting married. But this can be exhausting, obviously, and the idea of having to do it can mean that someone turns down the invitation. If the autistic person is close to the person getting married, they might be asked to help prepare for the wedding – something most people are happy to do, obviously, but which can again require masking as they interact with a range of people they don't know, such as other friends who are helping, or professionals like florists, hairdressers, or even their friends' family at the wedding rehearsal.

Most guests will not be invited to the stag or hen do, but there is still masking involved in attending a wedding. Choosing an outfit can often feel like the start of building a mask for the day – making sure you are in the 'right thing' is important for everyone, autistic or not, but for an autistic person it can feel like the equivalent of armour, or camouflage. Having on something that does not make you stand out as different is the first stage in getting through the day successfully. Luckily, most people now have very clear outlines of what will happen on their wedding day, with timings, that they send out with the invites and things like meal choice requests (though it depends on the type of wedding!). That can be really helpful for an autistic wedding guest and reduce their anxiety about what to expect from the day, as can the ability to choose food, or at least know what the food will be, before they go. Once they get to the wedding, however, there is still a significant amount of masking that can happen. Weddings often mean getting together lots of extended family members who have not seen each other in a long time, and who do not know each other very well (such as Felicity's two cousins, both seen at weddings only!). In this case, despite being family, these people can effectively feel like strangers who you can only do small talk with, meaning that most autistic people will automatically use their mask to get them through the interaction.

There are also 'standard' emotional reactions that people expect to see at certain points in a wedding – gasping or crying when the bride walks into the ceremony for the first time, laughing at the right point in the speeches, generally being excited and happy all day. Autistic people often express their emotions in different ways to non-autistic people (Eack, Mazefsky & Minshew, 2015), and non-autistic people are not good at interpreting these (Brewer *et al.*, 2016). This can lead to pressure to mask and show the 'right' emotions at the 'right' times, otherwise an autistic person might worry that they will be challenged for not being happy enough for the couple and by implication not caring about them enough.

There is, obviously, another side to a wedding – that of the people who are actually getting married! All of the above points about dealing with people you don't know in the planning process, worrying about doing the 'right' thing, the emotional pressures and expectations, and even the small talk with extended family members apply for the couple too. Some autistic people getting married will feel comfortable enough to build a wedding that works for them, such as refusing to invite people they don't feel close to, or skipping parts of the 'standard' day which will trigger their sensory sensitivities, but many will still feel they are expected to have a day that follows the traditional patterns. While they will hopefully not feel the need to mask with their partner, or their closest family and friends, there

146

are still all sorts of ways in which they may mask both in the run-up and on the actual day.

Informal social events

Beside these well-defined and more formal social events, there is a whole world of informal social events that we all experience in our lives. In adulthood there are a whole range of situations where people are socializing without clear structures or an expected flow of events, and often fewer exceptions or excuses are made for adults who 'get it wrong' than are made for children or even teenagers.

Pubs, bars and drinking alcohol

One such situation is going to the pub – a very common occurrence, in the UK at least. As a nation, the UK has thousands of pubs and bars, and 40 per cent of British adults report going to the pub at least once a fortnight with friends, colleagues, on dates and generally to socialize. Nearly one in ten go once a week, both for drinks and food (Lock, 2020). With often dozens of people in a pub engaging in those different social situations, it can feel daunting for an autistic person to navigate the space in combination with whatever purpose they have in being there. This high social load can lead to autistic people relying on their mask, even if they are with people who they feel comfortable with, because they do not know how other people in the pub are going to react to them. Equally, if it is a work outing or a big gathering, it is possible that there are people in the group who they do not know very well and so they do not feel safe to drop their mask and act more naturally because of how they may be perceived by those people.

However, there are some norms around pub behaviour that can help an autistic person be confident and enjoy the situation – for example, the 'rounds system' is usual in British pubs, where someone buys a drink for everyone, and then next time people need a drink the next person buys for everyone. This continues until each person has bought a round, or is continued the next time they get together, so that it works out fairly evenly over time. It is considered normal to ask for help to carry the drinks, so an autistic person would not appear unusual if they asked someone to go with them to the bar (if they are uncomfortable dealing with a crowd at the bar on their own, for example) or even giving money to someone to go up for them – the key is to pay for the drinks, not necessarily physically be the one to deliver them. Similarly, it is normal to stick to your own group, who will generally be sat at a table either inside or outside. While small talk with other people waiting to be served is common at the bar itself, this tends not to happen between tables (unless watching a sports event, where discussing the game is seen as natural).

We all carry expectations about how people behave while they are drinking alcohol. Laughing more, being more outgoing and lowering inhibitions are all considered signs of being tipsy or 'buzzed', terms associated with having consumed a small to medium amount of alcohol. As people drink past this point, they are generally considered to be 'drunk', which can also be associated with having fun, but is more likely to be seen negatively if you are on a work outing, or if someone becomes aggressive or extremely emotional (e.g. crying), or is 'blackout' drunk when they lose control of their faculties and do not remember things the next day. Learning how much alcohol it takes to reach each of these states is a highly individual process – there is no rule as to how many drinks make you tipsy, or drunk. It changes depending on what and whether you have eaten, or how hot the day is, for example.

The early stages of behaviour under the influence of alcohol are often viewed positively, such as being fun, 'the life of the party', and finding it easier to talk to people. Alcohol consumption tends to reduce social anxiety, a condition that up to 70 per cent of autistic people struggle with (Hollocks et al., 2019). So it makes sense that some autistic people talk about drinking to help them cope with social situations, as it reduces their anxiety, and provides the cover of 'being drunk' for potentially unusual behaviours if they let their mask slip. People who are thought of as being 'a good time' are likely to get positive reinforcement from those around them, making friends, being invited to events, and generally being included in the social life of their group. Considering the difficult social experiences many autistic people have as children and teenagers at school, the ability to drink once they are 18, especially for those who go to university where there is often a strong drinking culture, may feel like a 'cheat code' to access friendships and relationships.

These positive experiences, combined with the way alcohol itself makes you feel, can combine to create the potential for autistic people to drink in a problematic way or even become addicted to alcohol. This is what happened to Matthew Tinsley, as he recounts in the book he wrote with Sarah Hendrickx (Tinsley & Hendrickx, 2008), until he was at the point of drinking before he went to work in the morning simply to feel he was on a par with his colleagues in terms of social skill and anxiety level. At a broader population level, recent work has suggested that autistic adults who drink heavily do so for some of the same reasons as non-autistic adults (such as thinking it will have a positive effect on their behaviour). However, autistic adults also reported some autism-specific motivations and expectations around drinking, such as alcohol making verbal communication easier. They also reported that they were more likely to drink for these social reasons, and to make them feel good, rather than to fit in with other people or as an emotional crutch (Brosnan & Adams, 2020). This fits with the idea that autistic people may be less likely to give in to peer pressure, but also means that they may be more at risk of developing a dependency on alcohol in social situations.

It is worth noting that a clear majority of autistic people can and do drink in a healthy way. For example, in a study with autistic university students (a population we would expect to show high levels of drinking whether they are autistic or not), only 5 out of 25 participants reported high levels of drinking even in the period which covered Freshers Week, and this number was slightly lower across the rest of the academic year (Scott & Sedgewick, 2021). Even fewer participants reported using illegal substances recreationally, with just two saying that they had done this at any point across the

12 months of the study. Importantly, for most students who took part in this study, levels of alcohol and drug consumption stayed fairly stable across the academic year (despite the advent of COVID-19 and the national lockdown, where levels of alcohol consumption increased generally). There was no correlation between alcohol consumption and levels of anxiety or social anxiety, suggesting that at least in this sample, autistic people were not using alcohol as a coping mechanism for the anxiety they experienced, which is positive for their long-term physical health.

House and dinner parties

Another informal social situation that often comes up for adults is house or dinner parties. As a gross generalization, house parties tend to be more common in early adulthood (university and the few years after), and more alcohol focused, whereas dinner parties tend to be associated with people in their late 20s onwards and have a more defined focus on food – although plenty of alcohol is often still consumed. Both can feel like a cross between hanging out with close friends – you normally know at least one person well, often the host – and being around strangers, as it is common not to necessarily know every person at the party. This can feel like a strange mix for an autistic person in terms of masking, as they may not feel the need to mask with some people present but absolutely feel the need to mask with others. However, because these events take place in someone's home, and with a smallish group of people who the host at least knows well and likes, they are usually relaxed events where individual eccentricities are likely to be respected. This means that while masking and making small talk might feel necessary on the night, things like dietary preferences and sensory sensitivities can be taken into account in advance by the people making the food.

There are some norms around dinner parties, just as there are for the pub, and knowing these can help an autistic person feel more comfortable going into the situation. For example, most people take some kind of gift or offering if they are a guest – if they drink alcohol, or know that the host does, a bottle of wine is common; flowers or

WHY DO PEOPLE MASK? AND WHERE?

chocolates are popular choices as alternatives. Equally, depending on the group of people, offers to contribute to the meal in some way can be welcome. It can be helpful for the hosts to be able to specify what individual guests should bring, so they can keep an overview of what food there will be, and that the different foods go together, rather than guests bringing something that doesn't fit the rest of the meal. If a guest has specific foods that are the only things they can eat, allergies or dietary needs, or are uncomfortable with other people making their food, which means that they will take their own food, it is polite to let the host know in advance. Otherwise, it can look like they are being rude about the quality of the food the host has made and do not think it is worth eating. However, with friends an autistic person should not need to mask their way through eating foods they really do not like, and should be able to have those conversations openly!

Large events

There is another category of social events which is important to consider. While traditional thinking about autism has assumed that autistic people will inherently dislike and avoid large events, this was based on things like difficulties with the sensory aspects of noisy and close crowds, and a lack of interest in situations with lots of people present. However, we now know that this is not always the case at all, and while some elements of these events may involve masking, many autistic people actually feel that they provide socially acceptable opportunities to stop masking altogether.

Large events can be anything from music concerts to sports matches, from going to the theatre to going to marches. With such a range of activities, and with autistic people's preferences being so individual, we aren't going discuss them in the same detail as some of the other social situations described earlier on. Instead, we're going to think about some of the ways people can still mask – and not mask – in these larger-scale situations.

A lot of masking takes place in situations where an autistic person is dealing with one, or a few, other people who are paying them enough attention that they feel it will be noticeable if they act in a way that is outside the neurotypical 'norm'. This applies much less at large events, because when there are lots of people in a crowd or an audience, it is less likely that any one person (other than the people you have gone with, if you are in a group) will pay that much attention to you. Despite this, a lot of autistic people feel they still need to mask in these situations. This can be because it is so automatic to mask outside their own safe spaces that they feel vulnerable without the mask, or because it can still be possible to be singled out in a crowd if someone with malicious intent sees you as 'different' somehow.

There are often also formal 'steps' to go through to get into large events, and people can mask to get themselves through these. Things like collecting your tickets, or presenting them to an entry steward, finding your seat or spot, buying refreshments... These all involve interacting with other people, who are probably non-autistic and unlikely to have much knowledge about autistic people's needs and differences. It makes sense, therefore, for autistic people to mask through these interactions to smooth their way into the event they want to go to. This can especially be the case for large events centred around a shared interest or passion – sports teams, bands, a cause (think Pride or a political march). Most people attending will share that interest, often including the staff, and they may to use it to start casual conversations as they look at your ticket/hand you a drink/ point you to your seat. For many non-autistic people, these short conversations about the event are fun, improve the formal functions being performed, and give them a chance to share their excitement (or disappointment, if their team has lost!) in a brief and casual way. For autistic people, they can still present a challenge, as although you may share an interest, these conversations do not fit with all the standard social rules in the standard ways – they are technically small talk, but about something that may be a special interest; they take place in the context of a specific function, so should be formal, but are often treated informally by the other person. This can cause anxiety because they feel less predictable, and so it can be easier to watch how other people are handling them and simply copy their interactions – another type of mask.

Saying all this – what about not masking at large events? In a large crowd, you don't stand out so much so you can potentially let your guard down and express yourself more authentically – including dropping the mask. It is normal for everyone present to be more emotionally expressive, whether cheering on their team, or getting caught up in a play, or overjoyed to be seeing their favourite band live for the first time they've toured in four years. Some autistic people, therefore, feel comfortable enough to stop masking their emotional responses. In a large crowd people are less likely to notice stimming behaviours, or in a dark theatre they may not see them at all. Waving your hands around, screaming, jumping up and down... None of these are going to make you seem any different to anyone else in the front rows of a gig, or in the stands of a rugby ground as your team heads to the try line for the winning points. Being caught up in the moment and the intensity of the event can be a freeing experience for anyone, autistic or not, and this can lead to anyone and everyone there dropping at least some of their behavioural inhibitions.

The sensory immersion aspect of large events can also be an important part of not masking for autistic people. Far from being overwhelmed by the sensory elements of these events – loudspeakers, crowd roar, orchestral music, even precisely timed silences in theatre plays – these can all be an opportunity to revel in sensory experiences, rather than the opposite. That doesn't mean every sensory aspect of every or any large event will be pleasurable. You can love the feeling of concert-size bass speakers pounding through your body while still hating the scratchy feeling of the gig wristband on your skin, obviously. But many autistic people seek out sensory experiences in day-to-day life, just as much as avoiding others, and large events can be an opportunity to find the most intense version of those good sensory experiences. If you want to read more about this, try Georgia Harper's blog post 'I'm not breaking down, I'm breaking out: why sensory overload isn't linear' (Harper, 2019). She talks incredibly eloquently about going to a Muse concert, the inconsistencies in autistic sensory profiles and the joy that these gigs bring her.

The other aspect of large events that can make them good spaces for autistic people to drop the mask is that they are, as we said above, generally based around special interests. There aren't many people who spend (sometimes a lot of) money on gig/play/match tickets, go through the travel to get to the venue, and then commit to at least a couple of hours of whatever is going on, if they aren't pretty interested and potentially passionate about it! This means that an autistic person knows they are in a space where most other people share their interest, will understand them wanting to talk about it, and it makes sense for them to talk about it – and people are likely to respect and approve of the autistic person's in-depth knowledge, even if (and sometimes especially if) the autistic person knows more than them. It's also generally easier to start interactions in these settings if you want to, as the 'introduction' element isn't required. Instead, conversations can start with direct opinions like 'Blimey, that was a good game' or 'That was their best performance ever!', and generally the other person will simply respond with their opinion rather than thinking this is unusual.

Considering how we know that including special interests in the classroom can help autistic children do well at school, both academically and socially (Wood, 2019), it is no surprise that autistic people can thrive in environments based around those same special interests. It can be easier to talk to people when there is a shared focus (such as the stage or the pitch) and a shared understanding to base conversation on (the band's back catalogue, players' form, the playwright's last showing). This means that autistic people can feel more comfortable interacting with the people they meet at large events, can express their joy and their knowledge in 'socially acceptable' ways, and can potentially drop their mask to display more of their authentic selves – and gain positive reactions from people around them for doing so.

Case study: A comparison of difficulty at a large event

Helen's experience of a rugby match

My special interest is rugby union and I've been lucky enough to have attended dozens of matches at various locations over the last few years, and while each match brings me a lot of autistic joy, there are also many challenges that present reasons for me to mask my true reactions and needs. Probably the best example of a day when my mask was sorely needed, tested and eventually destroyed was a visit to Sandy Park in Devon in 2017; my team were there to play an away semi-final fresh off the back of another final that had brought us a shiny trophy. I'd been to the ground once before and not had a great time thanks to an awful combination of a bad sensory environment and a not pleasant attitude from the home fans towards my team/fellow supporters, so I wasn't feeling particularly optimistic on this trip. My mask was very firmly in place on arrival at the ground, full-on body armour too with my 'battle uniform' of club colours on display and a nervous stim in my hands being supressed by holding a pint of cider. The sensory experience was even worse this time, probably because I was anxiously anticipating it and because the home crowd could sense blood in the water as my team were fatigued and carrying little injuries from the previous weekend, whereas the home team had not played for a week so were fresh and focused. The rolling chants echoing through the stands were like a pulse being aimed at my head, echoing inside my skull and causing a 'bouncing pain' sensation where the pain spikes were moving continually around my head, from stabbing pains behind my eyes one minute to a crushing feeling on the top of my head the next. Even my face was hurting by the end of the first half, although some of that was down to clenching my jaw tightly and grinding my teeth to stop myself from screaming at people around me.

Trying to get to the ladies at half-time at any ground can be a bit of a nightmare, but when already very shaky and struggling to hold the mask in place it's even worse. Comments aimed at me like 'Cheer up love, you ain't lost yet' let me know that I was losing my battle to keep my facial mask in place. The eye roll I got from a female supporter in the queue as I stumbled of out the portacabin could have meant anything, but in my precarious mindset I took it as a personal slight and walked back to my seat feeling incredibly anxious and scratching my arms uncontrollably.

The match ended in a rapid flurry of point scoring, unfortunately not to our benefit, and suddenly it was over and we had lost. My mind was in chaos at this point. I desperately wanted to escape but was trapped in the middle of a row and had lost all sensation to my legs. The home crowd were reacting with gusto and the tannoy system was joining in at full volume. I could feel my eyes tearing up as the sensory overload threatened to overwhelm me and I knew I didn't have much of a mask left. I needed to find my ride home, but we'd ended up sat in different places so I was stumbling around on very shaky legs with tears slowly trickling down my face for several minutes. The looks and comments I got aimed at me by some of the home fans made me feel humiliated and exposed; I could tell they thought I was crying because we had lost and weren't going to the final.

I was so grateful at this point to have a lift home with people I trusted. I honestly don't know how I would have coped with any form of public transport that day, much less the lengthy train journey to get back to Hertfordshire from Devon. The family whose car I was in were amazing, they'd helped me through post-meltdown and trying-to-avoid meltdown situations a few times over the season and knew exactly what to say and do to allow me to reconstruct my mask as we headed home; the full meltdown was supressed until I got home and could sob my pain into my pillow.

Felicity's experience of a university debate

In my first year at university I joined the Union – at Cambridge, this isn't the student union bar but the debating society. I never got up and took part (I was far too shy back then) but I went and listened to lots of debates on all sorts of topics, and I loved it. There was one time, though, that I had a bad experience. It was about two-thirds of the way through a guest speaker talking about her time as a mental health nurse, and I suddenly felt quite faint. It hit me from nowhere, and I'd never felt like it before, so I didn't know what was happening – I just felt hot, and dizzy, even though I was sitting in exactly the same position as five seconds earlier. And then I fainted. In the middle of a wooden bench, between my friends, for no apparent reason. My friends got me out of the room, and a steward came to see if we were okay. I was able to talk and hold myself upright again by then, and was desperate not to make a scene (remember the shyness). So I tried to make myself seem okay – joking about it, answering all their questions, telling the others to go back inside as I just needed some fresh air. In reality, I felt scared and disoriented, the lights were too bright, and I just wanted to call my parents to reassure me. So that was the first 'mask' related to the situation. My parents, naturally, were worried, and told me to go to the GP about it, so I did. This led to me having to hide how I was really feeling a second time – she informed me that I 'must have been drunk and just been too hot', and that was why I fainted. She ignored me telling her that I had only had one drink, that the temperature was fine and the fainting incident felt significant because nothing like it had ever happened before. Again, I was left feeling upset, dismissed, and far from reassured, but I hid it behind politeness – I didn't feel there was anything else I could do. She was the doctor, and I just had to wait and see if it would happen again, when she might take it more seriously. Between not wanting to stand out at the Union event (because of all the people who would be looking at me) and not wanting to be difficult with the doctor (because I didn't want to be rude), I ended up 'masking' my physical and sensory reactions, as well as my emotions. But this was very much a one-off in my life, around specific experiences, and I have learned to manage the triggers differently and more successfully since.

Reflections on the two sets of experiences

As demonstrated by the two examples, the way autistic people and non-autistic people mask when at a large social event like a sports match can have a lot of similarities, such as trying to hide your emotional reactions so that you aren't an obvious target for comments from other people, or trying to hide how you are feeling to put other people at ease. In a situation like a sports event, where men usually outnumber women (and both authors in these case studies are women), this can feel especially important because it can be uncomfortable (and feel threatening) to be the focus of men's attention if you are on your own. Equally, both autistic and non-autistic people can mask their true reactions to placate someone who has more authority than them, because it feels like it will cause more difficulties to insist on your authentic response being recognized. The differences between these examples, though, are the intensity of the sensory experiences we describe, and the impact they had – Helen was already struggling hugely before things went wrong for her team and her mask, whereas Felicity didn't have any sensory issues until right before she fainted. Equally, those sensory difficulties are not something that Helen can simply adapt to, get over, or learn techniques to remove (autistic people can learn to manage their sensory experiences and environments, but this is not removing the experience entirely). In contrast, Felicity has learned how to manage when she feels faint, how to avoid getting to a point of feeling faint, and how to get other people to react if she does. So her 'masking' around the early instances is not ingrained, but was situational, and her fainting was not linked to the situation in the way masking is for autistic people.

Not masking with autistic people

Autistic people often comment that they often find other autistic people much more relaxing to be with than non-autistic people.

There are a variety of reasons for this, but a lot of it seems to come from the fact that when autistic people are together, they feel safe to 'drop the mask' as much as possible. This makes spending time together less effortful, less stressful and more fun. This section delves into some of the conversations around this phenomenon.

Not masking, and accepting each other

As camouflaging and masking became recognized in the autism literature, and the ways in which masks are used by autistic people started to be researched, there has also been an interest in the opposite – when, how, and with whom autistic people are *not* masking. One recent study that Felicity was involved in asked autistic people about their communication preferences in different settings (e.g. at school/work, when dealing with services, or with friends/family), both getting them to rank their preferences (e.g. phone, email, face to face) and to give an explanation for their choices. In most contexts, autistic people chose email or live text chat as their preference, except when it came to family and friends, where they preferred face to face. When asked to explain why they had given these answers, masking came up repeatedly. Participants talked about how in formal encounters, or with people they do not know well, they feel that they are:

performing neurotypicality to put others at ease.

[having to do an] emotional performance with my face.

One participant said that:

the more neurotypical they are, the harder it is to communicate. (Quoted in Howard & Sedgewick, 2021)

In stark contrast to these quotes, the descriptions of communicating with other autistic people emphasized how little masking people felt they needed to do, often describing it as 'finding my tribe'. When talking about being with autistic friends and family, or people who knew them well and accepted them as they were, people said things like:

No masking, all fun!

[it] allows me to relax, be able to communicate effectively and honestly. (Quoted in Howard & Sedgewick, 2021)

The same sentiments have been seen in other studies where autistic people are asked about their friendships, and about feeling comfortable with other people. A piece of research that asked 12 autistic adults (10 women) about their friends found that across-neurotype difficulties and within-neurotype ease were two key themes from the interviews. For example, when autistic people were socializing with non-autistic people they found it much more difficult to read their expressions and know what the unwritten social rules were, which made the time with those people more effortful even if they liked them:

I'm tired afterwards. It's not that it is bad, it is just tiring. It takes effort to be around them. I am always thinking 'Should I speak now, what should I say, has this moved on? Is this okay, is that appropriate, will that offend someone? And who is speaking, and what are they saying, and do they really mean that?' (Quoted in Crompton *et al.*, 2020a, p. 1442)

In contrast, the same participants said they felt much more comfortable and at ease with autistic friends and family members. They listed factors such as shared communication styles and flexible understandings of 'good' interactions, and therefore feeling able to stop masking and be more authentically themselves:

You can let your guard down, you can let your mask down. You don't have to be a certain way with them, because they totally get it. (Quoted in Crompton *et al.*, 2020a, p. 1443)

With autistic people, I have a much better idea of what people are doing, what they mean, and picking up on things. (Quoted in Crompton *et al.*, 2020a, p. 1443)

These sentiments were echoed by the contributors to this book, who also felt that they were able to drop the mask and communicate if they were in majority autistic – or actively and explicitly autism-accepting – situations. We asked what an environment that doesn't require masking might look like, and these are some of the answers people gave:

I need people who can either pretend to be, or learn to become, comfortable and calm around stimming. It's my way of managing emotional regulation. (Cassie, autistic woman, 34)

Other autistic people. No neurotypical expectations. Sensory needs are met. Fidget toys/able to stim. Promotes being unique and yourself. Accepting. (Isabella, autistic woman, 24)

With people who accept me regardless. For example, in my flat with my partner and my cats. Or when I meet up with my best friends and I can just say or be whoever I want. (Hannah, autistic woman, 31)

It is interesting how often the importance of being able to stim freely came up in people's descriptions of what a masking-free environment might look like. The ability to express yourself physically, and respond to the situation naturally, has been highlighted as central to many autistic people's conceptions of what true autism acceptance would look like (Kapp *et al.*, 2019). This idea of being able to be who you really are is core to why so many autistic people say they prefer socializing with others who they feel understand them well, and it is natural to feel that people with a similar neurotype understand you better. Below we outline some of the theoretical reasons behind the differences in how autistic people can feel when socializing with autistic versus non-autistic people.

Autistic-to-autistic communication
and the double empathy problem

Autistic people often say that one reason they mask around non-autistic people is because it helps them be understood by those non-autistic people, and avoids misunderstandings. In contrast, autistic people often say that they don't need to mask around other autistic people because there is less chance of misunderstanding. Recently, some innovative research has provided scientific evidence for this. Led by Catherine Crompton (Crompton *et al.*, 2020b), and co-produced with autistic people, this research explored communication styles in autistic and non-autistic people. The researchers asked groups of people to share information with each other, and measured how effective this communication was. One person was told a story and asked to then retell it to the next person, who retold it to another person, and so on down a chain of 8 people. The researchers then measured how accurately core details of this story were maintained from the start to the end of the chain. In one condition, the chain was made up of just non-autistic people; in another condition, the chain was made up of just autistic people. In the final condition, the chain alternated between autistic and non-autistic people.

The research team found that communication within the chain of autistic people stayed relatively accurate, to the same degree as the chain of non-autistic people. However, the chain that was made up of autistic and non-autistic people was much worse at keeping core details in the story, and participants in this chain felt less comfortable with each other than either of the other conditions. These results are fascinating because they challenge traditional ideas that being autistic in itself makes communication automatically harder. The group of autistic participants performed *just as well as* the group of non-autistic participants. Instead, it seems that combining autistic and non-autistic people leads to more misunderstanding and poorer communication. To be clear, we are not saying that it is the presence of autistic people that made the communication worse, as the autistic-only group were just as good at retelling the story. It is when autistic and non-autistic people try to communicate with each other, in both directions, that misunderstandings can arise.

These findings support a theory suggested by sociologist Dr Damian Milton (2012), the double empathy problem. This theory proposes that difficulties in communication between autistic and non-autistic people are not just due to autistic people being 'bad' at communication and empathy generally, but are also a result of non-autistic people failing to communicate effectively with autistic people. In contrast to the old (and disproven) idea of autistic people lacking empathy, the double empathy problem suggests that non-autistic people often lack empathy towards autistic people, and this might be the cause of many difficulties experienced by autistic people. This has implications for masking, as it suggests that masking might arise as a result of this bidirectional lack of understanding; autistic people mask because non-autistic people are bad at communicating with them.

There is a growing body of work that supports this theory, not just the excellent research by Crompton and her team. For example, a study that followed autistic young people who did online gaming together found that as a group, they created their own norms for communication which would have seemed odd to outsiders, especially non-autistic outsiders. They found that the autistic young people had what was described as 'a generous assumption of common ground that…led to rapid rapport' and 'a low demand for co-ordination that ameliorated many challenges' (Heasman & Gillespie, 2018). Essentially, because everyone involved knew that they were autistic and had common aims in the game, they made more allowances for atypical communication and were more comfortable with people having separate conversations alongside/within the group communication channels, so that people felt they were able to talk to each other as and when they wanted about what they wanted. This flexibility also meant that when someone did say something out of turn, the group worked around it rather than demanding the person fit within a specific pattern of communicating, and meant that people were less likely to be upset by misunderstandings.

Understanding someone's emotions and how they are feeling is crucial to making and maintaining successful friendships and relationships. This skill underlies knowing what makes someone happy or upset, and gives you clues as to how to fix things if something goes wrong. It has been shown that non-autistic people are worse at reading autistic people's emotions than they are at reading other non-autistic people's emotions. This may be because autistic people display emotion differently in terms of the facial expressions they use, and there is indeed a suggestion that their facial expressions may be more individualized, rather than falling into 'typical' facial expressions. Interestingly, this study found that autistic people were also better at correctly reading the emotions of non-autistic than autistic people, but it is unclear whether this is because the way autistic people show their emotions on their face is more idiosyncratic, or whether this is almost a 'practice effect'. There are more non-autistic than autistic people in the world, so it may be that even autistic people are more used to looking for the standard emotional signals (Brewer *et al.*, 2016).

Recent studies suggest that people who are more similar in terms of both being autistic, or both having similar levels of autistic traits, have better friendships – rating them as closer, more helpful and, importantly, more accepting. This was true regardless of age, sex/gender or how long the two people had known each other. It might be that finding someone whose autism 'fits' with your own is why some autistic people make and find autistic friends more easily than they do with non-autistic people (Bolis *et al.*, 2021). It has also been suggested that autistic adolescents may want slightly different things from a friendship than non-autistic teens do (e.g. they value a friend who likes the same things as they do much more, and have different preferences around how much physical contact they want from friends) (Finke, McCarthy & Sarver, 2019). This means that it may be easier to maintain a friendship with another autistic person than a non-autistic person, simply because they are more likely to want a similar type of friendship and will therefore be more compatible. Other work has supported this idea, finding that autistic adults say they are more interested in spending time with each other, and tell each other more about themselves in short interactions, than they do with non-autistic adults (Morrison et al., 2019a).

This finding has been seen in multiple studies, with one interesting addition coming from a study where people were initially unaware of the diagnostic status of the person they rated (De Brander et al., 2019). What the team found was that when non-autistic adults were told they were rating an autistic person, they improved their scores, but autistic adults did not change theirs (which were already more positive). This implies that autistic adults may have in some way 'recognized' each other without being explicitly told, and instinctively felt more warmly towards those people. The team also found in another study that the key factors in how people rated each other lay with the rater, not the rated (i.e. it matters what the person doing the scoring thinks more than how the person being scored behaves). Their analysis showed that people with more autism knowledge, and less autism stigma, rated autistic people more positively even when they were not told that person was autistic – again suggesting that people may be picking up on clues they are not consciously aware of (Morrison et al., 2019b).

Of course, there can be times when an autistic person wants to mask around other autistic people, for their own sake or for the sake of the other autistic person, or is expected to be the one who can be the 'bridge' between an autistic group and any non-autistics they are interacting with:

> As an autistic person who is so used to masking, I feel like others subconsciously expect me to mask even in autistic spaces, so that I am able to act as the 'token non-autistic person' and help others. For example, I'm usually the person that people assume is co-ordinating where we're going to dinner after a conference and ensuring that everyone is invited. (Tori, autistic woman)

Another such example is discussed in the personal piece from Carly Jones below, talking about masking her own distress so that she can focus on her daughter's needs. We talk about autistic families and autistic parenting a bit more in Chapter 5.

Personal Piece: Carly Jones, on masking, parenting and assistance dogs

I often think of a family circuit as a bit like a circuit board or the inside of a plug. You have the grounding, well-insulated earth wire; the active wire; and sometimes a live wire. Even if before having your own family you were more of a natural live wire, life with your own family means putting your own wants, thoughts, feeling and sometimes, if possible (it isn't always), your own reactions last. It's one thing for our own reactions to blow up, but when you are an autistic parent of an autistic child, your focus every day is putting their health and happiness first, so the environment is as calm and serene as possible for them.

A natural live wire develops ultra-masking, to become the circuit's grounding earth wire instead. Although emotionally difficult, it is physically easier than I'd imagined to mask my own autistic needs in a crisis when my love for my autistic child and her needs comes first. We can often kid onlookers, our child and, to a degree, ourselves that we are the calm not-fussed adult handling the situation. We are handling it much like a swan, graceful above the water, paddling like crazy underneath the surface. Obviously, although this helps your autistic child to have a happy, serene environment, it takes its toll, and sometimes as an autistic parent you need an evening or afternoon off just to unmask and peel off that insulation. This paddling is exhausting.

I tell you who you can't trick though: assistance dogs.

My daughter has an assistance dog. He's a collie Lab cross with more emotional support skills than most humans I have met. He doesn't just care if his human is in distress, he warns her first. This is a godsend! He will apply deep pressure when he feels she is anxious and will make certain warning sounds and movements if he is unsure of a stranger approaching us on walks.

He will also attempt to comfort anyone he thinks is in quiet distress.

So, imagine the scene:

Daughter is in distress, and I'm masking my distress at perhaps the same bright light on the train we are sat on, and the dog picks up on us both. That's an issue – he's not my assistant dog, he's my daughter's. I can't fake an 'I'm fine, please assist my daughter instead' to a dog as he just knows when things are wrong. He's left confused who to sit on. Then my daughter isn't supported by her dog quick enough, which is not what I want.

So, I have no choice but to simply NOT feel anxious. Sounds impossible, and actually it is. So this has led to life changes. Being more organized with what I take in my bag to support my child's and my own autistic needs out of the house. Limiting what I say 'yes' to, if it will create unbearable anxiety. In the past, I'd say 'yes' and let myself suffer. Now it's a 'no'. Not putting myself or my daughter into environments and situations where her needs will escalate, resulting in my needs being insulated and masked and us both having to recover afterwards. Really thinking about what is important for us all and putting that first.

Other things to think about: When you need to mask with autistic people

Of course, not all autistic people are automatically going to get on with each other and be comfortable around each other simply because they share a diagnostic label. It is possible for there to be personality clashes between autistic people just as much as between non-autistic people, or for two autistic people to have different accessibility or sensory needs, or upset each other, or any number of things to cause tension in an interaction or relationship. This has also been acknowledged in research, although it is much less discussed or investigated.

One example of when things can go wrong is that the honesty autistic people often display can be hurtful, even if that isn't the intention of someone's words. Equally, a participant in an interview study described how they can find other autistic people's stims or behaviours unpredictable, which causes them anxiety:

> Being with autistic people I don't know, who may exhibit unpredictable behaviours, can be more difficult than being around neurotypicals that I already know. It's about pre-dictability, if I know what to expect then I find things easier. (Crompton *et al.*, 2020a, p. 1443)

One contributor to this book shared the ways in which they can also find themselves changing their behaviour to be around different people, regardless of whether those people are autistic or not:

> Like talking with one friend about a topic they like and not about something they don't. Or me not making certain jokes with one friend as they don't like that humour. Sure, that's me acting differently for them, but at least with friends, I can be closer to my true self. (Loren, autistic non-binary person, 27)

This highlights the distinction between masking and adapting to the social situation – doing or talking about things to make your friends feel happy and comfortable is something that everyone does, both autistic and non-autistic. This is different to masking all your autistic traits or trying to appear non-autistic, and is more like being polite. It may be that difficulties recognizing this distinction, or making allowances for it, are behind some of the challenges autistic people can have inter-acting with each other when they have opposing needs in an environment, and this would be worth further consideration both in research and in everyday life.

Saying that, we are not advocating for masking just to be polite! Asking for accommodations or changes to the environment, or the communication mode, or whatever is relevant is generally the right thing to do, as most people will want the others around them to be comfortable if possible. It is just that these things have to be negotiated, because someone else in the situation may have a different need, and those will have to be balanced. The same goes for socializing – it is important for autistic people to find people with whom they can drop the mask and be their authentic selves, but this does not mean that one person in the situation gets to do or say whatever they want regardless of how that impacts the other person. It can take a while to learn how to offset this, and it might be different with different people, but it tends to result in the best experience for everyone once it has been discussed.

It can also be upsetting for an autistic person to find that they do not feel totally relaxed or comfortable with other autistic people, and so they do not feel able to drop the mask with them. If someone has spent a lot of their life feeling like they need to mask their true self around non-autistic people because they are different, then finding the group they are meant to be the same as and still needing the mask can be a real emotional and psychological blow. These people are meant to be their tribe, why is it not all super-easy and straightforward?

> It's so hard having to be the one in the room who keeps their mask in place because I'm running the meeting so I have to stay professional. There are times I want to scream, 'I'm autistic too you know, so stop making me want to cry!' But I know that would only make things worse, so I grit my teeth and carry on, knowing how badly the suppressed reaction will hurt later when I can safely de-mask. (Anonymous, autistic female)

Other contributors to this book also talked about these difficulties in professional settings:

> I was in a room with a dozen or so other autistic people, and someone asked for the strip lights in the room to be turned off, Next thing I know everyone else seems to be agreeing and saying that 'fluorescent lights aren't autistic friendly' and the lights are turned off. Well, great, I'm the autistic in the room who needs lots of light to be able to see and concentrate properly so now I'm getting eye strain trying to read the paperwork and my brain is trying to make me fall asleep because it's really dim without the lights on. (Anonymous, autistic female)

Some autistic people may even question whether they are autistic, or whether they are the 'right type' of autistic, when faced with this situation. The fact is, though, that because autism is such a varied and individual condition, autistic people are bound to differ from each other in lots of ways. Some of those ways can add up to one or both people in an interaction feeling like they need to keep their mask on in order to get through the interaction. That doesn't mean that either person is wrong, or being ableist, or being inconsiderate – sometimes, keeping the mask on can be the easiest way to facilitate communication because otherwise your needs would clash too much or someone would feel hurt. Understanding how and when to use the mask for strategic purposes, even with other autistic people, is a skill that is important to develop so that you can use it to your advantage, rather than being lost in the mask or feeling controlled by it.

CHAPTER 4

What Are the Consequences of Masking?

In this chapter, we are going to look at both the research and the personal accounts autistic people have shared around the consequences of masking. A lot of this has been hinted at in other chapters – difficulties with mental health is central to the discussion, and so we will start there, then think about things like burnout and the practical effects these can have.

Research into masking and mental health

From the earliest research studies asking autistic people about their experience of masking, the association with mental health problems has been raised. We will discuss how masking is related to specific mental health problems, but for many people it is less clear how their masking leads to anxiety in some cases, or depression in others. Many autistic people feel that because masking is a part of their general way of being in the world, its impact on their mental and physical health can't be separated. However, to summarize the research into masking and mental health, we will look at different aspects of mental health separately.

Please note that in this section we include quotations from people talking about their own experiences of mental health problems, including suicidal thoughts. Feel free to skip to 'Other things to think about: Are neurotypicals masking too?' at the end of this chapter if this isn't something you want to read about.

Anxiety

Some studies have suggested an association between masking and anxiety or stress, for instance showing that autistic people who mask a lot across different situations have higher levels of anxiety than people who do not mask much. This is supported by interviews with autistic people, who describe how masking makes them feel anxious both while they are masking and afterwards as they recover. One participant in a study described how they feel constantly stressed trying to keep track of everything needed while they mask:

> Constant overthinking of possibilities of what to say, how it will come across, what others are and are not saying, the connotations of every word, sentence structure, emphasis, body language... (Quoted in Livingston *et al.*, 2019, p. 771)

The exhaustion and burnout often associated with masking (which will be discussed in more detail later on) might partially result from high levels of anxiety around masking, particularly when it involves a lot of very conscious and effortful aspects. As one participant has said:

> It's very draining trying to figure out everything all the time, everything is more like on a manual, you've got to use one of those computers where you have to type every command in. (Quoted in Bargiela, Steward & Mandy, 2016, p. 3287).

A recent study conducted by Laura and colleagues (Hull *et al.*, 2021), based on Lily Levy's master's thesis, found that the amount of masking reported by autistic adults positively predicted their level of anxiety symptoms. In this study the researchers looked separately at general anxiety symptoms (symptoms shown by people with a generalized anxiety disorder, who feel anxious across various different situations and settings) and social anxiety symptoms (symptoms shown by people with social anxiety disorder, who feel anxious in social situations in particular). They found that the more people masked, the more likely they were to show symptoms of both general and social anxiety, to the point that they would be diagnosed with an anxiety disorder. Importantly, this study did not find any difference in the association between masking and anxiety between women and men. Non-binary people were also included in the study, and also demonstrated positive associations between masking and anxiety symptoms. In another study led by Eilidh Cage, people who masked across multiple different situations reported more anxiety than people who did not mask (Cage & Troxell-William, 2019).

However, other studies have not found a relationship between masking and anxiety, whether they were looking at general anxiety or more specifically at social anxiety. For instance, in one study there was no difference in the level of anxiety between autistic adults who spontaneously described masking and those who did not. In studies using a 'discrepancy' approach to measure masking (looking at masking as the difference between how autistic someone feels and how autistic they look to other people), no association between amount of masking and social or general anxiety has been found.

Studies looking at children also seem to show contradictory results – in one study by Lucy Livingston and colleagues, children who mask to a 'high' degree (as categorized by the researchers) reported higher levels of anxiety than children who mask to a 'low' degree. But when these children's parents were asked to evaluate their child's level of anxiety, no difference was found between 'high' and 'low' maskers (Livingston et al., 2019). Another study, led by Blythe Corbett, found that children's self-reported anxiety was the same regardless of how much they masked, but observers reporting on the child's anxiety thought that the children who masked more were more anxious (Corbett *et al.*, 2021). The stress that this causes can lead to physical health problems, as discussed in the section 'Physical health' below.

Depression and low mood

Many of these studies also looked at the association between masking and depression or low mood. Again, some studies have found that masking is associated with higher levels of depression or distress in autistic adults. The study that we described earlier by Laura and colleagues (Hull *et al.*, 2021) found that masking predicted higher levels of depression symptoms for both men and women, and for non-binary people. Another study, led by Jonathan Beck, has suggested that this relationship might only occur for people who mask to a high degree – although this study only included women (Beck *et al.*, 2020). Other studies have found that this might differ based on sex or gender. For instance, a study led by Meng-Chuan Lai found that masking was associated with depressive symptoms in autistic men but not women (Lai *et al.*, 2019). And Cage and Troxell-Whitman (2019) found no difference in the level of depression for autistic adults who masked at high or low levels.

A more consistent, and concerning, finding is that high levels of masking might be associated with suicidal thoughts and actions. Research from Sarah Cassidy and her colleagues, including Mirabel Pelton *et al.* (2020), has shown that masking is one of the strongest predictors of suicidal thoughts in autistic adults, and suggest that this might be because masking reduces feelings of reciprocity during social interactions (Cassidy *et al.*, 2020). They suggest that autistic people who feel an expectation or pressure to mask might feel like they are being less authentic and so less accepted by other people, and as a result experience loneliness and a lack of belonging that can lead to suicidal thoughts. This is reflected in what one contributor to our book said:

> People don't know me for who I really am: I don't feel authentic.
> (Olivia, autistic woman)

This is reflected in the descriptions of masking by autistic people: one person described how 'I feel sad because I feel like I haven't really related to the other people. It becomes very isolating because even when I'm with other people I feel like I've just been playing a part' (quoted in Hull *et al.*, 2017, p. 2529). This is an example of how masking can feel like pretending to be someone you are not, and feeling that the only way to be accepted by other people is to mask your autism. Another participant in a different study described how masking (which they called 'compensating') had such a negative impact on their relationships that they had considered suicide.

> I have planned three methods for my own suicide... I have lost great people in my life and destroyed previous careers and relationships. All of this, I put down to compensating. (Quoted in Livingston *et al.*, 2019, p. 772)

For some people, the effort of masking might become so extreme that suicide seems like a possible 'way out' of the pressure to mask. As one contributor to our book said:

> It led me to have a mental health breakdown. At 15 I ended up trying to kill myself because I saw no way of living as the real me. I knew difference wasn't good and I was so scared of not fitting in. I think it built up over a long period of time until I became more aware and more unhappy. It didn't feel fair. By 13 I was self-harming to cope with the feeling I had and by 15 I was admitted to a young persons' mental health unit. Only once I reached breaking point and had given up completely did I start behaving naturally and not masking. (Isabella, autistic woman, 24)

If you or someone you know are experiencing thoughts of suicide, or of hurting yourself, you can contact the Samaritans by phone or email, both of which are free. You can also contact your local healthcare service in the UK by calling 999 for immediate medical assistance, or 111 to be put in touch with trained crisis counsellors.

To summarize, the majority of evidence suggests that masking is associated with mental health problems, and that the more someone masks, the more likely they are to experience mental health problems. It's important to note that the research has not yet been able to prove that masking leads to mental health problems; the associations that have been found so far are correlational rather than causal. This means that the relationship could, in theory, work the other way around – autistic people who have higher levels of mental health problems might mask to a greater degree. This might very well also be true; some autistic people describe how they find themselves masking more when they are experiencing low mood or anxiety, in order to get through the situation more quickly. However, in general the descriptions given by autistic people suggest that most people think that their masking contributes to mental health problems.

Researchers need to study the impact of masking over a long time (several years) to test this scientifically; some studies are already attempting this but have not yet finished collecting data. If researchers can find evidence that masking causes mental health difficulties for autistic people, this should make it easier to advocate for support in stopping or controlling masking as part of mental health and wellbeing provision. For instance, counselling or therapeutic support could be provided as part of healthcare provisions for autistic people following diagnosis, and funding could be given for interventions that try to make environments more autism-friendly, to reduce the need to mask.

As we have mentioned previously, the impact of masking is different for each individual, and there are some people who may not experience any mental health consequences of masking. Some people might even find that masking improves their mental health in some situations! We therefore need to be careful not to assume the impact of masking for any one person, and instead learn from them about their own experiences of masking and how it makes them feel. This might be a long process which involves a lot of reflection; there are some suggestions for how this could be done in Chapter 5, in the section 'Guidance for healthcare professionals'.

There are many potential consequences to long-term masking, including identity issues, imposter syndrome (see below) and many mental health issues (such as eating disorders, depression, dissonance and self-harming), all of which contribute to the higher-than-average suicide risk in autistic people.

> Masking is the most exhausting aspect of being autistic for me personally. I find it really ironic that I used masking as a coping mechanism because I was terrified of failing to fit in, yet masking is also what fuelled my mental health breakdown. If I'm honest, masking destroyed my mental health. (Isabella, autistic woman)

Impostor syndrome

Identity is a key concept when exploring mental health issues in relation to autistic masking. As the great philosopher Socrates once said, 'know thyself, for once we know ourselves, we may learn how to care for ourselves'. It can be very hard to have a healthy self-esteem, ego, and outlook on life if you do not feel like you have a firm grasp on who you are and what your true personality is. One of our contributors discussed this, saying:

> I think that not having safe spaces where you don't have to mask can really lead you to question who you are. It can also make you wonder if you are lying to people because of their misconceptions of what masking means, and your own subconscious internalization or judgement of those misconceptions. This can create doubt about whether anyone could ever accept the real you. That is if you could

even work out who that was consistently enough to be that person more often. (Tori, autistic woman)

Imposter syndrome is the term used to describe when an individual doubts something about themselves (skill, achievement, identity) and has a recurring fear of being exposed or 'discovered' to be a liar/fraud. Imposter syndrome is not unique to autistic people, but can be a side effect of long-term masking. If someone is conscious of masking, they can feel like they are lying to people (as discussed above) and be scared that they are going to be 'found out' as not the person they have been presenting as.

Some autistic people also face impostor syndrome around their autistic identity. There is research on the idea of 'coming out' as autistic (e.g. Davidson & Henderson, 2010; Smith & Jones, 2020). In these studies, participants have described feeling disconnected from the diagnostic label because they were not 'autistic enough' or did not fit the stereotypes they were used to seeing. This is often especially the case for autistic women and non-binary people, as the stereotype of autism as a male condition is deeply culturally ingrained. Especially if those people mask in most of their interactions, other people may be more likely to judge them as not 'really' autistic, or as 'less' autistic than other people they know on the spectrum who have more visible difficulties. If even other autistic people, or family members of autistic people, can struggle to see past some masks, it says a lot for how entrenched the mask can be.

Physical health
There is to date no medical or psychological research on the links between masking and physical health, although there is a wealth of work on the links between mental health and physical health. Considering what we know about the negative impact of masking on mental health, and mental health on physical health, it is reasonable to assume that there may be an association between more masking and worse physical health – even if this is mediated by mental health experiences.

Some autistic people, anecdotally, feel that masking plays a role in their physical health. They often put this down to the stressful nature of masking as an autistic person living in a majority non-autistic world. For example, one of our contributors said:

> Your body keeps the score. I have so many health issues now, all related to stress. (Laura, autistic woman)

Minority stress theory states that people with minority identities (being non-white in white cultures, being non-male, being LGBTQIA+, being neurodivergent) experience more stress than those who fit with the cultural majority (white, male, straight, neurotypical) (Meyer, 1995). Those who fit into multiple minority groups (e.g. being female and autistic, or black and gay) experience much more stress, and this takes a toll on their mental and physical health (Cyrus, 2017; Hayes *et al.*, 2011).

The principles of this theory have been applied to autistic people when exploring identity, stress and mental health, and it has been found that autistic people do indeed experience stress that directly impacts their mental health because of their autistic identities (Botha & Frost, 2018). We can therefore speculate that the same is true for physical health, although this needs research.

Masking can also be about physically controlling movement; stopping yourself from fleeing a sensory overloading environment, repressing a stim, forcing a smile, for example. These things can cause acute tension in the body which can lead to cramps, muscle spasms and joint pain. This side of masking is also yet to be explored, but will be a valuable and important area of study in the future.

Risks arising from masking

Masking carries a lot of risks in and of itself, as we have seen above – worse mental health is the one that is currently best understood by researchers, and most talked about, but there are others.

This section will look at some of the risks arising from masking, rather than the risks of masking.

'Risky behaviours'

One of these risks is that of engaging in 'risky behaviours'. In research and policy, 'risky behaviours' are things like smoking, taking drugs, engaging in early or unsafe sexual behaviours, or physical violence scenarios. Non-autistic people who are keen to fit in, especially teenagers, are more likely to take part in all these 'risky behaviours' – in order to seem cool, to fit in, to be accepted, to feel wanted...the reasons we are all familiar with. Adopting these behaviours can help to create a persona that gets you friends, even if they lead you down a dangerous path.

The same thing is true for autistic people too. While autistic people do seem less likely to give in to peer pressure (Yafai, Verrier & Reidy, 2014), they are not immune to wanting to fit in and be accepted – that is a lot of what masking is about. This can lead to autistic people adopting these 'risky behaviours' to fit in with a group who also take part.

Equally, some autistic people may turn to things that are socially acceptable 'crutches' to get them through situations where they feel they need to mask heavily. Drinking alcohol and smoking are the most obvious and common of these. It is very normal for people to relax and lose their inhibitions a bit when they've had alcohol, and so autistic people may feel reassured that they are not the only ones who have said something wrong or done something odd when surrounded with others drinking, or that they have the excuse of being drunk (Brosnan & Adams, 2020). Similarly, and especially since the smoking ban was brought in, there is an accepted norm of social interaction around being outside in the smoking area of a pub – a bit like talking about your special interest at a large event, it is common for people to strike up casual conversations in the smoking area. It is also a socially acceptable reason to leave a conversation or social gathering to go outside for a cigarette, and people are less likely to think going frequently is odd, as they might if you said you were going to the loo every time. This means that it provides an autistic person with the opportunity to go and have a moment to themselves, without standing out.

Seen in this way, adopting so-called 'risky behaviours' even in adolescence makes logical sense. However, these behaviours can have long-term consequences, especially for physical health, and although they may help to maintain a mask at the time, there can still be the 'social hangover' alongside an actual hangover the next day.

Vulnerability to exploitation

Sadly, on top of the risks we have already discussed, masking can contribute to making autistic people more vulnerable to exploitation by people around them. We will discuss two potential forms of exploitation here, but will not go into detail. If reading about this is likely to upset you, feel free to skip this section.

VULNERABILITY TO MATE CRIME

We have briefly mentioned mate crime elsewhere in this book – the phenomenon of someone either being the victim of crime, or manipulated into committing a crime, by people who are pretending to be their friends because they see them as vulnerable (Quarmby, 2011). Disturbingly, mate crime also covers the perpetrator committing acts of cruelty towards the person, humiliating them and forcing them into servitude, alongside exploiting them and stealing from them.

People with learning difficulties are often targeted, as are those on the autism spectrum, because they are more likely to believe the lies these people tell them. The only study to date of this happening to autistic people was carried about by Amy Pearson and her team (Forster & Pearson, 2020). This study found that the perpetrators of the mate crime specifically use aspects of autism to take advantage of the autistic person, such as their desire for friends (but difficulty making them), their potential lack of knowledge of normal social rules (e.g. not knowing that it is not normal to give a friend all your money), and the contrast between these behaviours and what they had been taught was bullying:

> It's probably worse, like bullying is generally pretty direct, but this is like…tricking you into thinking that you are a friend. It's more like manipulation and it's worse because you're doing it deliberately. (Quoted in Forster & Pearson, 2020, p. 1115)

This abuse of trust is central to mate crime, and to the harm it causes. Alongside the material and potentially physical harm done to the autistic person, there is damage caused to their trust in people, something which can already be relatively fragile. It can also damage people's sense of self, and some indicated that they would feel ashamed of having been tricked in this way:

> Most people would not get themselves into such a situation, so I would feel more ashamed of it. (Quoted in Forster & Pearson, 2020, p. 1115).

Shame is an element of the stigma that many autistic people are faced with when they approach the world as their authentic selves, because the stigmatizing reactions cause them to feel ashamed of their behaviours. They therefore build up masks to avoid that stigma, but in doing so can end up being more vulnerable to exploitation because people underestimate the difficulties they experience and the challenges they have in interpreting the social world around them.

VULNERABILITY TO SEXUAL VICTIMIZATION

Another situation where the mask can be unhelpful and lead to being more likely to be victimized is in the area of sexual victimization. While there is little work currently published on this topic (most work on sexual violence and autistic people focuses on autistic men as perpetrators, or on victims in instutionalized settings), Felicity is leading some preliminary work to better understand these experiences, with the goal of being able to better support autistic people and to reduce their victimization rates. It is important to note that autistic people (and non-autistic people) of all genders can be victims of sexual violence and exploitation, but it happens more frequently to girls and women, who make up the majority of victims and the majority of participants in the research discussed below.

Autistic people report higher levels of sexual assault than non-autistic people across the lifespan, including in childhood (Ohlsson Gotby *et al.*, 2018; Weiss & Fardella, 2018). Research, including work from Felicity's PhD, shows that up to 80 per cent of autistic women have been victims of sexual assault, rape or domestic abuse (Sedge-wick *et al.*, 2018). These are higher rates than for physically disabled women (Coker, Smith & Fadden, 2005) and up to ten times higher than the general population (Office for National Statistics, 2018).

Among non-autistic people, understandably, both sexual vic-timization and domestic abuse have long-term negative impacts on mental and physical health, and quality of life (Draper *et al.*, 2008; Jordan, Campbell & Follingstad, 2010). These experiences are likely even more devastating for autistic people, who can struggle with social communication and emotion recognition/expression, and especially for late-diagnosed autistic people who spend years feeling they are responsible for problems in their lives (Kanfiszer, Davies & Collins, 2017; Sedgewick *et al.*, 2018).

What little has been directly researched about autistic people's experiences of sexual exploitation suggests that this is the case. In Felicity's most recent study, which is yet to be published, 25 autistic adults (7 men, 16 women, and 2 non-binary people) who had gone through some form of sexual victimization or domestic abuse were interviewed about their experiences. Without sharing details, rough-ly half had first been victimized in childhood, including some by teachers: 'he knew I was different somehow, and that he could take advantage of that' (anonymous, autistic man). Others discussed how their abuser took advantage of their social naivete, by telling them that this was just how relationships were, something that has been seen in other work with autistic victims of interpersonal victimiza-tion (Pearson, Rees & Forster, 2020).

As we discussed earlier in the book, autistic people are often taught by the world around them that their reactions to things are wrong or should be ignored, and this played a role for these autistic adults:

> I didn't like it, but I was being told I should like it, I did like it, and there was something wrong with me if I didn't like it... So I went along with it and pretended, put on a mask of enjoying it to not be difficult. (Anonymous, autistic non-binary person)

For women who were victimized in their teens and in adulthood, the role their mask played could be quite obvious to them in hindsight. One acknowledged that:

> I didn't send the signals of 'No', and I might have sent some signals that most men would assume was a 'Yes' – I thought I was being polite, but I'm often told I'm being flirty when I'm just being what I think is normal, because that's who you have to be when you're a woman working in nightclubs. And then if my 'No' verbally doesn't match the signals he thinks he's been getting, that's his excuse to ignore it. (Anonymous, autistic woman)

This does not mean that their victimization was in any way their fault, or the fault of them masking. It is just that sometimes, the masks women in particular build to get through a world which normalizes low-level sexual harassment mean that men who want to abuse them can find excuses, which are often believed by other people.

Not being believed was another problem that many autistic participants reported, because they did not present themselves the way people expected them to as victims of a crime:

> I wasn't crying or screaming or losing it, I was very calm and very precise, so the police thought I was making it up because if you're that upset you should be struggling with their questions. But the questions were all I could focus on – I couldn't have made a cup of tea if I'd tried, but I could remember everything. (Anonymous, autistic woman)

This ties in with other research we have discussed about how autistic people may display their emotions differently to non-autistic people, how non-autistic people are bad at reading autistic people's emotions, and the double empathy problem (Milton, 2012; see Chapter 3, section 'Autistic-to-autistic communication and the double empathy problem'). Considering that it is already vanishingly rare for victims of rape and sexual exploitation to see their abuser come to justice (1 in 60 cases lead to a charge in England and Wales: Barr & Topping, 2021), autistic victims may be even less likely to see this outcome, because they do not fit with stereotypes about victimhood. In this way, masking contributes to them being victimized twice – first by the perpetrator, and second by the justice system. Despite these challenges, it can still be important to report victimization, both in terms of trying to bring the perpetrator to justice and in terms of accessing support. It is worth noting, however, that you can get support from a number of charities following victimization without filing a police report.

Burnout

If you type 'autistic burnout' into Google Scholar, you get one paper that looks at burnout among autistic adults, and then several pages of papers about burnout in teachers of autistic children, carers of autistic people and parents of autistic people. This section focuses on what we know about burnout in autistic people, not in the people around them.

Burnout is the concept of reaching your limit, emotionally, physically and mentally, in response to long-term stress that is not being addressed or resolved. It was first discussed in relation to people in high-flying professional jobs who were overworked to the point where they stopped being able to work at all, or were 'burned out'. It isn't necessarily a pleasant term, but it is a widely used one, including in the autism community.

When autistic people talk about burnout they are more often talking about trying too hard to fit into the expected patterns of non-autistic life, and having to mask intensively to make this happen, over long periods of time. One contributor talked about it like this:

When you're wearing one of your masks it's similar to having all apps open on your smartphone – the battery drains much quicker and if you're not careful, physical symptoms (like the phone getting hot to hold or slow) will start to show through – the most common thing to 'slip through the cracks' is facial expressions or stim movements. When extremely tired or overloaded while masking it's possible for the mask to suddenly 'fall off' entirely, as if the straps holding it to the face have suddenly disintegrated – which is essentially what has happened, just that the 'straps' are representative of a huge amount of subconscious and conscious effort and energy expenditure. (Anonymous, autistic woman)

Burnout can cost people their jobs, their livelihoods, their relationships and their mental health. In the one paper that discussed autistic burnout currently published (as of early 2021), a group of autistic and non-autistic researchers worked together to analyse 19 public documents on the Internet (such as blogs) and 19 interviews with autistic people (Raymaker *et al.*, 2020). They found that autistic burnout was characterized by chronic exhaustion, a loss of skills people previously had, and a reduced ability to tolerate things like sensory triggers. For those who had experienced burnout, this happened because immediate stressors had been added on top of the general stress they were already experiencing, and they were unable to get support with this, which made the expectations they faced overwhelming. A lot of this is similar to burnout in non-autistic people, bar the sensory sensitivity element. Where it differs is in the difficulty of having the burnout recognized and validated by others – while workplace burnout is culturally understood, autistic burnout is generally unfamiliar to people outside the autistic community. This means that it is that much harder to get support, and therefore to recover, so the negative effects of burnout can last longer and be more wide ranging.

It is not easy for anyone of any neurotype to recover from burnout, because it occurs when they have depleted all the resources available to them in terms of their coping ability. Building this back up takes a long time and often conscious effort – it isn't as simple as taking a car to the garage to get an engine mended. It often requires a complete break from the main cause of the excessive demands and stress, though this can be difficult if it is workplace related. Raymaker and the team explicitly discussed 'unmasking' as a burnout recovery strategy for autistic people:

> The biggest thing of all you can do to prevent, or at least mitigate burnout, is to start identifying what you do when you Mask and stop. Even just little things like eye contact, which so many of us do, or least pretend to do. Allow yourself not to be sociable if you don't want to be. (Raymaker *et al.*, 2020, p. 138)

Burnout is another area in which more research is needed, especially on the links between autistic burnout, masking and suicidality. The wealth of community voices on the topic emphasize its importance, and researchers are beginning to catch up as they adopt community priorities in guiding their studies.

In conclusion to this chapter...

In this chapter we have looked at some of the darker sides and outcomes of masking, particularly masking long-term and without relief. While there are many sad and worrying things in those discussions, they also hint at some of the solutions – having time and space to unmask, learning to be your authentic self, acceptance from others and having a choice over whether to mask all have the potential to significantly improve autistic people's lives. In the next chapter, we will give some advice for specific people and situations as to how to try to build those safe spaces for autistic people and the people around them.

Other things to think about: Are neurotypicals masking too?

Non-autistic people will often relate to an autistic person's explanation of masking by talking about having a different persona at work to at home, or different ways of acting with friends versus older family members. These things are not the same though – and the differences come down to how long the mask remains in place and to what extent the mask wearer feels they have a choice about masking. Here we look at how a day presenting at a conference is experienced by both Helen and Laura, to look at some of these differences.

Case study: A comparison of a day presenting at a conference

We wanted to reflect a little on our own different experiences of masking, in light of our discussions in the book about masking, reputation management and how both autistic and non-autistic people can use these. As we all go to and present at conferences, we thought this would be a good comparison point. Laura and Helen have described their days at a conference below and you can see the similarities – and the differences.

Laura's experience of a conference

I love being at conferences. I write this having not been in the same room as other autism researchers or experts in over a year – so maybe that makes my memories a little more rose-tinted! But I enjoy the opportunity to meet people, to talk about research that fascinates me, and to catch up with colleagues I rarely get to visit.

When preparing for a day at a conference, I will think carefully about what I am going to wear and how I will do my make-up. I want to look professional (relatively modest clothing, smarter than I would usually wear to work; make-up that will last throughout the day) but be comfortable (layers, so I can take something off when I start getting warm; flat-heeled shoes for all the walking and standing around I will do). I usually travel to the conference venue with colleagues, so we discuss the talks we are looking forward to and any particularly interesting people we want to meet. I feel relaxed when I'm talking with close colleagues – I might joke with them or share some personal information such as what I did the previous weekend. When we arrive at the conference venue I put on a slightly more professional 'face', smiling at people I walk past, and I'm less likely to share personal information with those around me. However, I don't feel like I'm changing or hiding anything about myself – I still feel like I am being authentic and I don't think about my facial expressions or body language. I trust that I will be able to communicate a relaxed and composed manner to those around me, without having to think about it. This doesn't feel like a mask to me, since I'm expressing how I genuinely feel to people around and I feel authentically myself. It feels more like a slightly edited version of myself, where I automatically 'know' which parts of myself are most appropriate for the situation, and I don't feel the need to share other parts of myself that might not be relevant. I think this is because I know that people tend to respond positively to me when I am being myself, so I haven't had to learn to change anything about the way I act.

If I am giving a talk at the conference, of course I'll be nervous! I might spend five minutes in the toilets before the time for my talk, checking my make-up and clothes look okay and doing some deep breathing. As I walk up to speak I will try to smile at the people in the audience, to thank them for paying attention to me. I'm lucky that I don't have any fear of public speaking, but for the first few minutes of giving my (well-rehearsed) talk I often feel anxious. I will listen to myself speaking, making sure that I'm not talking too fast or forgetting to breathe. However, as I get into the talk I will relax and stop thinking much about what I am doing – instead, I focus on the information I am sharing and how the people in the audience respond to it. If people are looking interested and nodding, I know they are paying attention and I can focus on the content. On the other hand, if people look bored or are paying more attention to their phones than my slides, I will try to put more intonation in my voice and maybe walk around a little, to get their focus onto me!

I keep my face and tone of voice slightly more formal than in everyday conversations, but I also allow my real feelings and emotions to come through. For example, if something goes wrong with the presentation display, I might laugh at myself. I wouldn't show people if I felt frustrated or annoyed, because I want to convey the impression that I am confident and in control (even if I'm not!). Throughout the whole talk I am still being myself, just a slightly edited version. Importantly, I'm only slightly aware of the way I am editing myself; it doesn't feel like it takes much effort. When my talk finishes and I am answering questions I will allow myself to relax a little more, and might laugh or joke a bit more than during the talk. However, I would make sure that I am still polite, even if I disagree with the person asking the question. Afterwards I can relax properly, and I'm often aware of feeling more tired than I was during the talk. I still feel like I can listen to other people's talks, make conversation with colleagues and engage with the material – I might just need to sit down and have a cup of tea first.

At the end of the conference day I feel tired but happy. Usually there will be a meal or drinks with colleagues, which I enjoy. At this stage I'm often even more relaxed, but I can still easily switch between talking to a friend (where I might joke about things that happened during the day) and talking to a more senior colleague (where I might discuss the potential for a future collaboration). No matter who I'm talking to, I feel like I'm being my genuine self and I don't have to make any effort to hide parts of myself or consciously think about what to do in the situation. Again, this is probably because people usually respond positively when I'm being my authentic self – the way I present myself and the things I do and say are considered 'normal' and appropriate by other people without me having to think about it. Of course, my behaviour is different when talking to my colleague compared to my friend, but it doesn't feel like an effortful change, and I still feel like I am being myself in both of those situations. I'm naturally quite introverted so a conference day will take a lot of energy from me, but I will probably sleep well that night, and then wake up ready to do it all again soon!

Helen's experience at a conference

My 'day' doesn't start when I wake up that morning, in all practicality it started several days or even weeks earlier when I first began preparations for the day by looking into my travel arrangements. Where possible I will have booked a hotel for the night before, especially if I am speaking before lunchtime, as I am always very anxious about travel problems making me late for a speaking slot.

I'm also not a fan of travelling in my 'speaker outfit' as I start to get nervous from the moment I get dressed, so it's best for me if I can be in the outfit for the minimal amount of time possible prior to going onstage (or the equivalent for the event).

My outfit is a huge part of my preparations for any speaking engagement, or anything that is a majorly important work-related event, as I need to know that it's an outfit I feel comfortable in, but also feel 'professional' – generally I stick to a basic staple of a sleeveless black dress and a coloured jacket. The colour and style of jacket will depend on the season and the 'level' of event, while the shoes I wear will be very much led by if I'm going to be at a podium presenting or not. I'm only 5 feet 3 inches, so heels are definitely needed for most situations, as podiums and mics are generally set for those with a little bit more height than me!

Having a 'uniform' of sorts for presenting helps alleviate a lot of the pre-event stress, as it removes the need for decisions in the morning, although I always have a backup outfit chosen just in case, and often spare tights and a cardigan with me as well.

I'll also generally have 'post-talk' things with me – a soft jumper or hoody to put on over the dress, and flat shoes – little things that help me be less recognizable in the breaks as a speaker if I choose, along with changing my hairstyle and putting my glasses back on (Clark Kent taught me a lot as a child!).

The morning of the event I will be a bundle of nerves, no matter how much I am looking forward to my talk, and will often skip breakfast and avoid talking to people as much as possible. This isn't always possible with conferences though, especially if you aren't the opening speaker, and I'll find myself masking heavily to even my closest friends as I'm unwilling to admit to myself at this point just how scared I am.

The 'pre-talk' hours are exhausting, and trying to 'people' in those pre-hours is incredibly difficult as I feel like I only have about 20 per cent of my brain available. So much of it is preoccupied with the running internal commentary: going through my talk script (not necessarily written down but certainly prepared), alongside various plans for what to do if things go wrong (how to deal with an aggressive audience member in the Q&A after, what to do if the tech fails, etc.), reminders to myself of when to take water-intake pauses, and how to stay 'on script' for each slide so I don't get confused mid-talk.

I'll find myself staring at other people's outfits when in this state, fixating on sparkly jewellery or pretty colours, trying to claw some calm from focusing on one sense and fading away the rest. Of course, this rarely works, as anyone who looks at me will think I need help as I'm just standing/sitting there silently staring at something, so I inevitably then have to respond 'appropriately' to show I'm 'okay' to the other person, hiding behind my 'polite and smiley' mask and dragging out the old 'small talk' scripts so I appear engaged with them and not lost in my own head like I want to be.

But it is important to mask heavily at this point, and even lie through my teeth, as the last thing I want is any kind of verbal acknowledgement of my anxiety – it's the elephant in the room that I'm doing my best to ignore and squash, as that's the best coping method available to me at that point.

The minutes leading up to my talk are pure hell generally, no matter where I am or how much I trust the people I am with. There is simply nothing they can do to stop the awful churning in my stomach, the tension in my muscles, the pain behind my eyes. The internal voice has vanished now, and is paralysed in a fear too terrible to speak; my mind is almost blank and I'm moving on a form of autopilot, able only to follow clear instruction that's said loudly enough to hear over the booming sound of my own frantic heartbeat. My breathing is shallow to the point of barely happening, and my facial expression is frozen in what I hope is a warm smile. All I can think about at this point is how to make myself move; walking feels like wading through jelly, and I'm terrified my ankles will give way.

My hands will be clenched around the items I'm taking on-stage with me – my notes, my sand frog (a favoured sensory aid), a tissue or two (praying a sneeze won't happen) and maybe a bottle of water or diet cola. This is why I prefer a lectern/podium (even though they require me to wear heels to be properly seen by the audience), as I need surfaces to put things on and to hold on to in those initial moments as I'm adjusting to the lighting and seeing my audience in front of me.

It takes my breath away for a moment to see all those faces and eyes looking at me. My mouth goes drier than a desert and all I want to do is make an inappropriate profane joke to try to calm myself down! Once I've started talking, though, I find myself calming with every word I speak. I know the subject I'm presenting on and I have a quiet confidence about being able to handle any small stumbles as I've had so much experience in that department. Occasionally my brain will go faster than my mouth, especially if I know I've only got a short time slot, and a word or two will get mangled or replaced with a similar one ('neurodiverse' and 'neurological' are common ones for me), but as long as I don't pause long enough to let my internal voice get started I can normally keep going and make it to the end of the talk successfully.

The audience questions are always incredibly nerve-wracking

as I don't know what I'm going to be asked. The hardest questions are the ones asking for my advice on a specific situation or the 'it's more of a comment' that generally come from fellow autistics wanting to share their stories – I don't know what I'm meant to do in those situations as I want to interrupt and say, 'This is my talk, not yours, and this time is for questions, not comments.' But, at the same time, I'm super-aware that everyone is looking at me and I need to stay professional and polite, faking a pleasant interested expression as my mask while trying to work out what I'm supposed to say once they've finished speaking.

Post-talk I'm a strange combination of a wobbly wreck and someone on an endorphin high; my heartbeat is a fast fluttery feeling in my chest and my face feels like it's burning hotter than the sun. I crave sugar at this point, either from a soft drink or a cup of tea, and I have just a few minutes before a ravenous hunger will set in, although savoury is safer than sweet to avoid a nasty crash later.

My first action will be to head for the ladies. Not only are toilet cubicles often visually bland but they are generally kept at a cooler temperature and allow me a moment of peace to regain control of my mask and temper down my pulse rate and stomach cramps, holding my wrists under the cold tap and revelling in the pleasant sensory input from the feel of running water on my skin.

At this point I'm through the worst of the day, although the inevitable consequence of my stomach's reaction will show up later – how much later will depend on what I eat next and if anything else upsets me during the day. Listening to other speakers can cause me a great deal of distress if they are talking about a sensitive topic or are very medical-model based or behaviourist – my hold on my mask is fragile at this point so it takes less than normal to upset me and I'm far more obvious in my emotional response.

In terms of 'peopling': I'm tired at this point but buzzing with confidence. I want to run away and sleep while simultaneously wanting to bask in the praise and thanks being directed my way by the audience, my low self-esteem and flagging energy levels craving the boost. So I reinforce my mask, shoring it up by digging deep into my reserves, knowing that it's a forward payment that will be covered by the incoming deposits. And as they come the mask will fade a little, my tiredness will start to show through and I become less filtered in my verbal responses and facial expressions, but by this point I'm in a social situation where I can get away with it a bit. The talk I've just done will no doubt have been about autism and so any audience member I encounter will hopefully be more understanding of any faux pas I make, or respectful enough of my status as a speaker to not point it out!

In fact, I tend to do so much social interaction after a talk that by the time I get home I am out of words. It's like I've used up my quota, not just for that day but the next too! The following day is often spent hibernating, a desperate need for quiet and stillness to regain an equilibrium of sorts, a day where I wear no mask and have no expectations placed on me, the perfect counterbalance to such a high-anxiety day before.

Reflections on the two sets of experiences

As demonstrated by the two examples, the way autistic people and non-autistic people mask in public, react to stressful situations and are affected afterwards is very similar superficially but miles apart in terms of long-term impact and energy requirements. For non-autistic people, their 'masking' still feels as though they are being their authentic and genuine selves, as opposed to an entirely different character (complete with different reactions, emotions and mannerisms). There are also far less – or no – consequences for most non-autistic people to the conference day and having slightly different versions of themselves on display in the different settings of the conference. In contrast, although Helen will seem to those who do not know her well to have gone through the day just as calmly and successfully as Laura, she will then spend a day or two recovering from her 'performance' because it requires a lot more intense effort.

CHAPTER 5

How Can One Help around Masking for Different Groups?

This chapter aims to share some suggestions for the families of autistic people, partners of autistic people, education and healthcare professionals working with autistic people and employers of autistic people, on how to understand and support the autistic person in their life in masking less. We know, however, both from lived experience and from research, that it is unlikely that anyone falls into just one of these categories. These are intersecting identities, and there is a high chance that more than one section is relevant to you. They are not meant to be exclusive, or to imply that one is more important than another. We are also not trying to tell anyone how to be a parent, or a partner, or an employer – these are potential support options and suggestions that might help, not a prescription for what anyone should or should not do. Each autistic person, and the situations they are in, is too individual for one book, fixed at the point of publication, to guess at, let alone make the rules for managing!

Equally, we are not trying to tell any autistic person how to be autistic, when and whether to mask, or whether it is right or wrong to mask. Autistic people also have these intersecting identities, and may face dealing with clashing needs and masks within their family or workplace – we cannot give any kind of absolute guidance on how to manage that, nor would we want to. Everything below is very much a suggestion, something to think about and decide for yourselves if it might be useful, or even bits of it might be useful, in your situation.

Guidance for parents, siblings and wider family members

Thinking about who autistic children and young people, and many adults, spend the most time with – and therefore might mask around a lot of the time – the answer is family. Most family members would hope that their autistic child, sibling or relative would feel comfortable enough around them not to mask, obviously. And in many families that will be the case – home will be a safe, secure, supportive environment where they can relax and be their authentic self. But there can still be times when an otherwise little-masking autistic person may put the mask back on with their family, for various reasons, and this section is to help you think about the ways to make them more comfortable so these can be minimized.

One of the big things can be that, even if the immediate family know that the person is autistic and give them the space and support to express themselves, wider family may not know (if they have not been told) or may be less accepting. As they do not spend as much time with the autistic person, they may be more judgemental of their quirks and needs, or they may know less about autism overall and so be more confused or even worried by their behaviours. Therefore, in a situation with wider family members, an autistic person may feel the need to mask more than they do with just the people who know them well, similar to when they are meeting strangers or going into a formal situation.

Equally, an autistic person (whether a child or an adult) might feel the need to mask if they are getting tired, frustrated or overwhelmed.

Even in a normal day, any autistic person (anyone, autistic or not, really!) can reach 'the end of their tether', and this can lead to behavioural changes which are generally frowned on, like being snappy, or being quiet and withdrawn. For non-autistic people, it often feels relatively easy to say that they are tired, or can't face watching that movie, or that they have a headache. For autistic people, this can be much harder, either because they find it more difficult to interpret the signals from their bodies (DuBois *et al.*, 2016) or because they feel that it goes against the social rules they have worked so hard to learn and stick to. In these situations, an autistic person is likely to bring their mask into play, so that they can hide their discomfort behind it and not let other people know that they are finding things hard. This can be especially likely if they want to avoid upsetting the people around them by stopping or changing something that is going on, such as a family movie night or an excursion.

There can be all sorts of reasons why an autistic person might feel the need to mask with close family members, though they are less likely to maintain the mask seamlessly simply because of the amount of time people spend with their families and the fact that family often see each other at their best and worst (early mornings, sad news, happy news, funny moments...). If they want to mask less with family, or you independently want to make changes that might encourage this, we give some general ideas below. Remember, of course, that different things work for different families, as every family has their own dynamic and set of relationships that everyone is working with – the best first step is always finding ways to talk about what you and the autistic person want, what will suit them, and what is realistic with your lifestyle.

- *When with wider family members:* If it is an option that you and your autistic family member are comfortable with, it can be a good idea to tell wider family members about their diagnosis. While some people may not be supportive at first, we've talked elsewhere about research that shows that disclosure often leads to more acceptance and better attitudes over time (see Chapter 3, sections 'Masking at university' and 'Masking at work'). It can be an opportunity to educate these family members about autism in general and about the specific needs of your autistic child or sibling. Preparing other people for what to expect can be just as important in reducing negative interactions as preparing an autistic person to reduce their anxiety. Over time, this could lead to better relationships for the family as a whole, as it reduces awkwardness or reticence when talking about family life.

- *When they're just not up to it:* As we have emphasized many times in this book, listening to autistic people about what they find difficult and when, and responding to those needs, is central to helping them feel comfortable and able to drop the mask. Even for parents or siblings who know an autistic person really well, it can be difficult sometimes to spot the signs that they are struggling, although you are likely to know these signs better than many other people in their lives. Reassuring someone that if they are feeling overwhelmed, or need to leave, or change something about the environment, then this is okay, and they can and should tell you so that you can help, can build a track record of them knowing that their experiences will be respected so they can drop the mask. If you are in a situation that is more difficult for you to change or control (say, out of the house, or in a larger or more formal social situation) then establishing codewords that they can use to let you know that they are finding it difficult can also be useful. Having codewords, using them, and responding actively when they are used again helps build that understanding that you will do what you can to make them comfortable to the best of your ability at the time.

- *Ways to make your family a safe space to drop the mask:* These will differ for every family, as we have said above. Good communication is central (and this does not just have to be verbal – responding to behavioural cues from your autistic family member is also crucial). Building an environment where they know that they are valued for the person they are, that being autistic is not a bad thing, and that they can be proud of their strengths and supported in their difficulties – all of this will make your family feel like a safe and accepting space where the parts of the outside world that are too difficult don't have to apply. Doing this can also help to make the outside world easier, as having a secure base to return to at the end of the day makes it easier to cope with challenges. Similarly, normalizing conversations about why people do things that might be confusing can help build social insight and skills that your autistic family member can then use in their other interactions.

Families containing autistic people are not just made up of non-autistic parents of autistic children, obviously. Neurodiverse families come in all sorts of combinations, and the ways in which reduced masking can be supported will differ depending on the precise make-up of each. Below, we have a fascinating reflection on masking as an autistic parent in a majority non-autistic world.

Personal piece: Sarah Douglas, on masking and parenting

As I sit here gathering my thoughts about my experiences of being a parent I realize that this will be something of a double retrospective. First because my son, at 23, has survived my attempt at raising him and is now a man, but also because up until 2012, when I received my ASC diagnosis, I had no idea that I was autistic, let alone that I was unconsciously and constantly camouflaging my true neurodivergent self. This then will be both a few of my reflections on parenting a young adult through the perspective of a growing awareness of my diagnosed autistic self, but also through the lens of the confusion of knowing that I was somehow different and 'other' during his infancy and early years, but not understanding why.

I didn't think that I would ever be a parent. Growing up, babies were not on my radar, as I was the youngest in my family and I didn't really register small people. The day I found out that I was pregnant, having done a test in the loos at work following a week of feeling a bit 'off', was the first time in my life that I had ever held a baby. One of the admin women who was on maternity leave was visiting the office and I was offered a cuddle with her offspring. It was a terrifying combination of paranoia that I was going to drop this precious bundle and a growing terror that in approximately eight months I was going to be given one of these myself. The fact that I had only been married for two months and had handed in my notice a week before finding out my happy news and therefore wouldn't be eligible for company maternity pay only added to this anxiety.

As I understand it, masking as an autistic person is not simply the social camouflaging that most people deliberately and occasionally employ in order to make a good impression. Instead, it is an unconscious and constant attempt to fit in with everyone and with every situation and is hampered by not understanding the social rules or why people behave the way they do. Of course, until my son was 14, I had no idea that this is what I was doing, but looking back, it is clear that masking was my social default setting. I was trying to hide my difference, blend in and avoid the bullies, of which there had been many.

Masking is a survival strategy, but can come at a huge cost to mental health because of the relentless social hypervigilance and fear of 'getting it wrong'. Growing up undiagnosed in a world that was not designed for me, as well as struggling with a traumatic upbringing, meant that as I was preparing to become a parent, I had already unwittingly packed in 27 years of masking, which had manifested itself in my triple Dementors of anxiety, panic disorder and depression. I was diagnosed with postnatal depression shortly after my son was born and was then on Prozac for the next 16 years. I was an apparently functioning ball of tension, fear and inner sadness who had no idea of how to look after a helpless infant. I had learned from my mother that women were ornamental and were expected to be cheerful and smiley, so that is what I did. I put on a happy smile and pushed through the sensory and social hell that was sleepless nights, breastfeeding and carer and baby groups.

I hated the feeling of obligation of going to groups and being thrown together with other people whose only common ground was that we had had babies all at the same time. The utter torture of feeling that I had to make shiny, happy, small talk when I was both sleep deprived and not giving a shit about the sorts of things that 'normal' new mothers talk about was a horror that I could well have done without, as was the overwhelming noise, busyness and god-awful baby smells. How anything so small can produce such copious foulness is beyond me. Having undiagnosed sensory sensitivities to the smell and texture of vomit and ripe bums was horrendous. The sheer effort that it took me to smile, look concerned and come out with supportive, clucking mum wisdom when what I really wanted to do was rock in the corner with my hands over my ears was, looking back, beyond human endurance. My autistic masking 'super-power' (sarcasm!), however, made it possible, as did finding another mum who was equally curmudgeonly, but less secret about it than I was and, I suspect, possibly also neurodivergent, and we have remained best friends to this day.

My son, though, was everything. The intensity of the love I had for him was completely overwhelming and from day one I made a conscious decision to bring him up very differently to how I was raised. He would know that he was loved, cherished and valued for who he was, and I think that this mission and him became my long-term hyper-focus, my intense interest. I have no regrets about this and am assured by him that I didn't become a (s)mother and that his memories of growing up are good. He has become the quietly confident, secure-in-his-own-skin man that healthy and loving attachments produce, so hurrah for autistic passions and the right kind of perseverance!

Not so much hurrah, though, for my continued and continual masking. Years of learning social skills by copying others and trying to feign interest in the things that I thought I 'should' be interested in, like shopping and holidays, resulted in my needs being squashed and having no sense of my own identity. I was a mish-mash of all the people I had studied and had no idea of who I was and what I liked or disliked. This is what years of masking did. It didn't just try to hide my autistic core self from others, it also hid me from me. Other people's expectations and needs were my priority, and self-care and self-knowledge were very low on my list.

As my son grew older I started a job, oddly enough as a learning support assistant for an autistic child, at the local primary school that he attended. To this day I find it bizarre that at the time I had no idea that I was also autistic, but I couldn't possibly be as I was female, chatty and amiable, with a profound dislike of all things to do with trains. That happens when your very obviously autistic brother drags your young self around freezing, boring stations for 'fun'.

I felt completely out of my depth and overwhelmed by the sights, sounds and smells of the school environment. I also felt very cowed by some of the teaching staff, but the saving grace of the job was that it enabled me to avoid the social and political hell that was the Parent Teacher Association and parent support groups. As an employee of the school, I could get away with saying that to be involved would be a conflict of interests, and so could avoid having to volunteer for whatever group was being set up. The unmasked truth, of course, was that I was autistic and too much peopling, even though some of the parents were lovely, was just too much.

When my son became a teenager and went to high school, the primary school-style social pressure diminished and as I was now a total embarrassment to him, the more hands-on parenting that accompanies younger children also changed. He was naturally doing more of his own thing with his mates, and school involvement was only really parent's evenings and the occasional drinkies or meals with parents, which I could just about deal with as long as they were on an infrequent basis. My mental health was just as bad and I had shocking social anxiety, but on these occasions put on a 'brave' masked face and pushed through. I hated it, but because I believed that it was expected, I made myself put on the show with a lipsticky smile and forced humour. My relationship with my son, however, was solid and loving and when we clashed, we quickly made up and I think we learned from each other. I learned to trust him and allow him to grow and myself to let go. Of course, none of this would have been possible without my husband's love and support, and he was invaluable when my many insecurities frequently showed up along the way.

When I was 42 and my son was 14, I was diagnosed – but it took until he left for his gap year in Africa and Europe for me to allow myself to start learning about what autism meant for me. I guess my monotropic mind wouldn't allow me to focus on more than one thing at once and his welfare was my priority. Having an answer as to why I had felt so different for all those years started to make sense. I began counselling and started to realize that whoever I was had become very hidden beneath countless layers of camouflage. This had affected not just my own mental health and wellbeing but also, to an extent, my ability to enjoy being a parent. I had put my heart and soul into making sure that my son knew that he was loved and valued and that he could always depend on his mum and dad, but because I was constantly on high alert, doing what I thought was expected of me socially, and ignoring my own needs, there was no room for simple enjoyment and being. So if there are any parenting regrets, that would be it. Masking has taken its toll, but I consider myself fortunate that the masked version of myself was still enough for my son to be healthy and happy, and our relationship only gets stronger as I learn to peel off those layers and learn to be more authentically, autistically me.

Four o'clock time bomb

Parents of autistic children can struggle to get school support for seeking diagnosis, often because the school is seeing very different behaviour from their child, and so teachers do not recognize autism, especially in girls (Whitlock *et al.*, 2020). A child who is perfectly behaved all day in front of other children and their teachers may come home and have a meltdown – known colloquially as the '4 o'clock time bomb'. This is effectively a rapid and intense dropping of the mask they have worked hard to maintain all day at school, now that they are home and in a safe place.

This pattern has an impact not only on the autistic child and their parents, but also on siblings. Generally, siblings of autistic children report that their relationships are good, saying things like:

> He is my family, autism cannot change that. You need to love your family. It's part of who you are, you know.

> My sister has a talent for completing beautiful colour patterns... I am not sure if that is autism or it's her. I would like to think it's just my sister. I don't live with autism. I live with my sister. (Quoted in Pavlopoulou & Dimitriou, 2019, p. 7)

Generally, the mental health of siblings of autistic children is fairly good, although many acknowledge that having an autistic sibling can be stressful for them, as they are often pulled into helping to care for them alongside their parents (Watson, Hanna & Jones, 2021). Siblings can also end up on the sharp end of the after-school meltdown, especially if the children are a bit older and get home before their parents finish work, so they are the only people around when it happens. This is something Helen and her brother experienced:

> Looking back now I can't believe the way I used to treat my brother after school. Rows over the TV remote or seating arrangements would get physical, and I was often seething with jealousy over him having friends who wanted to come round or invite him over to their

houses. I couldn't work out why I didn't have friends like that, or why I kept trying to pick fights with the most important person in my life as soon as I saw him. But I did know that I needed to be good when Mum got home as I didn't want to make her cry. If I saw her get upset, I got a weird sick feeling in my stomach and would start to panic.

It can be important to think about everyone in the family when looking to support an autistic person, as the whole family are impacted by their needs, just as they are by the needs of anyone else. Creating ways for an autistic person to drop the mask and be their authentic selves consciously, rather than forcibly dropping it through a meltdown, can be beneficial for everyone.

Guidance for partners/spouses and children (autistic and non-autistic)

It can be hard for the partner of an autistic person to learn that they have been masking. First, it can be upsetting to learn that the person you love has been struggling or unhappy, and that they have hidden that from you. This is particularly difficult if the person themselves did not realize how much they have masked, and you are both trying to process the impact of masking for the first time. Second, if the person masked for a long time, their underlying autistic characteristics might not be obvious to those around them. Some partners might have only known the autistic person while they have been masking, and so might feel like their loved one is changing when they drop the mask. Finally, we have discussed in detail how exhausting and often distressing masking can be. It can be hard for non-autistic partners in particular to understand how much effort masking takes, and to be as patient and understanding as is needed.

Having said that, being the partner or spouse of an autistic person who masks can also be a privilege. If your partner feels supported and accepted by you when they are their authentic, non-masked self, you can provide a safe space for them to drop the mask and recover.

The importance of this support in a relationship was talked about by several of our contributors, including the story below:

> I'd been staying in Manchester with my fiancé, an amazing but very busy city. After two days of crowds, and a very large concert, I was at the end of my coping. When we got to the train station, there were significant delays, meaning the platform was packed with a swarm of people. I felt myself going towards meltdown, while a staff member regularly shouted for everyone to squash closer together... The crowd was so big I got separated from my fiancé... By the time I got back to my partner I was in meltdown, crying hysterically and trying to cover my ears. I grew more nervous when I saw the police passing through the station, knowing the stories of arrests or questioning that autistic people are often met with during meltdown. My partner thankfully realized quickly and grabbed hold of me so that the most visible factors of my meltdown were shielded. (Melissa, autistic woman, 26)

This shows how important both emotional and practical support from partners can be for autistic people who are trying to mask less, or when the mask fails due to a stressful experience. Being there for a partner, recognizing the signs that they need your help, and respecting the ways that they need that help to happen (e.g. some people will want to be touched during a meltdown and others will hate it) are all crucial, and are the sorts of things that good communication can establish. Of course, this is not just true for relationships where one or both people are autistic – good communication is important in all relationships – but it can be especially important when natural communication styles differ, as between an autistic and a non-autistic partner.

Partners can also support autistic people as they reflect on and evaluate their use of masking, and help them find a balance that works for them. How and when this happens will depend on individual relationships and circumstances: how long you have known each other, whether you are both autistic and/or neurodivergent, and your ability to communicate with each other in an honest and caring way will all influence how a partner can support someone who masks. However, we have a few general tips below.

For partners of those who are just beginning to learn about their masking (including people who are diagnosed or identify as autistic later in life):

- Listen without judging. This is probably the most important advice in the whole book! Your loved one is the best expert on their own experiences, including how much they mask and the impact it has on them. Particularly at the start of their reflection on masking, they might describe sensations or experiences that seem to go against what you know of them, such as wanting to avoid talking about topics that they were always interested in before. Try to remember that the way they experience a situation is true for them at that moment, and they might appear to contradict themselves a few times before they figure out what feels authentic and appropriate for them.

- Let them come to their own sense of how they mask. It's true that, with an external perspective, it can often be easier to see changes in someone's behaviour. But pointing out every time your partner masks or doesn't mask might put pressure on them or make them feel more self-conscious. Instead, ask if they would like your perspective on specific situations, and, if they agree, try to describe what they are doing in neutral terms, without assuming what is a masked versus an authentic behaviour.

- Do some reading. We might be a bit biased, considering we wrote this book on masking, but seeking out other sources of information can be helpful to you and your partner. While they are the experts on their own experiences and needs, they are not representative of all autistic people, and may not be able, or want, to be responsible for teaching you everything about masking at the same time as working things out for themselves. Reading about masking in general, or other people's experiences, can help give you insight without solely relying on your partner.

For partners of those who want to reduce how much they mask:

- Provide gentle and honest encouragement when you see your partner unmasking, without making it a big deal. For instance, if you see them start to stim in public when feeling excited about something, this hopefully means they feel comfortable enough to let this out. You could encourage this by passing them a stim toy (if they enjoy these), or saying privately to them how happy you are to see them stim.

- Allow them to choose when and where they mask. It's not easy to suddenly drop all parts of masking, particularly those that are automatic or unconscious. Even if your partner wants to reduce their masking, there might be some situations where they feel they need to keep masking, for safety or because they aren't sure what to do instead. You might be able to help by noticing how your partner or other people responded to them masking (or not masking), but not everyone finds it helpful to have that feedback.

- Work on making the spaces you go to together 'safe' for them to unmask. If you, as a couple, know what sorts of environments enable your partner to drop their mask and you are comfortable trying to make changes, go for it. This can be things like choosing to meet friends in smaller numbers so that they are having to manage fewer social interactions at once, asking for specific tables in restaurants that cater to their sensory needs around lighting or sound so that they can relax that part of their mask (or even ask for the music to be turned off altogether), or telling the people you are with what would make your partner more comfortable. Autistic people are capable of asking for these adjustments themselves, of course, but it can feel intimidating to have to do so, and having someone on your side who will deal with these things can take a lot of the pressure off. That can then help someone use their mask less because they walk into a situation knowing that it has been made as welcoming as possible.

Guidance for education professionals

The clearest way masking impacts autistic young people (and potentially those with other forms of SEND) in education is that it stops their needs being recognized and supported. If someone, especially an autistic girl, is masking at school, then that whole set of professionals may not be seeing the difficulties they are having just getting through each day. A child who appears calm, quiet and focused on their work rarely raises alarm bells for a teacher in the same way as another child who is disruptive, loud or distracted. But it can be these quiet children who are experiencing the worst mental health effects of masking, as they spend significant amounts of energy each day on simply fitting in 'enough' to get by without drawing negative attention from their peers or the staff. This leads, as we have seen, to anxiety, depression and exhaustion, none of which are what anyone would want for a child. We have discussed in Chapter 4 how longer and more intense masking is linked to worse mental health outcomes, and this relationship seems to start early in life. With evidence that autistic girls mimic the linguistic patterns of their non-autistic peers in primary school as a type of 'vocal mask' (Parish-Morris *et al.*, 2017), we can surmise that there are potential negative consequences from very early on.

The personal piece from Jodie Smitten at the end of this section talks in detail about lots of the ways in which the school environment actively teaches autistic children to mask, from early years onwards. Even well-meaning interactions ('don't cover your ears, the music isn't that loud, you'll enjoy it if you give it a chance') can undermine an autistic child's sense of their own bodily reactions, and starts teaching them that they should at least appear to like and dislike the same things as other people. School rules around where lunch must be eaten establish the idea that a child's sensory and social overwhelm doesn't matter and must be hidden, otherwise they will go hungry. Peers – especially bullies – repeatedly send the message that if you do anything 'odd', you stand out, and that makes an autistic child an easy and obvious target for a whole host of other unpleasant things, many of which teachers and even parents will brush off as 'just being kids' or 'a misunderstanding', no matter how upsetting it may be for the child. That isn't because they don't care, but it can be hard for adults to understand how something feels or is experienced by children in general, harder when that child is autistic and even harder if they do not know that child is autistic.

Research has shown that teachers are less likely to think a girl is autistic than a boy even when they show the same number or rate of autistic traits (Whitlock *et al.*, 2020), which means that they are less likely to support a referral to an educational or clinical psychologist. This is important, because most psychologists require evidence from more than one setting (e.g. from both home and school, not just home or just school) in order to take on the case. So if an autistic child is masking and seemingly 'coping' at school, but then is melting down at the end of every day from exhaustion, it is more likely that this will be labelled and investigated as a problem at home rather than being seen as a wider set of needs. This delay to the diagnostic process, which can already take several years through the public options, or be very expensive privately, delays access to support. This is crucial for any child with any developmental condition, from autism to dyslexia to ADHD. Decades of studies have shown that early interventions, targeted at specific skills and areas, have the most positive impacts on long-term outcomes for non-neurotypical children. This is the case for autistic children – the earlier their individual differences and needs are recognized and respected, the better time they have at school, the better they do in education. We've discussed in Chapter 3 (sections 'Masking at university' and 'Masking at work') the extensive evidence for how awareness and acceptance of autistic people can improve mental health, and this is likely to have knock-on positive effects on things like school engagement, grades achieved and even employment in adulthood. But if no one knows to give a child that extra space and support, they don't get those benefits.

So, how can education professionals – teachers, teaching assistants, playground monitors, everyone – spot a child who is masking their way through school?

- Look out for the quiet kids. Masking is not always about being quiet – a social butterfly can be masking too, by hiding their lack of close friends behind lots of acquaintances – but it is more common for children and young people who are masking to end up on the quiet side of the equation. They are often trying not to draw attention to themselves because they fear that attention will be negative, so try to blend in and appear as 'average' as they can. Especially if a child seeks out spaces which have fewer sensory stimuli (eating their lunch in a classroom versus in the lunch hall, for example) or spends most of their unstructured time in solo activities, it can be worth keeping them in mind and remembering this if you are ever asked to provide an opinion on whether they should be referred.
- Think about how to engage them in ways that require the least masking. If there is a child who you think may be autistic and masking as much as they can, try to think about ways in which to make the environment feel safer for them so that they can drop the mask, even a little bit. That short respite has the potential to really help them as a short relief from keeping up the façade, and will let them know that they are valued and valid as they are, not just for the face they present to everyone. Chatting in a quieter space where they don't need to control their sensory reactions so much can be a huge help, asking them about things you know they like (or asking what they like to find out!), and being positive in your response (no comments about whether it is childish, for example, but asking why they like it or what they like best) can all show

that you are considerate of their needs without making a big deal out of it.

- Remember, it isn't your job to decide if they are or are not autistic. Some school staff can feel worried that they are overstepping their role by suggesting a child may be autistic and masking. Others might be concerned that they don't know enough about autism to give a proper opinion that a child is autistic, so they don't want to support the referral that parents are seeking. The important thing here is that it isn't meant to be your job to work out if a child is autistic, and that your comments alone will not be the thing that makes that call. If you are concerned that child is not getting the support they need from the school for any reason, speak to your SENCO (special educational needs co-ordinator) or whoever is responsible for children with additional needs in your setting. They will know what the best next steps are, and are highly unlikely to ask you to talk to parents on your own, for example. Equally, if you are approached to give your thoughts on a child by an educational or clinical psychologist, be honest about your impressions and the things you have noticed – don't hold back just in case you're wrong. They will be collecting comments from lots of people to build up a wider picture of the child, and you are just one part of it. What would be worse is saying that a child is definitely not autistic simply because you haven't seen what you think of as the traditional behaviours – try to give a fair and balanced account, regardless of your own opinion.

- Look at the resources. There are a growing number of brilliant resources out there to help educators and school staff understand the autistic children they work with, resources which go far beyond the half-an-INSET-day of training a lot of us get! The Autism Education Trust have specific information for teachers, aimed specifically at early years, primary, secondary and post-16 staff. There are videos on YouTube about autism in school (we suggest the National Autistic Society channel in general, and searching for 'autism what I wish my teachers knew' as a starting point), including lots from autistic people themselves about what they wish their teachers had known and what would have helped them. The University of Bath has put together a free course, hosted on FutureLearn, called Good Practice in Autism Education, which specifically sets out to teach people how best to support the education of autistic children and young people – it takes roughly four weeks (though you learn at your own pace) and covers a whole range of topics and recommendations for best practice.[1] See what is out there and what works for you, but definitely take a look at resources beyond this book to build up your knowledge and skills.

Personal piece: Jodie Smitten, autistic autism consultant, on children masking at school

Children receive messages from the world around them from birth, through others' reactions, responses, comments and body language. A subtle look or comment of annoyance from an auntie when they have been repeatedly twirling in circles on the washing line very quickly gives the child a message that this behaviour is not okay. This can cause a child to stop, they receive the message that this will upset others and so they are made to feel that the intense enjoyment they receive from the spinning isn't acceptable despite the fact they are doing no one any harm. A nursery worker who suggests that a child remove their hands from their ears as the group's singing isn't 'that loud' tells a child the pain they feel from this sensory experience doesn't matter.

So before a child has even started school it is likely that they have already been fed the idea that some element of their being is wrong.

Then school starts! A child enters an environment full of

---

1   Available at www.futurelearn.com/courses/autism-education, accessed on 23 May 2021.

unwritten rules and expectations around what they should be doing and when: 'wash your hands', 'show good listening', 'quiet hands'. You experience this early on; the child who doesn't sit still and quietly on the carpet gets told off. For an autistic child who is sensitive to tone of voice, the feelings of others and threats of uncertain punishments, the fear is intense. The result is they mask and supress their need to move. They subconsciously use all their energies to follow the unwritten rules, sink into the background, listen, suppress their true selves and do as they are told straight away. A perfect, dream student (from a neuro-normative perspective).

Masking is further compounded by reactions from peers, being included or excluded in play for example. Maybe an autistic child becomes excited and jumps and flaps with enjoyment, a motion that others may not have experienced and hence don't understand. The child quickly learns that in order to be accepted by and have friends they have to mimic those around them or supress natural reactions; often children will mimic those they deem more popular.

Observing and mimicking others, hiding distress and suppressing natural reactions is exhausting. The suppression is held until a child reaches their safe place or people. Some parents see this the second their child reaches them in the playground, when the child 'overflows' with emotion; some children will wait until they have reached the safety of their home. These emotional outbursts can be filled with anger, frustration and aggression towards self or others. After some time, the parents may approach school with their concerns; school are dismissive and describe the child as an 'ideal student' who has friends, listens well in class and completes all their work. The parents start to believe or are led to believe that their parenting is to blame. The parents are advised to 'toughen up' on a child, and give consistent boundaries; sadly this only exacerbates the distress for the child and can sometimes lead to the child internalizing and masking at home.

When I describe the concept of masking to parents who have

failed in attempts to access support, their relief is immense. Finally, they think, they can introduce this concept to school and things will start to change. Unfortunately this isn't always the case, due to school resources being so stretched and with limited understanding of masking. Educators must be aware of autistic masking and how to work collaboratively with parents in recognizing the signs. I have had the privilege of working with many children who can eloquently talk about this experience and how they simply 'act' or 'pretend' their way through the school day. Yet due to fear of the system and nobody actually asking these children, their true voices and feelings are simply not heard. Equally, for many this instinctive response is so ingrained that they are simply completely unaware of its occurrence. The mental health implications of this lack of knowledge about masking and the resulting unmet needs in autistic children can be drastic and tragic. Children can become school phobic, unable to leave the house, get dressed or access any form of education because they are in autistic burnout and have suffered years of trauma, and this can even lead to suicidal thoughts.

I have worked collaboratively with Kieran Rose and Dr Pooky Knightsmith to develop courses to support understanding of masking in autistic children. Both courses are invaluable as the positive mental health of autistic children relies on this knowledge becoming mainstream.[2]

How can we best support a child who masks?

All professionals must work collaboratively with parents. It's incredibly stressful for parents who are continually doing all they can at home to manage the expression of distress that has been

---

2   Autistic Masking: The Basics & Beyond. Available at https://theautisticad-vocate.teachable.com/p/autistic-masking-the-basics-and-beyond, accessed on 23 May 2021; Understand Autistic Masking. Available at www.creativeed-ucation.co.uk/courses/understand-autistic-masking, accessed on 23 May 2021.

bubbling all day while advocating for their child outside of the home and not always feeling listened to or believed.

The whole community that the child resides in (e.g. school, family) should have knowledge, understanding and acceptance of autistic difference. Autistic norms such as stimming, differences in communication, sensory processing differences and so on should be normalized within non-autistic spaces, allowing an autistic person the safety to be themselves without fear of victimization or discipline. So many children are deemed to be defiant or daydreaming, as they may find it easier to listen and process instructions if they are looking out of the window or doodling rather than showing 'good listening' (non-autistic expectations!).

Autistic children benefit greatly from being introduced to their 'tribe'. Opportunities to meet other autistics, both adults and children and in particular those with similar interests, can do wonders for positive self-identity. True self-identity is negatively impacted when you spend considerable time suppressing yourself.

Guidance for healthcare professionals

The most obvious way that masking can affect people in healthcare settings is that it impacts their ability to receive appropriate support. This could be because their masking means it is harder for them to receive an accurate diagnosis of autism, or because their level of other needs and difficulties is not being recognized. For instance, many autistic people have said that because they mask their autistic characteristics when meeting new or important people (sometimes without even realizing), they do not 'look autistic' to doctors or teachers. This means that they might not be referred on for formal diagnostic assessment, or might not be given adjustments they need in class. Healthcare professionals in all disciplines should be aware when assessing or supporting an autistic person that they might not 'look' autistic in a stereotypical sense. However, this does not mean that the person doesn't experience difficulties because of their autism, or that they do not need the same support as someone else who 'looks' more autistic.

Healthcare professionals who are involved with autism assessment should be particularly aware of this. An autistic person might be able to present a very neurotypical mask for a short time, for instance during a ten-minute chat. If the person or those around them report having autistic traits, these should be taken seriously, even if they are not visible straight away. By asking explicitly about masking, looking at the impact that socializing has on a person and evaluating how they act across different situations, healthcare professionals can begin to see under the mask and will be able to evaluate the person's needs properly.

However, as has been described in Chapter 4, masking itself can also have a direct impact on people's wellbeing. Healthcare professionals should be aware that autistic people who mask are likely to also experience burnout, exhaustion, anxiety and issues around self-esteem and identity. In addition to actively looking out for signs of these issues in their autistic patients, healthcare professionals can share this information. Colleagues working in mental health, social care, paediatrics and general medicine would all benefit from learning about masking and the impacts it can have for the autistic people they work with.

Autistic people who experience these negative impacts because they mask may need different types of support compared to other people. For instance, someone who experiences burnout because of long-term masking needs support that helps them reduce their masking strategies, whereas someone who experiences burnout because of working in a stressful environment needs support in changing the characteristics of their working environment. In contrast, some people might develop depression or anxiety because their lack of masking means they find it difficult to make friends. They would benefit from support in developing appropriate masking strategies (or support in finding friends without having to mask, depending on their preference), whereas other people with these mental health conditions might benefit from pharmacological interventions.

Another thing to note is that some people might want support from healthcare professionals to better control their masking. This could involve reducing how much they mask and the strategies they use, or receiving guidance on how to mask more effectively when they want to. It is important for healthcare professionals to understand that masking is an individual behaviour, and only the person themselves can decide how much masking (including no masking) is best for them. This might also change over time and across different situations.

It is also important to remember that there are some autistic people who don't, or can't, mask. They might experience unique difficulties as a result of this – for instance, they might be seen as more difficult than other patients or service users because they don't adapt their behaviour to neurotypical norms. Some people might want to mask more, because they feel masking would help them form friendships or get through job interviews. If they specifically request support with masking, it is important to evaluate the benefits and disadvantages of all masking strategies, including how their impact changes over time.

A fantastic new resource that has been co-developed by autistic adults, clinicians and researchers is *Psychological Therapy for Autistic Adults* by the Authentistic Research Collective (Stark *et al.*, 2021). This is a freely available guide on how to adapt cognitive behavioural therapy (CBT) to be relevant for autistic adults. The guide acknowledges that masking can impact autism assessment, and makes the great point that healthcare professionals are likely to have already been working with autistic adults who may not yet be diagnosed or even aware they are autistic. Masking is therefore something to consider regardless of whether or not the individual you are working with has a formal diagnosis of autism.

The members of this group emphasize that in some cases masking can still be helpful to them, and so urge healthcare professionals to talk to the individual before assuming that they want to stop all masking. However, they also state that feeling authentic, accepted and safe is a crucial part of the therapy process, and so high levels of masking during therapy may impact its effectiveness. Some group members describe masking during therapy in order to seem more likeable to the therapist, or because they felt it was necessary in order to be seen as engaging with the support. Instead, healthcare professionals should explicitly discuss the concept of masking with those they work with, and emphasize that therapy is a safe space in which to drop the mask even if it changes the way that the autistic person presents themselves. This might involve retraining for the healthcare professional, to change what they think 'effective engagement' looks like with a certain therapy.

How can healthcare professionals support autistic people who mask? The best answer is to ask the person themselves, and work with them to identify, evaluate and manage their masking behaviours. Tools to measure masking can be used to provide specific examples of masking strategies. If someone wants to reduce how much they are masking, a healthcare professional could work with them to identify individual strategies and develop a plan to practise not using those strategies, perhaps starting in situations where the person feels relatively safe and accepted. Alternatively, if someone would like support in developing their masking strategies (for example, putting on a welcoming smile when meeting someone new), the healthcare professional could take time to practise the strategies with that person and offer constructive feedback. Specific examples of strategies are proposed by the Authentistic group in their summary document (Stark *et al.*, 2021).

At this stage of learning about masking, we still don't know how it impacts everyone. We therefore would caution healthcare professionals not to assume that strategies which are effective for some people will work for others, or conversely that strategies which are harmful for some will also harm others. The best approach to supporting someone who masks is to follow their lead, and make gradual changes to any existing behavioural strategies so that the person has time to adapt.

As we mentioned Chapter 1, we still know very little about if and how much masking is done by autistic people with an intellectual disability and limited spoken or written language. However, that doesn't mean that healthcare professionals working with these individuals should assume they do not mask at all. Autistic people with high support needs might still mask aspects of their autism, and might still experience some of the negative consequences of such masking. In particular, there is a risk that autistic people with high support needs will mask parts of their experiences that they might need additional support with, such as sensory experiences. If someone expresses sensory discomfort by banging their head against a wall, they might be punished or prevented from doing this. While this stops them from hurting themselves, it doesn't address the sensory discomfort that led to the behaviour in the first place – although the individual might have learned to mask the response to it. The sensory experience might still cause them discomfort because others have not realized it was the cause of the behaviour, when it could be addressed. Healthcare professionals should be aware of non-verbal masking of autistic characteristics, such as a change in response to a certain situation, that might reflect expectations from others rather than a change in that person's true response to the situation.

On the other hand, autistic people with higher support needs might mask aspects of their autistic experience that bring them joy, because of the stigma of seeming different. For instance, an autistic adult with an intellectual disability might be told that liking the TV programme *In the Night Garden* is 'childish' or inappropriate, and so might hide their interest in and knowledge of the programme. They might not talk about it even though it's something that brings them a lot of joy, or they might pretend not to want to watch it because they are worried about others judging them. People with intellectual disability are very much aware of the reactions and prejudices of others, and there is a long history of research and activism around the stigmatization of intellectual disability among this community. It is therefore important for healthcare professionals working with autistic people with high support needs to be aware that their responses and those of others might influence people's masking, and that this might impact their wellbeing.

Guidance for employers

We've discussed some of the reasons why autistic people might feel the need to mask at work, and the ways this can impact their ability to get and succeed in a job, in the section 'Masking at work' in Chapter 3. Having read that, you can perhaps more easily understand why autistic people have among the lowest rates of consistent employment of any group of disabled people in the UK (Office for National Statistics, 2021) – masking can take up so much cognitive capacity that it makes doing a job to the best of your ability very difficult, even without things like sensory sensitivities also affecting you.

There are lots of benefits to having a diverse workforce – more creative thinking, different perspectives, greater resilience and experience handling a wider range of problems. Neurodiversity is just as important a part of building diverse teams as any other diversity category. So, if you want to recruit, retain and benefit from autistic employees, here are some of our suggestions.

In the recruitment and interview processes

- Make your job adverts clear and accurate: give a clear description of the job, and make your list of essential and desirable criteria easily accessible – preferably in the form of a bullet point list so that people have to do the least 'deciphering' possible.
    - Avoid standard requirements like 'good team player' if the job will not actually involve that much day-to-day team working. Team working is not the same as being in a team, and it is good to highlight where this is a specific expectation rather than a description of the way your company is organized.
    - Make clear whether and what flexible working arrangements are possible, as some autistic people are highly competent at a specific role but may prefer working from home (where they can control their

sensory environment) – making this option clear would encourage those people to apply and may improve your candidate pool.

- Design a supportive interview approach: this does not mean an interview that is set up so that everyone looks brilliant – but it does mean an interview that is set up so that everyone can give a fair account of their capabilities.

  - Simple things like providing interview questions in advance can allow all your candidates to prepare their best answers and examples, rather than being a test of how well they think on the spot, and this will significantly reduce anxiety for your autistic candidates.

  - Ask about sensory needs before the interview so that you can turn off harsh strip lighting, or have made it clear that you are happy for someone to wear sunglasses, for example. This will help put an autistic person at ease so that they can perform to the best of their ability – and marks you out as an understanding and supportive employer they want to work for.

  - Try not to be swayed by eye contact and body language. Interviews are an anxious time for everyone, and autistic people especially may struggle to maintain their mask of 'normal' social behaviour on these points while under stress. Focus on how they are answering your questions and their skills and experiences, rather than assuming that awkwardness in the interview means that someone will not fit in well with others at the company. Often, once they are in a job and feel more comfortable, people become more relaxed, and it is that person you will be working with every day, not the version of them in the interview.

Supporting an autistic employee

Once you have hired an autistic person, there are a wide range of things you can do to support them to thrive in your employment.

This works out best for them and for you, and while reasonable adjustments are specific to each individual, we have some general ideas below.

- Have a comprehensive and organized induction: taking time to give someone a full and structured induction can have a massive impact on both their anxiety and their ability to get on with the job.
  - Things like giving them an induction timetable of who to meet, when, and why they are important can be great. It not only introduces your autistic employee to people, but gives them some social context before they go to the meeting so that they are prepared.
  - A tour of all the buildings or rooms in the workplace is a good idea, even if they aren't working in them directly, because it is surprising how often someone is asked to 'just pop over to X' and hasn't been shown where X is.
  - Creating a list of 'tips for working with us' can be beneficial for all new employees, not just those on the spectrum. These are the sorts of things that are not official company regulations, but are the 'unwritten rules' of your workplace: expectations around working hours or lunch breaks, dress code, a preference for a clear desk even if it isn't official policy.
  - Giving new employees a buddy – someone to go to with all the niggly questions that come up when you are in a job – is, again, helpful for everyone. It means that they know who to go to if they need to find a specific form, rather than either worrying about it on their own or asking someone inappropriate, for example. This ends up saving everyone time in the long run!
- Understand working and communication differences: it sounds obvious, but learning a bit about autistic people and their strengths and difficulties at work can save you a lot of time by preparing you for what to put in place, and can

save your employee potential anxiety or distress in having to repeatedly explain themselves.

- Expectations: Making your expectations around communication norms clear from the outset is important. If your company uses Slack (a proprietary business communication platform) rather than email, or is more of a culture where people go to each other's desks to check things, explain this. Some of these communication modes might not work for your employee, so give them the opportunity to say this and to find an alternative together, rather than expecting them to put on a mask of being fine with it and just coping.
- Managing the environment: Talk to your employee about their sensory sensitivities and (again) work together to find reasonable solutions. It is very common for autistic people to use noise-cancelling headphones, for example, and as long as this is not going to impede their ability to do the job, there is no reason for these to be forbidden in the office. Similarly, if particular lighting causes them pain, finding ways to mitigate this is usually possible. Try not to make assumptions about what their needs will be though – some autistic people can love working in an open plan office despite the noise and people, whereas others find it impossible to work in those conditions.
- Look into helpful technologies: Most workplaces use a significant amount of technology day to day, and a lot of jobs (as we have learned in 2020) can be done purely online. There are a lot of apps and organizational features out there now which can help an autistic person manage their time, prioritize tasks and generally do well at work. Everything from shared calendars and project trackers, to timing apps that encourage focus, to anxiety support apps that help people manage their

emotions through the day can and should be considered to make sure that someone is able to do the best they are capable of.

Guidance for autistic people

Helen's personal advice is 'Decide for yourself when and how you want to mask, have the confidence to be your authentic self but also don't put yourself down for strategically retreating behind the mask occasionally!' She also recommends Dr Camilla Pang's advice: 'My advice is to forget about perfect when it comes to new social and professional situations. Instead, focus on lowering your error count – and counting the little things you have achieved' (Pang, 2020, p. 223)

So, to sum up this chapter...

There are lots of things that anyone and everyone who knows, works with, socializes with or cares about an autistic person can do to help them feel safe and secure enough to drop the mask. We all could, and should, do what we can to make the environment and our interactions more comfortable. It is likely to be a long process – for autistic people who mask every day, stopping can be complicated and emotional – and it is not necessarily an easy one. But, as other sections of this book have shown, it is an important one, and so supporting them to do this is an invaluable step each of us can take.

Other things to think about: A brief overview of masking by other neurodivergent people

Throughout this book we have been focusing on autistic masking; that is, masking of characteristics associated with autism. As we said earlier, that doesn't mean that only autistic people mask. The concept of masking differences is common across a variety of neurodivergent conditions, such as ADHD, dyslexia and Tourette's. People with physical and mental health conditions also mask aspects of their conditions, such as pain, adaptations they have to make, or other symptoms. As many autistic people have other neurodevelopmental, mental and physical health conditions, it is important to be aware that their masking strategies might reflect those conditions at times. We don't have the space here to go into masking of other conditions in detail, but will give a few examples of other types of masking that might take place in two specific conditions: dyslexia and anxiety.

Dyslexia is often described as a learning difficulty, disability or neurodevelopmental condition. The most common characteristics of dyslexia are difficulties in reading and writing – for instance, struggling to put letters in the right order when reading or writing words, or taking much longer to read words than most people. Having a longer than average reading time is one of the key ways that dyslexia is identified, as the exact characteristics are still not agreed upon. However, some people who are dyslexic seem to be able to mask their dyslexia in certain situations, sometimes to the extent that their reading time is the same as non-dyslexic people. It has been proposed that this is because they find alternative ways to read words, which don't rely on the traditional processes of matching letter shapes to sounds ('phonological processing'). For instance, some dyslexic people might instead memorize the shape of different words, so they learn what an entire word 'looks' like and can identify it as quickly as others would do from combining the individual letters. Memorization requires more effort than the traditional approaches to reading, meaning that if the person is tired or has to process more information at the same time, they might struggle to use it as effectively. This has been described as a 'compensation' technique, which represents a similar concept to masking of autism. The underlying condition (dyslexia or autism) still exists, but because of the masking efforts of the individual (memorizing word shapes or what facial expressions look like), it's not always obvious to other people.

A similar strategy has been observed in people with anxiety, who use 'safety behaviours' as a way to avoid encountering the triggers that cause them anxiety – but without removing the anxiety itself. For instance, someone who has a phobia of dogs might avoid walking past a neighbour's house where a large dog often barks at her. This might be a conscious strategy, used even though it means the route to work takes five minutes longer. Alternatively, it could be unconscious, with the person not even realizing that on the days that she takes a different route she is calmer and doesn't have panic attacks.

Crucially, the difference between safety behaviours and adaptive coping strategies, which actually address and reduce the anxiety itself, is that safety behaviours often reinforce the association between the experience and anxiety. Because she avoids the dog, this person's family might forget that she is afraid of it and so be less patient with her when she does feel anxious. In the event that she couldn't avoid the dog – say, for example, she has to park her car outside the neighbour's house one day – her anxiety would be just as strong as it ever was, perhaps even stronger because she hasn't seen the dog in a while and isn't sure how aggressive it might be. If she was supported to use a more adaptive coping strategy, such as looking at pictures of dogs and listening to recordings of dogs barking while she felt safe and secure, she might in time feel less anxious when she sees the dog in real life. Safety behaviours in anxiety are not exactly the same as masking – for one thing, masking your autism doesn't make you more autistic over time! – but there are some common outcomes. In both cases, the difference or difficulty is still there, but might not be obvious to other people, and it might impact the amount of support or understanding a person receives.

These are just two brief examples, but they demonstrate

that people can mask things besides autism that can prevent them from getting support. If we consider that many autistic people have multiple co-occurring mental and physical health problems, it is likely that an autistic person wouldn't just mask their autism. When considering how much someone is masking and how it impacts them, it is important to think about their entire experience. If an autistic mask is 'lifted' it might reveal other difficulties or differences that even the person themselves is not always aware of.

Conclusion

In this book, we have tried to give an overview of every aspect of masking – from what it is, to who does it, to the impact it can have and how we can support autistic people in masking less.

We do not claim to have all the answers. The research on masking is incredibly new and does not cover everything we would want it to. The insights from autistic people themselves are incredibly valuable here, because autistic people have lifetimes of experience with masking, and that is why we have tried to share their voices throughout. Those voices, though, can only be a representation of a small number of people's experiences, and do not describe how everyone experiences or feels about masking.

What is a clear and consistent message from both the research and autistic people is that masking takes a lot of effort, feels like denying or hiding your authentic self and that effort has a negative effect on autistic people's mental health.

This does not mean that all masking, in every situation, by every person, is bad – or even equally bad. Different people have different experiences, and some autistic people find their masks incredibly useful. Masking is not a black-and-white behaviour, universally bad or universally good, even if it can be tempting to think about it that way. What is crucial is feeling that you are in control of that mask, that you are able to use it how you want, and that you are able to take it off when you want to. As we learn more about masking, it may well be that what we find is that this control of the mask, feeling like you can choose what of yourself to show to people and how, is what is linked to better outcomes for autistic people.

It is important to feel that you can be your authentic self and that your authentic self is valued, liked and respected by the people around you. This should be the focus of any and all support around masking that is developed and offered to autistic people. We should be working to enable autistic people to react well and safely to the situation in front of them, and remembering that this is likely to differ for each person and each scenario. Many social skills interventions that currently exist provide autistic children with rules for interacting with other people, but then researchers are surprised when these rules don't transfer to other settings than the one they set up. Interventions and teaching around masking need to avoid this trap and think about how to empower autistic people to make their own informed decisions about masking and not masking, and understand what that looks like for them.

To return to the elephant metaphor that we started with – what you think masking is will depend on which part of it you are looking at. To follow that idea through – you will behave differently depending on which part you are looking at as well. This holds true for masking, as you may have to behave differently depending on what situation you are in. Some situations will call for a 'professional' mask (which, as we've seen, even non-autistic people can have a version of). Other situations will call for parts of a mask (thinking about getting into a gig versus being free to express yourself in the middle of the crowd). And hopefully, autistic people will have other situations where they feel that no mask is needed at all. These are all 'parts' of the masking 'elephant', and are all legitimate responses to the situations autistic people find themselves in, especially if it helps them to stay safe.

There is another metaphor that might be useful when thinking about masking – seeing it as a piece of art. When you are close up (if you are masking intensely, for example, or in the middle of supporting someone who you know is trying to hide a meltdown), it can be hard to see how the bit you are looking at might make sense in the wider context. If you can find a way to step back, you can see the pieces of the picture coming together to make the whole artwork. This stepping back might be finding a safe space to relax the mask and slowly getting used to the sense of yourself that emerges without it. Stepping back could be talking to the people around you to work out how masking or not masking is affecting them as well as you (especially in settings where there is more than one autistic person, to check for clashing needs). Stepping back could be looking at the environment your autistic friend/child/partner is in, and thinking about how to make them more comfortable so that they don't need to mask, or at least not so much. Stepping back to think about the 'big picture' of masking and the impact it has is important in any autistic person's life, and the lives of anyone supporting autistic people.

We hope that this book has gone some way towards helping with those processes. And to mix our metaphors – we hope that it helps people to step back and see the picture of the whole elephant, rather than just the piece they are used to experiencing.

Glossary

accuracy How true or correct something is. In measurement, how much we can be sure it is definitely measuring what we want it to measure.

anorexia nervosa (AN) A mental health condition affecting around 1 per cent of the population. AN is an eating disorder which is characterized by very low body weight (BMI lower than 17.5), driven by a desire for thinness, and often accompanied by body dysmorphia which means that those with AN are unable to recognize the reality of their physical condition or their mental health.

applied behavioural analysis An approach based in behavioural psychology, pioneered by Lovaas in the 1960s and made famous by a 1987 study (Lovaas, 1987) where he found that autistic children's IQ scores improved following 40 hours a week of intense behavioural intervention. It focuses on using and changing visible behaviours, rather than exploring causes of behaviour, and uses a range of techniques to teach children to behave in desired ways. ABA is widely used across the world, especially in the United States, but is less used in the UK because of campaigning by autistic adults, who highlight that the process can be traumatizing. Historically, ABA used physical punishment to change behaviour, along with positive reinforcement.

While use of physical punishment is much more rare in the modern world, ABA still reinforces ideas that certain natural autistic ways of being are 'wrong', and therefore can undermine self-esteem and mental health.

Asperger's syndrome An old subtype of autism characterized by having average or above-average intellectual ability, and no language delay. Since 2013 Asperger's syndrome has been removed from diagnostic manuals, as it is acknowledged that there is no meaningful difference between people who meet the criteria for Asperger's and those who meet the criteria for autism. Some people prefer to use this term to describe themselves while others now reject the term due to revelations about Hans Asperger's personal history.

attention deficit hyperactivity disorder (ADHD) A neurodevelopmental condition which includes struggling to concentrate, being restless, and having creative and constantly changing thoughts.

autism A neurodevelopmental condition involving differences and/or difficulties in social communication, focused or repeated interests, actions or behaviours, and differences in sensory processing.

autism spectrum disorder The diagnosis given by clinicians identifying someone as autistic.

autistic traits Characteristics such as behaviours, ways of thinking or responses to the world that are commonly found in autistic people. Someone can have some autistic traits without meeting the diagnostic criteria for autism.

burnout A mental and physical state of exhaustion, often resulting from long-term unresolved stress or pressure. Originally discussed in relation to people who were 'burnt out' from intense professional situations, the term is now used to recognize the impact of chronic stress on people from any cause.

camouflage hypothesis A theory proposed by Lorna Wing in 1981 that clinicians might find it harder to identify autism in girls, because some autistic girls camouflage or mask some of their autistic characteristics.

camouflaging Another word for masking, which sometimes refers to strategies that allow someone to blend in and avoid attention from others.

Camouflaging Autistic Traits Questionnaire (CAT-Q) A self-report questionnaire measuring a person's use of masking (camouflaging) strategies.

catastrophizing Assuming that the worst possible outcome for any given situation is the most likely one, and proceeding both emotionally and behaviourally on the basis of that assumption. This is often regardless of how likely the imagined worst possible outcome actually is.

compensation Using alternative strategies to achieve a goal. For instance, using autistic strengths such as memory to interpret facial expressions that non-autistic people understand automatically.

disability A physical, mental or emotional condition that limits a person in terms of their movement, senses, experiences or activities, for whatever reason.

discrepancy method A way of measuring masking. The extent of masking can be measured by the difference (or discrepancy) between how autistic someone feels, and how autistic they look based on traditional behavioural assessments.

double empathy problem A theory proposed by Dr Damian Milton that misunderstandings and differences in communication between autistic and non-autistic people are the result of a failure by non-autistic people to empathize, rather than purely due to autistic people's 'lack of empathy'.

dyslexia A learning difficulty which affects literacy skills such as reading, writing and processing of words generally. It can occur in people of all intellectual ability levels, and is usually diagnosed when someone's literacy level is significantly below the levels of the rest of their cognitive profile, or when it is significantly below the average literacy level for those of their age and intellectual ability.

dyspraxia (also known as developmental co-ordination disorder: DCD) A learning difficulty which affects physical co-ordination, both at the fine motor (small movements, e.g. writing) and gross motor (big movements, e.g. walking) levels. It can occur in people of all intellectual ability levels, and is highly varied in how it presents. It is possible for someone's difficulties related to dyspraxia to change across the course of their lifetime.

emotional intelligence The ability to recognize, understand, manage and use your own and other people's emotions. Empathy is often included as part of discussions about emotional intelligence.

executive function A set of cognitive processes which play a central role in the cognitive control of behaviour. The three main areas of executive function are working memory (retaining new information, being able to manipulate information), cognitive flexibility (adapting to new information, creative problem-solving) and inhibitory control (setting priorities, resisting impulsive responses).

extroversion/extrovert A personality trait of enjoying active engagement with other people. Extroverts often describe themselves as gaining energy when interacting with others.

filled pauses Sounds that are used to fill gaps while speaking, often to indicate that someone hasn't finished speaking yet, e.g. 'um' or 'uh'.

flapping Moving fingers or hands rapidly back and forth in the air.

identity-first language Language that describes someone's disability or condition as an intrinsic part of their identity, for instance, 'autistic person'. See also **person-first language.**

impression management The conscious or unconscious effort to influence or control how others perceive you.

introversion/introvert A personality trait of preferring time alone, or with a few select people. Introverts often describe themselves as using up energy when interacting with others, which needs to be restored by time alone.

LGBTQIA+ Stands for lesbian, gay, bisexual, trans, queer, intersex, asexual + others. This is an acronym used to encompass those who are non-heterosexual or non-heteronormative in some way regarding their sexuality or gender identity.

linguistic camouflaging Masking by changing the way that you speak, for instance by using similar words or non-verbal cues to non-autistic people.

masking Hiding or suppressing autistic traits (whether consciously or not), often in order to appear less autistic and avoid negative reactions from others.

medical model A way of thinking about disability that places the disabling features of someone's life within their medical history and status; for example, a deaf person is disabled because their aural nerve was damaged, or an autistic person is disabled because they are over-sensitive to lights. It is often described as looking for what is 'wrong' with the person, in contrast to the **social model.**

mimicry Copying someone else's behaviour (whether consciously or not) automatically.

neurodevelopmental Associated with the development of the brain. This is generally used to describe conditions in which differences in brain development impact someone across the lifespan (rather than differences resulting from a specific illness or incident).

neurodiversity/neurodivergent Variation in brain development. An individual whose brain develops in a different way to most people could be described as neurodivergent. People with several different types of brain difference (including typical brain development) would be described as neurodiverse.

neuroticism A tendency towards negative emotions, being more likely to be anxious and/or depressed, and interpreting situations and interactions in a negative way. It is one of the Big Five personality traits (see Chapter 3), and exists on a spectrum rather than being categorical.

neurotypical Someone whose brain develops in a typical way; that is, someone who is not autistic nor has any other neurodevelopmental condition. Someone who is not autistic, but who does have ADHD, would not be considered neurotypical but would be considered neurodivergent.

obsessive compulsive disorder (OCD) A common mental health condition affecting around 1 per cent of the population. It is characterized by obsessive thoughts and compulsive behaviours, as well as intrusive thoughts (thoughts which appear into your mind suddenly with no trigger, which are often distressing). OCD can affect anyone, but usually starts in early adulthood, and can have a significant impact on daily life.

peopling A term used by many autistic people to describe the effortful nature of socializing, or spending time with other people.

person-first language Language which describes a person's disability or condition as separate to their identity or personhood; for instance, 'person with autism'. See also **identity-first language.**

phonological processing Refers to how someone converts the sounds they hear into words. Phonological processing is made up of phonological awareness (detecting and creating words, breaking words into syllables, etc.); phonological memory (retaining speech-based information – remembering what has been said to you); and rapid automatized naming (being able to identify and name a set of common stimuli like letters, objects or animals).

post-traumatic stress disorder (PTSD) An anxiety disorder which is caused by experiencing traumatic, stressful and/or frightening events. Someone with PTSD will often relive these events through nightmares and flashbacks, particularly in response to a 'trigger' which is related to the original event. Along with other physical and mental health symptoms, these can have a significant impact on a person's everyday life.

reliability How similar something is across different contexts. In measurement, how similar results are across different people, methods of measurements, or time points.

safety behaviours Strategies used to avoid or reduce triggers of anxiety.

safeguarding The obligation to protect or 'safeguard' children, young people and vulnerable adults from harm. This obligation applies to school staff, healthcare staff and a range of other professionals, and covers physical, sexual and emotional harms.

SEND Acronym standing for special educational needs and disability. This encompasses children with a wide range of needs and conditions, including autism, ADHD, mental health issues and dyslexia.

social hangover A term used by many autistic people to describe the after-effects of socializing, similar to the after-effects of drinking alcohol. This can include exhaustion and headaches, among a variety of other mental, emotional and physical impacts. It is usually managed by spending time alone, delving into special interests as a restorative practice, or through sleep.

social model A way of thinking about disability which places the disabling features of someone's life mostly with the society around someone with a potentially disabling condition. For example, a deaf person is disabled because there is no sign language interpreter provided to ensure they can take part, or an autistic person is disabled because people are not respecting their sensory needs and turning off the overhead lights. It is often described as looking for what is 'wrong' with the situation or society that leads to exclusion for disabled people, in contrast to the **medical model**.

social motivation The desire to interact with people and form relationships (friendships or romantic relationships).

social skills training/interventions Clinician-, parent-, teacher-, peer- or technology-led programmes aimed at improving the existing social skills someone has, or teaching them new skills they do not currently have. Social skills are often defined broadly, rather than having specific meanings, but can include things like turn-taking in conversation, understanding what is and is not appropriate to say, or how to make and maintain friendships.

stigma A strong sense of disapproval towards a characteristic of an individual, by most people in the relevant group or society, or in cultural norms. This can also take the form of stereotypes about a person or group of people who are seen as different in some way to the person judging them, or who are seen as different from the cultural majority.

stimming Moving parts or the whole of the body (often hands, fingers, head, legs or toes) in a repetitive way that can be soothing or express emotion. Some autistic people stim in order to calm themselves down, or to express strong feelings of happiness or excitement.

Contributors

A huge thank you to our contributors, both those who wrote longer pieces and those who filled out our online questionnaire about what masking means in their day-to-day lives. We thank people here according to their preferences in terms of name and identification.

Tabitha, autistic woman
Carly Jones, autistic woman
Jack Howes, autistic man
Nura Aabe, non-autistic woman
Sarah Douglas, autistic woman
Jodie Smitten, autistic woman
Helen, autistic woman
Olivia, autistic woman
Isabella, autistic woman
Cassie, autistic woman
Mark, autistic man
Allace, autistic woman
Maria
Laura, autistic woman
Paula Gizzard, autistic non-binary person
Cheyenne Thorton, autistic woman
Wendy, autistic woman

Jessica, autistic woman
Melissa, autistic woman
Tori Haar, autistic woman
Bella, autistic girl
Loren, autistic non-binary person
Hannah Belcher, autistic woman

Bibliography

Chapter 1

Anderson, J., Marley, C., Gillespie-Smith, K., Carter, L., & MacMahon, K. (2020). When the mask comes off: Mothers' experiences of parenting a daughter with autism spectrum condition. *Autism, 20*(6), 1546–1556.

Baldwin, S., & Costley, D. (2016). The experiences and needs of female adults with high-functioning autism spectrum disorder. *Autism, 20*(4), 483–495.

Bargiela, S., Steward, R., & Mandy, W. (2016). The experiences of late-diagnosed women with autism spectrum conditions: An investigation of the female autism phenotype. *Journal of Autism and Developmental Disorders, 46*(10), 3281–3294.

Cage, E., Di Monaco, J., & Newell, V. (2018). Experiences of autism acceptance and mental health in autistic adults. *Journal of Autism and Developmental Disorders, 48*(2), 473–484.

Cage, E., & Troxell-Whitman, Z. (2019). Understanding the reasons, contexts and costs of camouflaging for autistic adults. *Journal of Autism and Developmental Disorders, 49*(5), 1899–1911.

Cook, A., Ogden, J., & Winstone, N. (2018). Friendship motivations, challenges and the role of masking for girls with autism in contrasting school settings. *European Journal of Special Needs Education, 33*(3), 302–315.

Cook, J., Crane, L., Bourne, L., Hull, L., & Mandy, W. (2021). Camouflaging in an everyday social context: An interpersonal recall study. *Autism.* https://doi.org/10.1177/1362361321992641

Cresswell, L., & Cage, E. (2019). 'Who Am I?': An exploratory study of the relationships between identity, acculturation and mental health in autistic adolescents. *Journal of Autism and Developmental Disorders, 49*, 2901–2912.

Dean, M., Harwood, R., & Kasari, C. (2017). The art of camouflage: Gender differences in the social behaviors of girls and boys with autism spectrum disorder. *Autism, 21*(6), 678–689.

Gernsbacher, M. A. (2017). Editorial perspective: The use of person-first language in scholarly writing may accentuate stigma. *Journal of Child Psychology and Psychiatry, 58*(7), 859–861.

Goffman, E. (1991a). *The Presentation of Self in Everyday Life.* London: Penguin.

Goffman, E. (1991b). *Stigma: Notes on the Management of Spoiled Identity.* London: Penguin.

Holliday Willey, L. (2015). *Pretending to Be Normal: Living with Asperger's Syndrome* (expanded edition). London: Jessica Kingsley Publishers.

Hull, L., Lai, M.-C., Baron-Cohen, S., Allison, C., *et al.* (2020a). Gender differences in self-reported camouflaging in autistic and non-autistic adults. *Autism, 24*(2), 352–363.

Hull, L., Mandy, W., Lai, M.-C., Baron-Cohen, S., *et al.* (2018). Development and validation of the Camouflaging Autistic Traits Questionnaire (CAT-Q). *Journal of Autism and Developmental Disorders, 49*(3), 819–833.

Hull, L., Petrides, K. V., Allison, C., Smith, P., *et al.* (2017). 'Putting on my best normal': Social camouflaging in adults with autism spectrum conditions. *Journal of Autism and Developmental Disorders, 47*(8), 2519–2534.

Hull, L., Petrides, K. V., & Mandy, W. (2020b). Cognitive predictors of self-reported camouflaging in autistic adolescents. *Autism Research.* https://doi.org/10.1002/aur.2407

Jorgenson, C., Lewis, T., Rose, C., & Kanne, S. (2020). Social camouflaging in autistic and neurotypical adolescents: A pilot study of differences by sex and diagnosis. *Journal of Autism and Developmental Disorders.* https://doi.org/10.1007/s10803-020-04491-7

Kenny, L., Hattersley, C., Molins, B., Buckley, C., Povey, C., & Pellicano, E. (2016). Which terms should be used to describe autism? Perspectives from the UK autism community. *Autism, 20*(4), 442–462.

Kopp, S., & Gillberg, C. (1992). Girls with social deficits and learning problems: Autism, atypical Asperger syndrome or a variant of these conditions. *European Child and Adolescent Psychiatry, 1*(2), 89–99.

Lai, M.-C., Lombardo, M. V., Chakrabarti, B., Ruigrok, A. N., *et al.* (2019). Neural self-representation in autistic women and association with 'compensatory camouflaging.' *Autism, 23*(5), 1210–1223.

Lai, M.-C., Lombardo, M. V., Ruigrok, A. N. V., Chakrabarti, B., *et al.* (2017). Quantifying and exploring camouflaging in men and women with autism. *Autism, 21*(6), 690–702.

Livingston, L. A., Shah, P., & Happé, F. (2019). Compensatory strategies below the behavioural surface in autism: A qualitative study. *Lancet Psychiatry, 0366*(19), 1–12.

Moseley, R., Druce, T., & Turner-Cobb, J. (2020). 'When my autism broke': A qualitative study spotlighting autistic voices on menopause. *Autism, 24*(6), 1423–1437.

Parish-Morris, J., Liberman, M. Y., Cieri, C., Herrington, J. D., *et al.* (2017). Linguistic camouflage in girls with autism spectrum disorder. *Molecular Autism, 8*(1), 48.

Pearson, A., & Rose, K. (2021). A conceptual analysis of autistic masking: Understanding the narrative of stigma and the illusion of choice. *Autism in Adulthood.* https://doi.org/10.1089/aut.2020.0043

Robinson, E., Hull, L., & Petrides, K. V. (2020). Big Five model and trait emotional intelligence in camouflaging behaviours in autism. *Personality and Individual Differences, 152*(2019), 109565.

Schneid, I., & Raz, A. E. (2020). The mask of autism: Social camouflaging and impression management as coping/normalization from the perspectives of autistic adults. *Social Science and Medicine,* 112826.

Sedgewick, F., Crane, L., Hill, V., & Pellicano, E. (2018). Friends and lovers: The relationships of autistic and neurotypical women. *Autism in Adulthood, 1*(2), 112–123.

Sedgewick, F., Hill, V., & Pellicano, E. (2019). 'It's different for girls': Gender differences in the friendships and conflict of autistic and neurotypical adolescents. *Autism, 23*(5), 1119–1132.

Sedgewick, F., Hill, V., Yates, R., Pickering, L., & Pellicano, E. (2015). Gender differences in the social motivation and friendship experiences of autistic and non-autistic adolescents. *Journal of Autism and Developmental Disorders, 46*(4), 1297–1306.

Tierney, S., Burns, J., & Kilbey, E. (2016). Looking behind the mask: Social coping strategies of girls on the autistic spectrum. *Research in Autism Spectrum Disorders, 23,* 73–83.

Wing, L. (1981). Sex ratios in early childhood autism and related conditions. *Psychiatry Research, 5*(2), 129–137.

Chapter 2

Ahn, S., Amemiya, J., Compton, B. J., & Heyman, G. D. (2020). Children approve of lying to benefit another person's reputation. *Cognitive Development.* https://doi.org/10.1016/j.cogdev.2020.100960

Anderson, J., Marley, C., Gillespie-Smith, K., Carter, L., & MacMahon, K. (2020). When the mask comes off: Mothers' experiences of parenting a daughter with autism spectrum condition. *Autism, 24*(6), 1546–1556.

Bargiela, S., Steward, R., & Mandy, W. (2016). The experiences of late-diagnosed women with autism spectrum conditions: An investigation of the female autism phenotype. *Journal of Autism and Developmental Disorders, 46*(10), 3281–3294.

Baron-Cohen, S., Leslie, A. M., & Frith, U. (1985). Does the autistic child have a 'theory of mind'? *Cognition, 21*(1), 37–46.

Bellesi, G., Vyas, K., Jameel, L., & Channon, S. (2018). Moral reasoning about everyday situations in adults with autism spectrum disorder. *Research in Autism Spectrum Disorders, 52*, 1–11.

Bergstrom, R., Najdowski, A. C., Alvarado, M., & Tarbox, J. (2016). Teaching children with autism to tell socially appropriate lies. *Journal of Applied Behavior Analysis, 49*(2), 405–410.

Cage, E., & Troxell-Whitman, Z. (2019). Understanding the reasons, contexts and costs of camouflaging for autistic adults. *Journal of Autism and Developmental Disorders.* https://doi.org/10.1007/s10803-018-03878-x

Cook, J., Crane, L., Bourne, L., Hull, L., & Mandy, W. (2021). Camouflaging in an everyday social context: An interpersonal recall study. *Autism.* https://doi.org/10.1177/1362361321992641

Crompton, C. J., Ropar, D., Evans-Williams, C. V., Flynn, E. G., & Fletcher-Watson, S. (2020). Autistic peer-to-peer information transfer is highly effective. *Autism, 24*(7), 1704–1712.

Devita-Raeburn, E. (2016). The controversy over autism's most common therapy. *Spectrum.* www.spectrumnews.org/features/deep-dive/controversy-autisms-common-therapy, accessed on 23 May 2021.

Evans, A. D., & Lee, K. (2013). Emergence of lying in very young children. *Developmental Psychology, 49*(10), 1958–1963.

Fu, G., Evans, A. D., Wang, L., & Lee, K. (2008). Lying in the name of the collective good: A developmental study. *Developmental Science, 11*(4), 495–503.

Gillespie-Lynch, K., Daou, N., Sanchez-Ruiz, M. J., Kapp, S. K., *et al.* (2019). Factors underlying cross-cultural differences in stigma toward autism among college students in Lebanon and the United States. *Autism, 23*(8), 1993–2006.

Glätzle-Rützler, D., & Lergetporer, P. (2015). Lying and age: An experimental study. *Journal of Economic Psychology, 46*, 12–25.

Heinrich, M., & Liszkowski, U. (2021). Three-year-olds' spontaneous lying in a novel interaction-based paradigm and its relations to explicit skills and motivational factors. *Journal of Experimental Child Psychology.* https://doi.org/10.1016/j.jecp.2021.105125

Hull, L., Mandy, W., Lai, M.-C., Baron-Cohen, S., *et al.* (2019). Development and validation of the Camouflaging Autistic Traits Questionnaire (CAT-Q). *Journal of Autism and Developmental Disorders, 49*(3), 819–833.

Hull, L., Petrides, K. V., Allison, C., Smith, P., *et al.* (2017). 'Putting on my best normal': Social camouflaging in adults with autism spectrum conditions. *Journal of Autism and Developmental Disorders, 47*(8), 2519–2534.

Hwang, Y. I., Arnold, S., Srasuebkul, P., & Trollor, J. (2020). Understanding anxiety in adults on the autism spectrum: An investigation of its relationship with intolerance of uncertainty, sensory sensitivities and repetitive behaviours. *Autism, 24*(2), 411–422.

Jensen, L. A., Arnett, J. J., Feldman, S. S., & Cauffman, E. (2004). The right to do wrong: Lying to parents among adolescents and emerging adults. *Journal of Youth and Adolescence, 33*(2), 101–112.

Kupferstein, H. (2018). Evidence of increased PTSD symptoms in autistics exposed to applied behavior analysis. *Advances in Autism, 4*(1), 19–29.

Lai, M.-C., Lombardo, M. V., Ruigrok, A. N., Chakrabarti, B., et al. (2017). Quantifying and exploring camouflaging in men and women with autism. *Autism, 21*(6), 690–702.

Lee, J. Y. S., & Imuta, K. (2021). Lying and theory of mind: A meta-analysis. *Child Development, 92*(2), 536–553.

Leedham, A., Thompson, A., Smith, R., & Freeth, M. (2019). 'I was exhausted trying to figure it out': The experiences of females receiving an autism diagnosis in middle to late adulthood. *Autism.* https://doi.org/10.1177/1362361319853442

Lei, J., Jones, L., & Brosnan, M. (2021). Exploring an e-learning community's response to the language and terminology use in autism from two massive open online courses on autism education and technology use. *Autism.* https://doi.org/10.1177/1362361320987963

Li, A. S., Kelley, E. A., Evans, A. D., & Lee, K. (2011). Exploring the ability to deceive in children with autism spectrum disorders. *Journal of Autism and Developmental Disorders, 41*(2), 185–195.

Lynch, C. L. (2019). Invisible abuse: ABA and the things only autistic people can see. NeuroClastic. https://neuroclastic.com/2019/03/28/invisible-abuse-aba-and-the-things-only-autistic-people-can-see, accessed on 23 May 2021

Ma, W., Sai, L., Tay, C., Du, Y., Jiang, J., & Ding, X. P. (2019). Children with autism spectrum disorder's lying is correlated with their working memory but not theory of mind. *Journal of Autism and Developmental Disorders, 49*(8), 3364–3375.

Maggian, V., & Villeval, M.-C. (2014). Social preferences and lying aversion in children. *SSRN.* https://doi.org/10.2139/ssrn.2375706

Mandy, W., & Lai, M.-C. (2016). Annual research review: The role of the environment in the developmental psychopathology of autism spectrum condition. *Journal of Child Psychology and Psychiatry, 57*(3), 271–292.

Margoni, F., & Surian, L. (2016). Mental state understanding and moral judgment in children with autistic spectrum disorder. *Frontiers in Psychology.* https://doi.org/10.3389/fpsyg.2016.01478

McDonald, S., Bornhofen, C., Shum, D., Long, E., Saunders, C., & Neulinger, K. (2006). Reliability and validity of The Awareness of Social Inference Test (TASIT): A clinical test of social perception. *Disability and Rehabilitation, 28*(24), 1529–1542.

McGill, O., & Robinson, A. (2020). 'Recalling hidden harms': Autistic experiences of childhood applied behavioural analysis (ABA). *Advances in Autism.* https://doi.org/10.1108/AIA-04-2020-0025

McGowan, M., & Pezzullo, R. (2018). *Ghost: My Thirty Years as an FBI Undercover Agent*. New York: Macmillan.

Pang, C. (2020). *Explaining Humans: What Science Can Teach Us about Life, Love and Relationships*. London: Penguin.

Pearson, A., & Rose, K. (2021). A conceptual analysis of autistic masking: Understanding the narrative of stigma and the illusion of choice. *Autism in Adulthood*. https://doi.org/10.1089/aut.2020.0043

Ranick, J., Persicke, A., Tarbox, J., & Kornack, J. A. (2013). Teaching children with autism to detect and respond to deceptive statements. *Research in Autism Spectrum Disorders, 7*(4), 503–508.

Rogé, B., & Mullet, E. (2011). Blame and forgiveness judgements among children, adolescents and adults with autism. *Autism, 15*(6), 702–712.

Ruskin, M. (2017). *The Pretender: My Life Undercover for the FBI*. New York: Macmillan.

Sai, L., Ding, X. P., Gao, X., & Fu, G. (2018). Children's second-order lying: Young children can tell the truth to deceive. *Journal of Experimental Child Psychology, 176*, 128–139.

Sai, L., Shang, S., Tay, C., Liu, X., *et al.* (2021). Theory of mind, executive function, and lying in children: A meta-analysis. *Developmental Science*. https://doi.org/10.1111/desc.13096

Sedgewick, F., Crane, L., Hill, V., & Pellicano, E. (2019). Friends and lovers: The relationships of autistic and neurotypical women. *Autism in Adulthood*. https://doi.org/10.1089/aut.2018.0028

Sedgewick, F., Hill, V., & Pellicano, E. (2019). 'It's different for girls': Gender differences in the friendships and conflict of autistic and neurotypical adolescents. *Autism*. https://doi.org/10.1177/1362361318794930

Talwar, V., & Lee, K. (2008). Social and cognitive correlates of children's lying behavior. *Child Development, 79*(4), 866–881. https://doi.org/10.1111/j.1467-8624.2008.01164.x

Talwar, V., Zwaigenbaum, L., Goulden, K. J., Manji, S., Loomes, C., & Rasmussen, C. (2012). Lie-telling behavior in children with autism and its relation to false-belief understanding. *Focus on Autism and Other Developmental Disabilities, 27*(2), 122–129.

Taylor, M., Lussier, G. L., & Maring, B. L. (2003). The distinction between lying and pretending. *Journal of Cognition and Development, 4*(3), 299–323.

Tekola, B., Kinfe, M., Girma, F., Hanlon, C., & Hoekstra, R. A. (2020). Perceptions and experiences of stigma among parents of children with developmental disorders in Ethiopia: A qualitative study. *Social Science and Medicine*. https://doi.org/10.1016/j.socscimed.2020.113034

Tierney, S., Burns, J., & Kilbey, E. (2016). Looking behind the mask: Social coping strategies of girls on the autistic spectrum. *Research in Autism Spectrum Disorders*. https://doi.org/10.1016/j.rasd.2015.11.013

Van Bockstaele, B., Verschuere, B., Moens, T., Suchotzki, K., Debey, E., & Spruyt, A. (2012). Learning to lie: Effects of practice on the cognitive cost of lying. *Frontiers in Psychology*. https://doi.org/10.3389/fpsyg.2012.00526

van Tiel, B., Deliens, G., Geelhand, P., Murillo Oosterwijk, A., & Kissine, M. (2021). Strategic deception in adults with autism spectrum disorder. *Journal of Autism and Developmental Disorders*, 51(1), 255–266.

Xu, F., Bao, X., Fu, G., Talwar, V., & Lee, K. (2010). Lying and truth-telling in children: From concept to action. *Child Development*, 81(2), 581–596.

Chapter 3

American Psychiatric Association. (2013). *Diagnostic and Statistical Manual of Mental Disorders: DSM-5*. Washington, DC: American Psychiatric Association.

Anderson, A. H., Stephenson, J., & Carter, M. (2020). Perspectives of former students with ASD from Australia and New Zealand on their university experience. *Journal of Autism and Developmental Disorders*. https://doi.org/10.1007/s10803-020-04386-7

Antezana, L., Factor, R. S., Condy, E. E., Strege, M. V., Scarpa, A., & Richey, J. A. (2019). Gender differences in restricted and repetitive behaviors and interests in youth with autism. *Autism Research*, 12(2), 274–283.

Backer van Ommeren, T., Koot, H. M., Scheeren, A. M., & Begeer, S. (2017). Sex differences in the reciprocal behaviour of children with autism. *Autism*, 21(6), 795–803.

Baldwin, S., & Costley, D. (2016). The experiences and needs of female adults with high-functioning autism spectrum disorder. *Autism*, 20(4), 483–495.

Baldwin, S., Costley, D., & Warren, A. (2014). Employment activities and experiences of adults with high-functioning autism and Asperger's disorder. *Journal of Autism and Developmental Disorders*, 44(10), 2440–2449.

Baron-Cohen, S. (2002). The extreme male brain theory of autism. *Trends in Cognitive Sciences*, 6(6), 248–254.

Baron-Cohen, S. (2010). Empathizing, systemizing, and the extreme male brain theory of autism. *Progress in Brain Research*, 186(C), 167–175.

Baron-Cohen, S., Knickmeyer, R. C., & Belmonte, M. K. (2005). Sex differences in the brain: Implications for explaining autism. *Science*, 310(5749), 819–823.

Baron-Cohen, S., Wheelwright, S., Skinner, R., Martin, J., & Clubley, E. (2001). The Autism-Spectrum Quotient (AQ): Evidence from Asperger syndrome/high-functioning autism, males and females, scientists and mathematicians. *Journal of Autism and Developmental Disorders*, 31(1), 5–17.

Bauminger, N., Solomon, M., & Rogers, S. J. (2010). predicting friendship quality in autism spectrum disorders and typical development. *Journal of Autism and Developmental Disorders*, 40(6), 751–761.

BBC News. (2013). Paris Brown: Tweets were 'not meant to offend'. www.bbc.co.uk/news/av/uk-22058082, accessed on 16 June 2021.

Bennett, M., Webster, A. A., Goodall, E., & Rowland, S. (2018). Establishing Social Inclusion the Autism Way: Denying the 'They Don't Want Friends' Myth. In *Life on the Autism Spectrum* (pp. 173–193). Singapore: Springer Singapore.

Bewick, B., Koutsopoulou, G., Miles, J., Slaa, E., & Barkham, M. (2010). Changes in undergraduate students' psychological well-being as they progress through university. *Studies in Higher Education, 35*(6), 633–645.

Bird, R. B., & Smith, E. A. (2005). Signaling theory, strategic interaction, and symbolic capital. *Current Anthropology, 46*(2), 221–248.

Bolino, M. C., & Turnley, W. H. (2003). Counternormative impression management, likeability, and performance ratings: The use of intimidation in an organizational setting. *Journal of Organizational Behavior: The International Journal of Industrial, Occupational and Organizational Psychology and Behavior, 24*(2), 237–250.

Bolis, D., Lahnakoski, J. M., Seidel, D., Tamm, J., & Schilbach, L. (2021). Interpersonal similarity of autistic traits predicts friendship quality. *Social Cognitive and Affective Neuroscience, 16*(1–2), 222–231.

Bourdage, J. S., Wiltshire, J., & Lee, K. (2015). Personality and workplace impression management: Correlates and implications. *Journal of Applied Psychology, 100*(2), 537–546.

Brewer, R., Biotti, F., Catmur, C., Press, C., *et al.* (2016). Can neurotypical individuals read autistic facial expressions? Atypical production of emotional facial expressions in autism spectrum disorders. *Autism Research, 9*(2), 262–271.

Brosnan, M., & Adams, S. (2020). The expectancies and motivations for heavy episodic drinking of alcohol in autistic adults. *Autism in Adulthood, 2*(4), 317–324.

Cage, E., Bird, G., & Pellicano, E. (2016a). Reputation management in children on the autism spectrum. *Journal of Autism and Developmental Disorders, 46*(12), 3798–3811.

Cage, E., Bird, G., & Pellicano, L. (2016b). 'I am who I am': Reputation concerns in adolescents on the autism spectrum. *Research in Autism Spectrum Disorders, 25*, 12–23.

Cage, E., & Howes, J. (2020). Dropping out and moving on: A qualitative study of autistic people's experiences of university. *Autism.* https://doi.org/10.1177/1362361320918750

Cage, E., Pellicano, E., Shah, P., & Bird, G. (2013). Reputation management: Evidence for ability but reduced propensity in autism. *Autism Research, 6*(5), 433–442.

Cage, E., & Troxell-Whitman, Z. (2019). Understanding the reasons, contexts and costs of camouflaging for autistic adults. *Journal of Autism and Developmental Disorders.* https://doi.org/10.1007/s10803-018-03878-x

Carlson, J. R., Carlson, D. S., & Ferguson, M. (2011). Deceptive impression management: Does deception pay in established workplace relationships? *Journal of Business Ethics, 100*(3), 497–514.

Carroll, A. (2002). At-risk and not at-risk adolescent girls in single-sex and mixed-sex school settings: An examination of their goals and reputations. *Westminster Studies in Education, 25*(2), 147–162.

Chevallier, C., Kohls, G., Troiani, V., Brodkin, E. S., & Schultz, R. T. (2012). The social motivation theory of autism. *Trends in Cognitive Sciences, 16*(4), 231–239.

Connell, R. (2008). Masculinity construction and sports in boys' education: A framework for thinking about the issue. *Sport, Education and Society, 13*(2), 131–145.

Crane, L., Batty, R., Adeyinka, H., Goddard, L., Henry, L. A., & Hill, E. L. (2018). Autism diagnosis in the United Kingdom: Perspectives of autistic adults, parents and professionals. *Journal of Autism and Developmental Disorders, 48*(11), 3761–3772.

Crane, L., Hearst, C., Ashworth, M., Davies, J., & Hill, E. L. (2020). Supporting newly identified or diagnosed autistic adults: An initial evaluation of an autistic-led programme. *Journal of Autism and Developmental Disorders.* https://doi.org/10.1007/s10803-020-04486-4

Crompton, C. J., Hallett, S., Ropar, D., Flynn, E., & Fletcher-Watson, S. (2020a). 'I never realised everybody felt as happy as I do when I am around autistic people': A thematic analysis of autistic adults' relationships with autistic and neurotypical friends and family. *Autism, 24*(6), 1438–1448.

Crompton, C. J., Ropar, D., Evans-Williams, C. V. M., Flynn, E. G., & Fletcher-Watson, S. (2020b). Autistic peer-to-peer information transfer is highly effective. *Autism.* https://doi.org/10.1177/1362361320919286

Croson, R., Handy, F., & Shang, J. (2009). Keeping up with the Joneses: The relationship of perceived descriptive social norms, social information, and charitable giving. *Nonprofit Management and Leadership, 19*(4), 467–489.

Dean, M., Kasari, C., Shih, W., Frankel, F., *et al.* (2014). The peer relationships of girls with ASD at school: Comparison to boys and girls with and without ASD. *Journal of Child Psychology and Psychiatry, 55*(11), 1218–1225.

DeBrabander, K. M., Morrison, K. E., Jones, D. R., Faso, D. J., Chmielewski, M., & Sasson, N. J. (2019). Do first impressions of autistic adults differ between autistic and nonautistic observers? *Autism in Adulthood, 1*(4), 250–257.

Digard, B. G., Sorace, A., Stanfield, A., & Fletcher-Watson, S. (2020). Bilingualism in autism: Language learning profiles and social experiences. *Autism, 24*(8), 2166–2177.

Dreaver, J., Thompson, C., Girdler, S., Adolfsson, M., Black, M. H., & Falkmer, M. (2020). Success factors enabling employment for adults on the autism spectrum from employers' perspective. *Journal of Autism and Developmental Disorders, 50*(5), 1657–1667.

Eack, S. M., Mazefsky, C. A., & Minshew, N. J. (2015). Misinterpretation of facial expressions of emotion in verbal adults with autism spectrum disorder. *Autism, 19*(3), 308–315.

Eagly, A. H. (2013). *Sex Differences in Social Behavior: A Social-Role Interpretation.* London: Psychology Press.

Finke, E. H., McCarthy, J. H., & Sarver, N. A. (2019). Self-perception of friendship style: Young adults with and without autism spectrum disorder. *Autism and Developmental Language Impairments.* https://doi.org/10.1177/2396941519855390

Forster, S., & Pearson, A. (2020). 'Bullies tend to be obvious': Autistic adults perceptions of friendship and the concept of 'mate crime'. *Disability and Society, 35*(7), 1103–1123.

Fowler, K., & O'Connor, C. (2021). 'I just rolled up my sleeves': Mothers' perspectives on raising girls on the autism spectrum. *Autism, 25*(1), 275–287.

Fox, J., & Ralston, R. (2016). Queer identity online: Informal learning and teaching experiences of LGBTQ individuals on social media. *Computers in Human Behavior, 65,* 635–642.

Frith, U., & Frith, C. (2011). Reputation management: In autism, generosity is its own reward. *Current Biology, 21*(24), R994–R995.

Fu, G., Heyman, G. D., Qian, M., Guo, T., & Lee, K. (2016). Young children with a positive reputation to maintain are less likely to cheat. *Developmental Science, 19*(2), 275–283.

Goffman, E. (1963). *Stigma: Notes on the Management of Spoiled Identity.* London: Penguin.

Gould, J., & Ashton-Smith, J. (2011). Missed diagnosis or misdiagnosis? Girls and women on the autism spectrum. *Good Autism Practice (GAP), 12*(1), 34–41.

Greenlee, J. L., Winter, M. A., & Marcovici, I. A. (2020). Brief report: Gender differences in experiences of peer victimization among adolescents with autism spectrum disorder. *Journal of Autism and Developmental Disorders, 50*(10), 3790–3799.

Griffiths, S., Allison, C., Kenny, R., Holt, R., Smith, P., & Baron-Cohen, S. (2019). The Vulnerability Experiences Quotient (VEQ): A study of vulnerability, mental health and life satisfaction in autistic adults. *Autism Research.* https://doi.org/10.1002/aur.2162

Grossman, Z. (2015). Self-signaling and social-signaling in giving. *Journal of Economic Behavior and Organization, 117,* 26–39.

Guadagno, R. E., & Cialdini, R. B. (2007). Gender differences in impression management in organizations: A qualitative review. *Sex Roles, 56*(7–8), 483–494.

Gwal, R. (2015). Tactics of impression management: Relative success on workplace relationship. *International Journal of Indian Psychology.* https://doi.org/10.25215/0202.064

Hall, J. A., & Xing, C. (2015). The verbal and nonverbal correlates of the five flirting styles. *Journal of Nonverbal Behavior, 39*(1), 41–68.

Hampton, S., Rabagliati, H., Sorace, A., & Fletcher-Watson, S. (2017). Autism and bilingualism: A qualitative interview study of parents' perspectives and experiences. *Journal of Speech, Language, and Hearing Research, 60*(2), 435–446.

Harper, G. (2019). I'm not breaking down, I'm breaking out: Why sensory overload isn't linear. Mind the Flap. https://mindtheflap.wordpress.com/2019/09/17/im-not-breaking-down-im-breaking-out-why-sensory-overload-isnt-linear, accessed on 23 May 2021.

Harrison, A. J., Long, K. A., Tommet, D. C., & Jones, R. N. (2017). Examining the role of race, ethnicity, and gender on social and behavioral ratings within the Autism Diagnostic Observation Schedule. *Journal of Autism and Developmental Disorders, 47*(9), 2770–2782.

Hawk, S. T., van den Eijnden, R. J. J. M., van Lissa, C. J., & ter Bogt, T. F. M. (2019). Narcissistic adolescents' attention-seeking following social rejection: Links with social media disclosure, problematic social media use, and smartphone stress. *Computers in Human Behavior, 92*, 65–75.

Hayes, G. R., Custodio, V. E., Haimson, O. L., Nguyen, K., *et al.* (2015). Mobile video modeling for employment interviews for individuals with autism. *Journal of Vocational Rehabilitation, 43*(3), 275–287.

Heasman, B., & Gillespie, A. (2018). Perspective-taking is two-sided: Misunderstandings between people with Asperger's syndrome and their family members. *Autism.* https://doi.org/10.1177/1362361317708287

Hollocks, M. J., Lerh, J. W., Magiati, I., Meiser-Stedman, R., & Brugha, T. S. (2019). Anxiety and depression in adults with autism spectrum disorder: A systematic review and meta-analysis. *Psychological Medicine, 49*(4), 559–572.

Houghton, S. J., Nathan, E., & Taylor, M. (2012). To bully or not to bully, that is not the question. *Journal of Adolescent Research, 27*(4), 498–522.

Howard, P. L. & Sedgewick, F. (2021). Anything but the phone! Communication mode preferences in the autism community. *Autism.* June 2021. https://doi.org/10.1177/13623613211014995

Hwang, Y. I., Arnold, S., Srasuebkul, P., & Trollor, J. (2020). Understanding anxiety in adults on the autism spectrum: An investigation of its relationship with intolerance of uncertainty, sensory sensitivities and repetitive behaviours. *Autism, 24*(2), 411–422.

Ibrahim, M. B., & Abdelreheem, M. H. (2015). Prevalence of anxiety and depression among medical and pharmaceutical students in Alexandria University. *Alexandria Journal of Medicine, 51*(2), 167–173.

Jorgenson, C., Lewis, T., Rose, C., & Kanne, S. (2020). Social camouflaging in autistic and neurotypical adolescents: A pilot study of differences by sex and diagnosis. *Journal of Autism and Developmental Disorders, 50*(12), 4344–4355.

Kapp, S. K., Steward, R., Crane, L., Elliott, D., *et al.* (2019). 'People should be allowed to do what they like': Autistic adults' views and experiences of stimming. *Autism, 23*(7), 1782–1792.

Kelsey, C., Grossmann, T., & Vaish, A. (2018). Early reputation management: Three-year-old children are more generous following exposure to eyes. *Frontiers in Psychology*. https://doi.org/10.3389/fpsyg.2018.00698

Kopp, S., & Gillberg, C. (2011). The Autism Spectrum Screening Questionnaire (ASSQ)-Revised Extended Version (ASSQ-REV): An instrument for better capturing the autism phenotype in girls? A preliminary study involving 191 clinical cases and community controls. *Research in Developmental Disabilities, 32*(6), 2875–2888.

Lai, M.-C., Lombardo, M. V., Chakrabarti, B., Ruigrok, A. N. V., *et al.* (2019). Neural self-representation in autistic women and association with 'compensatory camouflaging'. *Autism, 23*(5), 1210–1223.

Lai, M.-C., & Szatmari, P. (2020). Sex and gender impacts on the behavioural presentation and recognition of autism. *Current Opinion in Psychiatry, 33*(2), 117–123.

Lei, J., Brosnan, M., Ashwin, C., & Russell, A. (2020). Evaluating the role of autistic traits, social anxiety, and social network changes during transition to first year of university in typically developing students and students on the autism spectrum. *Journal of Autism and Developmental Disorders*. https://doi.org/10.1007/s10803-020-04391-w

Lindsay, S., Osten, V., Rezai, M., & Bui, S. (2021). Disclosure and workplace accommodations for people with autism: A systematic review. *Disability and Rehabilitation, 43*(5), 597–610.

Lipson, J., Taylor, C., Burk, J. A., & Dickter, C. L. (2020). Perceptions of and behavior toward university students with autism. *Basic and Applied Social Psychology, 42*(5), 354–368.

López-Romero, L., & Romero, E. (2011). Reputation management of adolescents in relation to antisocial behavior. *Journal of Genetic Psychology, 172*(4), 440–446.

Lock, S. (2020). How often Brits eat and drink in pubs. Statista. www.statista.com/statistics/1101707/how-often-brits-eat-and-drink-in-pubs, accessed on 23 May 2021.

Lord, C., Rutter, M., DiLavore, P., Risi, S., Gotham, K., & Bishop, S. (2012). *Autism Diagnostic Observation Schedule Second Edition (ADOS-2) Manual (Part 1): Modules 1–4*. Torrance, CA: Western Psychological Services.

Maier, S. F., & Seligman, M. E. P. (2016). Learned helplessness at fifty: Insights from neuroscience. *Psychological Review, 123*(4), 1–19.

Manago, A. M., & Vaughn, L. (2015). Social Media, Friendship, and Happiness in the Millennial Generation. In *Friendship and Happiness: Across the Life-Span and Cultures* (pp. 187–206). Springer Netherlands.

Mandell, D. S., Richard, A. E., Ae, F. I., Levy, S. E., & Pinto-Martin, J. A. (2007). Disparities in diagnoses received prior to a diagnosis of autism spectrum disorder. *Journal of Autism and Developmental Disorders*. https://doi.org/10.1007/s10803-006-0314-8

Mandell, D. S., Wiggins, L. D., Carpenter, L. A., Daniels, J., *et al.* (2009). Racial/ethnic disparities in the identification of children with autism spectrum disorders. *American Journal of Public Health, 99*(3), 493–498.

Mandy, W., Chilvers, R., Chowdhury, U., Salter, G., Seigal, A., & Skuse, D. (2012). Sex differences in autism spectrum disorder: Evidence from a large sample of children and adolescents. *Journal of Autism and Developmental Disorders, 42*(7), 1304–1313.

Maras, K., Norris, J. E., Nicholson, J., Heasman, B., Remington, A., & Crane, L. (2020). Ameliorating the disadvantage for autistic job seekers: An initial evaluation of adapted employment interview questions. *Autism*. https://doi.org/10.1177/1362361320981319

Margoni, F., & Surian, L. (2016). Mental state understanding and moral judgment in children with autistic spectrum disorder. *Frontiers in Psychology*. https://doi.org/10.3389/fpsyg.2016.01478

Mason, D., Mackintosh, J., McConachie, H., Rodgers, J., Finch, T., & Parr, J. R. (2019). Quality of life for older autistic people: The impact of mental health difficulties. *Research in Autism Spectrum Disorders*. https://doi.org/10.1016/j.rasd.2019.02.007

McFayden, T. C., Antezana, L., Albright, J., Muskett, A., & Scarpa, A. (2020). Sex differences in an autism spectrum disorder diagnosis: Are restricted repetitive behaviors and interests the key? *Review Journal of Autism and Developmental Disorders, 7*(2), 119–126.

Milton, D. E. M. (2012). On the ontological status of autism: The 'double empathy problem'. *Disability and Society, 27*(6), 883–887.

Möller-Leimkühler, A. M. (2002). Barriers to help-seeking by men: A review of sociocultural and clinical literature with particular reference to depression. *Journal of Affective Disorders, 71*(1–3), 1–9.

Morrison, K. E., DeBrabander, K. M., Faso, D. J., & Sasson, N. J. (2019a). Variability in first impressions of autistic adults made by neurotypical raters is driven more by characteristics of the rater than by characteristics of autistic adults. *Autism*. https://doi.org/10.1177/1362361318824104

Morrison, K. E., DeBrabander, K. M., Jones, D. R., Faso, D. J., Ackerman, R. A., & Sasson, N. J. (2019b). Outcomes of real-world social interaction for autistic adults paired with autistic compared to typically developing partners. *Autism*. https://doi.org/10.1177/1362361319892701

Paquette, J. A., & Underwood, M. K. (1999). Gender differences in young adolescents' experiences of peer victimization: Social and physical aggression. *Merrill-Palmer Quarterly, 45*, 242–266.

Pisula, E., Pudło, M., Słowińska, M., Kawa, R., *et al.* (2017). Behavioral and emotional problems in high-functioning girls and boys with autism spectrum disorders: Parents' reports and adolescents' self-reports. *Autism, 21*(6), 738–748.

Ray, G. B. (2009). *Language and Interracial Communication in the United States: Speaking in Black and White*. New York: Peter Lang Publishing.

Romualdez, A. M., Heasman, B., Walker, Z., Davies, J., & Remington, A. (2021). 'People might understand me better': Diagnostic disclosure experiences of autistic individuals in the workplace. *Autism in Adulthood*. https://doi. org/10.1089/aut.2020.0063

Rosales, R., & Whitlow, H. (2019). A component analysis of job interview training for young adults with autism spectrum disorder. *Behavioral Interventions, 34*(2), 147–162.

Rowley, E., Chandler, S., Baird, G., Simonoff, E., *et al.* (2012). The experience of friendship, victimization and bullying in children with an autism spectrum disorder: Associations with child characteristics and school placement. *Research in Autism Spectrum Disorders, 6*(3), 1126–1134.

Rudman, L. A., & Glick, P. (1999). Feminized management and backlash toward agentic women: The hidden costs to women of a kinder, gentler image of middle managers. *Journal of Personality and Social Psychology, 77*(5), 1004–1010.

Salter, M. (2016). Privates in the online public: Sex(ting) and reputation on social media. *New Media and Society, 18*(11), 2723–2739.

Sasson, N. J., & Morrison, K. E. (2019). First impressions of adults with autism improve with diagnostic disclosure and increased autism knowledge of peers. *Autism*. https://doi.org/10.1177/1362361317729526

Scott, M., & Sedgewick, F. (2021). 'I have more control over my life': A qualitative exploration of challenges, opportunities, and support needs among autistic university students. *Autism and Developmental Language Impairments, 6*, 23969415211010419.

Sedgewick, F., Crane, L., Hill, V., & Pellicano, E. (2018). Friends and lovers: The relationships of autistic and neurotypical women. *Autism in Adulthood*. https://doi.org/10.1089/aut.2018.0028

Sedgewick, F., Hill, V., Yates, R., Pickering, L., & Pellicano, E. (2016). Gender differences in the social motivation and friendship experiences of autistic and non-autistic adolescents. *Journal of Autism and Developmental Disorders, 46*(4), 1297–1306.

Sedgewick, F., Leppanen, J., & Tchanturia, K. (2020). Gender differences in mental health prevalence in autism. *Advances in Autism*. https://doi.org/10.1108/AIA-01-2020-0007

Seers, K., & Hogg, R. C. (2021). 'You don't look autistic': A qualitative exploration of women's experiences of being the 'autistic other'. *Autism*. https://doi. org/10.1177/1362361321993722

Shaw, A., Montinari, N., Piovesan, M., Olson, K. R., Gino, F., & Norton, M. I. (2014). Children develop a veil of fairness. *Journal of Experimental Psychology: General, 143*(1), 363–375. https://doi.org/10.1037/a0031247

Smith, M. J., Ginger, E. J., Wright, K., Wright, M. A., *et al.* (2014). Virtual reality job interview training in adults with autism spectrum disorder. *Journal of Autism and Developmental Disorders, 44*(10), 2450–2463.

Sosnowy, C., Silverman, C., Shattuck, P., & Garfield, T. (2019). Setbacks and successes: How young adults on the autism spectrum seek friendship. *Autism in Adulthood, 1*(1), 44–51.

Sreckovic, M. A., Brunsting, N. C., & Able, H. (2014). Victimization of students with autism spectrum disorder: A review of prevalence and risk factors. *Research in Autism Spectrum Disorders, 8*(9), 1155–1172.

Storrie, K., Ahern, K., & Tuckett, A. (2010). A systematic review: Students with mental health problems – a growing problem. *International Journal of Nursing Practice, 16*(1), 1–6.

Stronach, S., Wiegand, S., & Mentz, E. (2019). Brief report: Autism knowledge and stigma in university and community samples. *Journal of Autism and Developmental Disorders, 49*(3), 1298–1302.

Tinsley, M., & Hendrickx, S. (2008). *Asperger Syndrome and Alcohol: Drinking to Cope?* London: Jessica Kingsley Publishers.

Thompson, A., Hollis, C., & Richards, D. (2003). Authoritarian parenting attitudes as a risk for conduct problems: Results from a British national cohort study. *European Child and Adolescent Psychiatry, 12*(2), 84–91.

Thompson-Hodgetts, S., Labonte, C., Mazumder, R., & Phelan, S. (2020). Helpful or harmful? A scoping review of perceptions and outcomes of autism diagnostic disclosure to others. *Research in Autism Spectrum Disorders.* https://doi.org/10.1016/j.rasd.2020.101598

Vannucci, A., Simpson, E. G., Gagnon, S., & Ohannessian, C. M. C. (2020). Social media use and risky behaviors in adolescents: A meta-analysis. *Journal of Adolescence, 79*, 258–274.

Vincent, J. (2020). Employability for UK university students and graduates on the autism spectrum: Mobilities and materialities. *Scandinavian Journal of Disability Research, 22*(1), 12–24.

Walton, G. M., Murphy, M. C., & Ryan, A. M. (2015). Stereotype threat in organizations: Implications for equity and performance. *Annual Review of Organizational Psychology and Organizational Behavior, 2*, 523–550.

Wang, M., Jegathesan, T., Young, E., Huber, J., & Minhas, R. (2018). Raising children with autism spectrum disorders in monolingual vs bilingual homes: A scoping review. *Journal of Developmental & Behavioral Pediatrics, 39*(5), 434–446.

Weijs, C. A., Coe, J. B., Muise, A., Christofides, E., & Desmarais, S. (2014). Reputation management on Facebook: Awareness is key to protecting yourself, your practice, and the veterinary profession. *Journal of the American Animal Hospital Association, 50*(4), 227–236.

West, A. L., Muise, A., & Sasaki, J. Y. (2020). The cost of being 'true to yourself' for mixed selves: Frame switching leads to perceived inauthenticity and downstream social consequences for biculturals. *Social Psychological and Personality Science.* https://doi.org/10.1177/1948550620944049

White, D., Hillier, A., Frye, A., & Makrez, E. (2019). College students' knowledge and attitudes towards students on the autism spectrum. *Journal of Autism and Developmental Disorders, 49*(7), 2699–2705.

Wood, R. (2019). Autism, intense interests and support in school: From wasted efforts to shared understandings. *Educational Review.* https://doi.org/10.10 80/00131911.2019.1566213

Zablotsky, B., Bradshaw, C. P., Anderson, C. M., & Law, P. (2014). Risk factors for bullying among children with autism spectrum disorders. *Autism, 18*(4), 419–427.

Chapter 4

Bargiela, S., Steward, R., & Mandy, W. (2016). The experiences of late-diagnosed women with autism spectrum conditions: An investigation of the female autism phenotype. *Journal of Autism and Developmental Disorders, 46*(10), 3281–3294.

Barr, C., & Topping, A. (2021). Fewer than one in 60 rape cases lead to charge in England and Wales. *The Guardian.* www.theguardian.com/society/2021/ may/23/fewer-than-one-in-60-cases-lead-to-charge-in-england-and-wales, accessed on 16 June 2021.

Beck, J. S., Lundwall, R. A., Gabrielsen, T., Cox, J. C., & South, M. (2020). Looking good but feeling bad: 'Camouflaging' behaviors and mental health in women with autistic traits. *Autism, 24*(4), 809–821.

Botha, M., & Frost, D. M. (2018). Extending the minority stress model to under-stand mental health problems experienced by the autistic population. *Society and Mental Health.* https://doi.org/10.1177/2156869318804297

Brosnan, M., & Adams, S. (2020). The expectancies and motivations for heavy epi-sodic drinking of alcohol in autistic adults. *Autism in Adulthood, 2*(4), 317–324.

Cage, E., & Troxell-Whitman, Z. (2019). Understanding the reasons, contexts and costs of camouflaging for autistic adults. *Journal of Autism and Developmental Disorders.* https://doi.org/10.1007/s10803-018-03878-x

Cassidy, S. A., Gould, K., Townsend, E., Pelton, M., Robertson, A. E., & Rodgers, J. (2020). Is camouflaging autistic traits associated with suicidal thoughts and behaviours? Expanding the interpersonal psychological theory of suicide in an undergraduate student sample. *Journal of Autism and Developmental Disorders, 50*(10), 3638–3648.

Coker, A. L., Smith, P. H., & Fadden, M. K. (2005). Intimate partner violence and disabilities among women attending family practice clinics. *Journal of Women's Health, 14*(9), 829–838.

Corbett, B. A., Schwartzman, J. M., Libsack, E. J., Muscatello, R. A., *et al.* (2021). Camouflaging in autism: Examining sex-based and compensatory models in social cognition and communication. *Autism Research, 14*(1), 127–142.

Cyrus, K. (2017). Multiple minorities as multiply marginalized: Applying the minority stress theory to LGBTQ people of color. *Journal of Gay and Lesbian Mental Health, 21*(3), 194–202.

Davidson, J., & Henderson, V. L. (2010). 'Coming out' on the spectrum: Autism, identity and disclosure. *Social and Cultural Geography, 11*(2), 155–170.

Draper, B., Pfaff, J. J., Pirkis, J., Snowdon, J., *et al.* (2008). Long-term effects of childhood abuse on the quality of life and health of older people: Results from the Depression and Early Prevention of Suicide in General Practice Project. *Journal of the American Geriatrics Society, 56*(2), 262–271.

Forster, S., & Pearson, A. (2020). 'Bullies tend to be obvious': Autistic adults perceptions of friendship and the concept of 'mate crime'. *Disability and Society, 35*(7), 1103–1123.

Hayes, J. A., Chun-Kennedy, C., Edens, A., & Locke, B. D. (2011). Do double minority students face double jeopardy? Testing minority stress theory. *Journal of College Counseling, 14*(2), 117–126.

Hull, L., Levy, L., Lai, M.-C., Petrides, K. V., *et al.* (2021). Is social camouflaging associated with anxiety and depression in autistic adults? *Molecular Autism.* https://doi.org/10.1186/s13229-021-00421-1

Hull, L., Petrides, K. V., Allison, C., Smith, P., *et al.* (2017). 'Putting on my best normal': Social camouflaging in adults with autism spectrum conditions. *Journal of Autism and Developmental Disorders, 47*(8), 2519–2534.

Jordan, C. E., Campbell, R., & Follingstad, D. (2010). Violence and women's mental health: The impact of physical, sexual, and psychological aggression. *Annual Review of Clinical Psychology, 6*(1), 607–628.

Kanfiszer, L., Davies, F., & Collins, S. (2017). 'I was just so different': The experiences of women diagnosed with an autism spectrum disorder in adulthood in relation to gender and social relationships. *Autism, 21*(6), 661–669.

Lai, M.-C., Kassee, C., Besney, R., Bonato, S., *et al.* (2019). Prevalence of co-occurring mental health diagnoses in the autism population: A systematic review and meta-analysis. *Lancet Psychiatry.* https://doi.org/10.1016/S2215-0366(19)30289-5

Livingston, L. A., Colvert, E., Bolton, P., & Happé, F. (2019). Good social skills despite poor theory of mind: Exploring compensation in autism spectrum disorder. *Journal of Child Psychology and Psychiatry and Allied Disciplines, 60*(1), 102–110.

Meyer, I. H. (1995). Minority stress and mental health in gay men. *Journal of Health and Social Behavior, 36*(1), 38.

Milton, D. E. M. (2012). On the ontological status of autism: The 'double empathy problem'. *Disability and Society, 27*(6), 883–887.

Office for National Statistics. (2018). Domestic abuse in England and Wales: Year ending March 2018. www.ons.gov.uk/peoplepopulationandcommunity/crimeandjustice/bulletins/domesticabuseinenglandandwales/yearendingmarch2018, accessed on 23 May 2021.

Ohlsson Gotby, V., Lichtenstein, P., Långström, N., & Pettersson, E. (2018). Childhood neurodevelopmental disorders and risk of coercive sexual victimization in childhood and adolescence – a population-based prospective twin study. *Journal of Child Psychology and Psychiatry, 59*(9), 957–965.

Pearson, A., Rees, J., & Forster, S. (2020). 'This was just how this friendship worked': Experiences of interpersonal victimisation in autistic adults. OSF Preprints. https://doi.org/10.31219/osf.io/amn6k

Pelton, M. K., Crawford, H., Robertson, A. E., Rodgers, J., Baron-Cohen, S., & Cassidy, S. (2020). Understanding suicide risk in autistic adults: Comparing the interpersonal theory of suicide in autistic and non-autistic samples. *Journal of Autism and Developmental Disorders*. https://doi.org/10.1007/s10803-020-04393-8

Quarmby, K. (2011). *Scapegoat: Why We Are Failing Disabled People*. London: Portobello Books.

Raymaker, D. M., Teo, A. R., Steckler, N. A., Lentz, B., *et al.* (2020). 'Having all of your internal resources exhausted beyond measure and being left with no clean-up crew': Defining autistic burnout. *Autism in Adulthood, 2*(2), 132–143.

Schuck, R. K., Flores, R. E., & Fung, L. K. (2019). Brief report: Sex/gender differences in symptomology and camouflaging in adults with autism spectrum disorder. *Journal of Autism and Developmental Disorders, 49*, 2597–2604.

Sedgewick, F., Crane, L., Hill, V., & Pellicano, E. (2018). Friends and lovers: The relationships of autistic and neurotypical women. *Autism in Adulthood*. https://doi.org/10.1089/aut.2018.0028

Smith, O., & Jones, S. C. (2020). 'Coming out' with Autism: Identity in people with an Asperger's diagnosis after DSM-5. *Journal of Autism and Developmental Disorders, 50*(2), 592–602.

Tierney, S., Burns, J., & Kilbey, E. (2016). Looking behind the mask: Social coping strategies of girls on the autistic spectrum. *Research in Autism Spectrum Disorders, 23*, 73–83.

Weiss, J. A., & Fardella, M. A. (2018). Victimization and perpetration experiences of adults with autism. *Frontiers in Psychiatry*. www.frontiersin.org/articles/10.3389/fpsyt.2018.00203/full, accessed on 23 May 2021.

Yafai, A. F., Verrier, D., & Reidy, L. (2014). Social conformity and autism spectrum disorder: A child-friendly take on a classic study. *Autism, 18*(8), 1007–1013.

Chapter 5

DuBois, D., Ameis, S. H., Lai, M. C., Casanova, M. F., & Desarkar, P. (2016). Interoception in autism spectrum disorder: A review. *International Journal of Developmental Neuroscience, 52*, 104–111.

Office for National Statistics. (2021). Disability and employment, UK: 2019. www.ons.gov.uk/peoplepopulationandcommunity/healthandsocialcare/disability/bulletins/disabilityandemploymentuk/2019, accessed on 23 May 2021.

Pang, C. (2020). *Explaining Humans: What Science Can Teach Us about Life, Love and Relationships.* London: Penguin.

Parish-Morris, J., Liberman, M. Y., Cieri, C., Herrington, J. D., *et al.* (2017). Linguistic camouflage in girls with autism spectrum disorder. *Molecular Autism, 8*(1), 1–12.

Pavlopoulou, G., & Dimitriou, D. (2019). 'I don't live with autism; I live with my sister'. Sisters' accounts on growing up with their preverbal autistic siblings. *Research in Developmental Disabilities, 88,* 1–15.

Stark, E., Ali, D., Ayre, A., Schneider, N., *et al.* (2021). *Psychological Therapy for Autistic Adults* (1st digital edn). Authentistic Research Collective. www.authentistic.uk, accessed on 17 June 2021.

Watson, L., Hanna, P., & Jones, C. J. (2021). A systematic review of the experience of being a sibling of a child with an autism spectrum disorder. *Clinical Child Psychology and Psychiatry.* https://doi.org/10.1177/13591045211007921

Whitlock, A., Fulton, K., Lai, M., Pellicano, E., & Mandy, W. (2020). Recognition of girls on the autism spectrum by primary school educators: An experimental study. *Autism Research, 13*(8), 1358–1372.

Glossary

Lovaas, O. I. (1987). Behavioral treatment and normal educational and intellectual functioning in young autistic children. *Journal of Consulting and Clinical Psychology, 55*(1), 3–9.

Index

Wiltshire, J. 88
Wing, L. 20, 235
Winter, M. A. 117
Wood, R. 154
work
  conference attendance 188–95
  'flirting' at 137
  masking at 133–7
  office politics 135–6
  recruitment/interview
      process 132–3, 222–3

supporting autistic
    employees 223–6
whether to disclose at 128–31

Xing, C. 137
Xu, F. 72

Yafai, A. F. 180

Zablotsky, B. 116